ENVY

ENVY

HAROLD N. BORIS

JASON ARONSON INC.
Northvale, New Jersey
London

This book was set in 10 point Baskerville by Lind Graphics of Upper Saddle River, New Jersey, and printed and bound by Haddon Craftsmen of Scranton, Pennsylvania.

10 9 8 7 6 5 4 3 2 1

Library of Congress Cataloging-in-Publication Data

Boris, Harold N., 1932–
    Envy / by Harold N. Boris.
        p.   cm.
    Includes bibliographical references and index.
    ISBN 1-56821-083-3
    1. Envy.   I. Title.
    [DNLM: 1. Emotions.   2. Interpersonal Relations.   BF 575.E65
B734e.   1994]
BF575.E65B67   1994
152.4—dc20
DNLM/DLC
for Library of Congress   93-24377

Manufactured in the United States of America. Jason Aronson Inc. offers books and cassettes. For information and catalog write to Jason Aronson Inc., 230 Livingston Street, Northvale, New Jersey 07647.

Contents

Foreword

Adam Phillips

It is one of the paradoxes of envy that people tend to write enviously about it. As in medieval accounts of the Seven Deadly Sins, tribute is paid to its pervasive influence only through caricature and disparagement. In the work of Melanie Klein—who first made envy thinkable from a psychoanalytic point of view—it is as though the theory, and the therapy that is its consequence, are somehow in competition with the envious part of the self that is being described. Its progress is to be sabotaged, its subtlety spoiled, with insight. Envy is eminently imitable, its own best enemy. In this extraordinary book Harold Boris has not exactly written a celebration of envy, which could only be triumphalist, but the next best thing, an appreciation: a sustained meditation on the state of mind that makes such meditation impossible. Seeing the senses of envy, as he puts it, "functionally rather than as a pathology or a moral failure we can see what envy contributes." In this book, he has done that most unlikely thing: he has made of envy an inspiration. The multiple ironies of this book cannot conceal the fact that it is written with a certain awe of the matter at hand.

If in Klein's writing envy often sounds like a relentless, rather narrow-minded ghost in the machine—what Henry James referred to as the "demon of envy"—in Boris's work the ingenuities of envy are more explicitly the solution to an existential crisis: not only an agent but an answer. How can I depend on what does not belong to me? How can I belong to what does not depend on me? These are the questions, once theological, that haunt the people who are the subjects of this book, those who are dominated by what Boris calls, "the wish . . . to own or replace the source." Boris is interested, in other words, not in what Freud called the preconditions for loving, but rather, the preconditions for survival: the kind of survival that might make loving possible. If desire guarantees, is the medium of survival, why is desiring so problematic? Or, why have we constructed it in such a self-defeating, indeed self-mocking way? By showing us the psychic work involved in making a world in which there is nothing worth desiring—the sheer scale of such projects—Boris suggests that envy is part of the problem and part of the solution of desire. In certain circumstances, he writes, "the infant cannot but feel that the 'role' of mother is wasted on the mother who occupies it."

It is the mother who, for good reasons of her own cannot receive— metabolize, in Bion's sense—the infant's most unbearable projected feelings, that leaves the infant with an impossible task. The infant then, in a sense, identifies with what he cannot dispose of. "The feeling of envy arises very early in life," Boris writes, "out of the infant's feelings of the dread that he or she is not meant to be." Boris's sense of envy in this book depends, ostensibly, on his treatment of certain kinds of patients: those people who are unwanted, who feel themselves to be the "runts of the litter"; those he keeps referring to as "conceived but not conceived of." These individuals, he writes, "have their jobs cut out for them if they are to bounce back rather than forthwith begin the job of dying." It is the unchosen that Boris has selected for attention.

But if Boris, in this book, has added a character to the landscape, the internal landscape, he has also provided us with the only useful kind of diagnostic category, one that, instead of labeling a person, extends the repertoire of parts of ourselves. He has described the unbearable recognition for which envy is the primitive cure, the recognition, however fleeting that there is no right in oneself to a life, that one might not make it, but apparently because, for an obscure reason, one was not supposed to. Boris redescribes the Freudian battle between Eros and Thanatos in terms of the Darwinian struggle between the selected and the unselected, and he manages to do this without producing the covert psychoanalytic Calvinism or sociobiology that is endemic to so much of contemporary object relations theory. If the title of this book, in a psychoanalytic context, inevitably allies Boris with a Kleinian object relations tradition of inquiry, the style of the book—the manner and the gist of its preoccupation, the mordant wit of it—links Boris more with the world of Kafka and Beckett and Bion (and perhaps Donald Barthelme: see the dialogue of mother and baby in Chapter 5): the world of unplaced persons. The people for whom good things are a terror.

The dread that one is not meant to be brings with it, with harsh Darwinian (and psychoanalytic) logic, the idea that there are those who *are* meant to be: the chosen who, in Boris's word, are free to be "choosy." Those supposedly good enough to get the goods. But Boris's vocabulary alerts us that ironies are rife, that envy always performs a paradox. "The nettle of envy," he writes, also "provides the sting that drives us to the top of the heap, where our biology wants us," mindful that it doesn't always, and that our "biology" doesn't, as the pun suggests, "want" anything at all from us. Though what we are talking about when we talk about envy is what we want.

Envy is a form of recognition and, as Boris reveals, it may be our most primitive or fundamental recognition of value, of the imagined good (tell me what you need to spoil and I will tell you what you want, what you think of as good). It is envy as radar, as a kind of sixth (aesthetic) sense that this book is so eloquent about. Though Boris continually acknowledges in his writing his debt to Bion, no one before has been able to describe from a psycho-analytic perspective just what a sophisticated epistemological and moral activity envying is: a recognition both of the good and of one's need for it, an ascription of essence (of essential, if fantastic, good) so overwhelming as to be unbearable, an assumption of hope that cannot be borne. And all this, as Boris makes clear, has significant implications for treatment. If the analyst has what Boris calls "designs" on the patient, then he is by implication offering the patient what he most dreads, because it is subject to envious attack — more better life. The analyst, Boris suggests, should dispense with the idea that "there is something wrong with the patient, and that there is a better he can get." The analyst, by definition, is a sitting target for the patient's envy. If envy attacks rival perspectives — and intrapsychically envy is the archenemy of points of view, making people dull and fanatical — it is because the envious part of the self knows better (and worse) than any other just how good another view might be. The malign visionary that is the anti-hero of this book — the envious self — has never been allowed before such lucid and radical complexity. If Klein made envy available to psychoanalysis, and Bion made thinkable envy's aversion to thought, Boris has been able to build out of this tradition — a tradition noticeably recalcitrant to innovation — his own unique aesthetic of psychic survival.

But this essentially psychoanalytic project has involved Boris in a marriage of improbables, a three-way marriage, so to speak. "What we are after," as he says, "is viewpoint," and the book consists, broadly speaking, of three viewpoints: the psychoanalytic, almost exclusively Freud and Bion; the Darwinian but not only natural selection in quite the conventional sense ("I am rather interested in the idea of parents choosing offspring"); and as a sleeping-partner, so to speak, an existentialism ironized by genetics and evolutionary theory (I am my choices I cannot help making). The building blocks of his theory are unconscious desire, dream-work, and preconceptions; natural selection as the struggle to survive and reproduce; and the choices that are to be made. Interestingly, Boris's paradigm for choice is the infant's (genetically programmed) ruly passions of selective attention: the existentialist as voyeur. These, though, are simply the ingredients, because the book is in no sense a synthesis. The voice in the writing is too distinctive for pastiche, and the commentaries on other texts are usually as idiosyncratic and remarkable as the texts themselves. Indeed his use of quotation is in itself interesting. Texts are woven in; quotations are like another voice in the conversation, rather than monuments we are supposed to stop and stare at. It is part of Boris's subtlety to have made these three viewpoints so mutually illuminating as to seem almost complementary. And ironically it is the concept of envy that is the link, or perhaps the key, to this unusual combination. But such mobile perspectives require a certain attentiveness in the reader: a willingness to suspend one's preconceptions about psychoanalytic writing. The kaleidoscope that Boris used as an image for his method in *Passions of the Mind* — and that Roland Barthes also uses, but as an image for the self — is, by the same token, a clue about how he should be read.

The resources of theory are inextricable from the resources of language. They *are* the resources of language. So it is entirely apt that a book on envy, a psychoanalytic book on envy, should be good at unobtrusively redeeming clichés and rooting for puns. Envy says, "There's nothing new [good] under the sun." Banal writing is an envious attack on the language; the bland is, in the terms of Bion and Boris, the denuded. When Boris, for example, adds as a footnote, "This is a poor pun, which nevertheless I mean seriously," we cannot help wondering what poverty is at stake, given that poverty is exactly what's at stake in envy: a state of mind in which one is *nevertheless* poor. Similarly, when Boris writes of charismatic leaders: "But the grace we give them is not perduring," we can hear the perjuring in perduring. And we may also hear in that grace the grace before meals, perhaps before the totem meal of Freud's primal father? Or an allusion to Klein's point in *Our Adult World and Its Roots in Infancy* (1959) about Christian grace before meals, "These words imply that one asks for the one quality — gratitude — which will make one happy and free from resentment and envy." There is, that is to say, a striking resonance to much of Boris's writing, the kind of texture — of echo and allusion — that we tend to associate with modernist writing (the reference to Joyce, and Boris's use of Eliot's *Four Quartets* are, of course, indications of affinities at work). Unusually for a psychoanalyst, Boris never pretends to conceal the fact that his essays are written.

Boris writes persuasively in this book about the "maneuver by which people try to mitigate their envy by converting differences into similarities." But language, of course, is constituted by difference. The relationship between envy and language is one of the unarticulated sub-plots of this remarkable book. Envy, of course, abhors distinctions, and the distinction

which distinctions signify. So it is clearly not incidental that this book about envy should be full of the finest and most intriguing distinctions: between hope and desire, between greed and appetite, between the Pleasure Principle and what Boris calls the Selection Principle, between the owned breast and the providing breast, between the therapeutic and the beneficial, between the scholar and the demagogue. And centrally, his own distinction between the Couple and the Pair as the fundamental vertices that organize his work. Each of these is subject here to lucid and quotable definition, and the quotable is ready to be used (and envied). It gives us something to begin with.

Inevitably, a book this engaging leaves one with many questions. Why, for example, is sexuality so suited to being a preemptive realization of preconceptions that cannot be borne (as in the so-called perversions in which it seems as if the *function* of sexuality is, in Boris's terms, to fill in the empty categories)? How much is the psychoanalytic tradition a consequence of unanalyzed (or unanalyzable) envy, something perpetuated every time a patient becomes a therapist? Or, given the intrapsychic dynamics of envy that Boris writes about so tantalizingly at the end of the book — "the subject self can envy the object self" — what are the subtler forms of envious self-predation? Perhaps it is worth considering, for example, envious attacks on the unenvious self for whom desiring is delight?

Genetic theory tells us that we are all unique; psychoanalysis shows us what we may have in common. At a time when most psychoanalytic theory is what Boris calls here, in a different context, "old whines in new battles," this book reminds us that psychoanalysis can provide an opening for the private and the political passions of the mind. And that the good life and the enviable life are not always the same thing.

Acknowledgments

Some people can think of a net as string knotted together to catch or hold something. Others can think of it as spaces created and linked by knotted string. Envy has long been considered one of the seven deadly sins, and no doubt it is. Blinded by our envy, we fail to see all that could make us thankful. "Like, I am not in Bosnia, don't have HIV, and am not starving," a patient ruminated with some bitterness, feeling so unenviable in his envy, wanting so much genuinely to feel happy he was not one of those starving children he was so often reminded he wasn't; envying so much those who could. The story goes (Bion 1980, p. 56) that Melanie Klein showed the manuscript of her book on envy to Elliott Jaques. After reading it, he said, "You've got the title wrong—it ought to be Envy *and Gratitude.*" My patient would have understood that: he had a ton of gratitude waiting to happen.

I wish, first, to express profound thanks to Arthur H. Feiner, Ph. D., Editor, and the Editorial Board of *Contemporary Psychoanalysis*, not only for permission to reprint the following papers but also for allowing me to write and publish them as an unfolding body of work designed to develop into this book: "Black Milk," "More of the Same," "The Equalizing Eye," "The Self Too Seen," "About Time." It is and was a generous act; I do not think I could have managed to build and elaborate my work without it.

"Tolerating Nothing" is also reprinted from *Contemporary Psychoanalysis*: it began life as a paper presented to Division 39 in spring 1988, under the Chairpersonship of Art Feiner and Darlene Bregman Ehrenberg, Ph.D.

"Hope" began as an invited presentation to what is now known as the Myerson Symposium at Tufts University School of Medicine. I thank the editors of *International Review of Psycho-Analysis* for permission to reprint it and "Identification with a Vengeance" here. Far too belatedly I want to rectify my egregiousness in failing to mention Karl Menninger's work on the subject of hope, to which his son Walter drew my attention soon after the paper was published.

The remaining material was prepared especially for this volume and is published here for the first time.

Writing is necessarily work done alone, but the sources for the experiences out of which the writing emerges are deeply shared. I learned much from what my patients and the members of the many groups I have in some sense conducted vouchsafed me. I learned from the supervisions and seminars I have given. And of course I learned from both the written and discursive works of my friends and colleagues. I want here once more to thank them all—and add to their roster Judy and Ted Mitrani, who have made my teaching visits to Los Angeles a warm and enjoyable experience.

I offer special thanks to Adam Phillips, who has kindly prepared the Foreword. Phillips drew my attention to the fact that in my correspondence with him I referred to what he was providing me as a "forward." So in a way it was.

Carol Lounsberry Boris has once more made the arduous ardor that any book requires possible. She has what is fast beginning to look like my undying thanks.

Few likely to be reading this will doubt that it takes a certain native familiarity with the subject to be able to—indeed, to want to—write a treatise on envy. But sometimes even the eye squinted to find fault cannot adequately do so: some people simply resist deprecation. Clara L. Hay, small-s social anthropologist, peerless story teller, enlivener and enricher of many lives—not least, lifelong, my own—is such a person. To her, with love and admiration, I dedicate this book.

Introduction

Envy is what in some measure the have-nots feel toward the haves. It arises out of a state of mind in which we scrutinize what others have in order to compare to what we ourselves possess. Through that other unwinking green-eyed monster, jealousy, our perturbed gaze goes to the intimacy others enjoy with one another, from which we are excluded. But when the eye of envy is agape, it is the *wherewithal out of which they have fashioned and enjoy* that intimacy that we canvass with awe or fear. Jealousy contemplates people in relation to one another in respect to who chooses whom; envy remarks only one's self and others as to who has what. This makes it necessary to consider envy *a relationship*. One person may well make such a relationship when the other does not. (A mother may be surprised that her infant envies her the breast. She may experience her breast as a conduit for her nurture and love, little knowing that her baby experiences it as an object he might prefer to possess rather than to receive from.) Nor need there be something in particular to envy: we can feel envy for a long time before realizing what exactly it is we envy.

Precisely because envy is so often one sided and isolating, it carries with it a particular sort of misery. Not only do we feel deficient and defective and filled with hate but in our aloneness, *by* our aloneness, we feel diminished, even humiliated. Others, by comparison, seem comfortably above the fray — and this burnished supposition adds insult to our injury and exacerbates our pain. It is not just that we are left wanting: it is as if we are judged and *found* wanting. We whisper to ourselves that it doesn't matter, that we have what it takes, that what the other has is worthless or worse, so that we are not consumed by the covet of it. But should separation or loss occur — sometimes if the other should so much as move — we experience an amputation or a disintegration, as if a part of our self is gone. To be sure there is consolation to be found in deriding and devaluing the other, particularly if we can find companions of like mind: What's there to envy? But should fortune later bestow upon us that same wherewithal, we are given that same comfort served cold; out of our continuing or remembered envy, we deride and devalue ourselves and fear the derision of our former companions. (So powerful can this become that entire lives are lived in ways calculated to avert a return of envy; the fear of incurring envy is a force to be reckoned with in an analytic therapy.)

Envy, then, is fundamentally a response to discrepancy; it floods in to fill the spaces variously of fall-short and short-fall. As a state of mind — as a way in which things appear to be related — it seems to have been formed in the Age of Scarcity: discrepancy equals disparity. In-coming supplies may ameliorate our envy and induce gratitude; such gratitude also lays the groundwork for our admiration of what others have. But even as we are provided for, we nevertheless covet the wherewithal by which we could supply ourselves — and others. (It is the infant who cannot, sooner or later, feed the hand from which it feeds that is the child who will then attempt to bite it.) If what others furnish us is plentiful and unstinting, we may experience gratitude sufficient to forgive them their wherewithal, indeed, to wish them the well of it. This enables us, in turn, to feel admiration. And when the two, gratitude and admiration, are both present, we can at last cherish a *vicarious relationship* with those upon whom fortune has smiled — at times, so much so that it hardly matters any longer which of us has the wherewithal, the important thing being that some of us have it, for when some of us have it, we all have it. (That one-for-all/ all-for-one quality marks our relations with our sports teams and culture heroes.)

Yet envy is such that we are bound to envy even what we don't admire. Or only perversely admire. The "bad" unsatisfying breast is as much a stimulus to envy as the "good." Since in the unconscious there is no such thing as nothing, only no-things, only presences of what is absent that are as impossible to ignore as hunger or thirst are, the presence of a no-thing exudes menace and power. These no-things assert hegemony over us. That hegemony is instantly enviable. If we cannot stand its potency, we attempt to reverse it, but if we cannot reverse it, we must either flee from it or destroy it. (Only relationships based on the mutual agitation of ongoing envy — like

that Albee evoked in *Who's Afraid of Virginia Woolf?*—have any staying power.) This makes envy peculiarly difficult to study psychoanalytically.

Such study is made even more difficult by the tendency of the envious to evade, abort, or obliterate any relationship that confers benefit upon the haves. The truly envious person, accordingly, does not apply for psychoanalytic treatment. If he looks for help at all, he is apt to seek self-help measures. If nevertheless he must turn to others, he is likely to seek out those practitioners who, out of their own envy, do not take human complexity seriously—so cannot take themselves seriously. If the very envious do seek analysis, they are disposed either to murder it outright or murder it chronically. An analysis can go on for years without anything much happening.

One reason for this is that envious people are commonly unable to feel empathy, except for the unenviable. That their analysts can feel empathy is a distinction that seems to them at once enviable and invidious. In so far as they are too ungrateful to draw benefit from their analyst's empathy, they set out spitefully to ruin it. They can cause such havoc in the analyst's analytic, or for that matter, extra-analytic, life that the analyst, deprived finally of his empathy, becomes himself envious of his patient—it being magnificent, in its way, to have the chutzpah to spoil the only chance one has to develop a fuller life. Understandably the analyst often remains unconscious of his envy (and furtive admiration) of the patient who can, with such reckless disregard, despoil what not only was the analyst's own (therapeutic) salvation but has become his profession and identity. The analyst continues to struggle to behave empathically, but since this now can only be by rote, it will cause him to lose intuition. For example he will lean over backward to be understanding—too often thereupon passively accepting the rather degraded material the patient is likely to be offering. In any case, an analyst who acts at being something he is not is no longer doing analysis. That the patient regards the consequent unempathic treatment as a victory rather than a loss only increases the analyst's sense of violation and outrage—or reaction-formations thereto. Understandably, if sadly for the study of envy, some analysts shrink from treating such patients analytically, employing instead measures that palliate the envy. (An analyst who does not do analysis does palliate the patient's envy; he surrenders important components of his therapeutic potency!)

Jealousy, that hallmark of the oedipal triangle, gave up most of its analytic secrets long ago. Envy has been rather more demure. Freud broke the ground with his work on penis envy. Adler added his idea of the masculine protest. Abraham and Klein broadened the purview of envy with their discovery that envy was something that inheres in all relationships at all stages. Bion, in his examination of the mind as an experience-fashioning entity, provided a meticulous exegesis of the function of envy in the uses of cognition and mentation. Sullivan and Kohut both extended the interactive, interpersonal dimension. Each of these contributions has, in turn, been modified relative to subsequent deconstructive and structural analyses, particularly concerning the theory and practice of the therapy of psychoanalysis as a cultural system. As a result of this community of work, we know a good deal about what stimulates and allays envy and how envy makes itself manifest, whether consciously felt or unconsciously covert.

All the same, a fairly central question remains: *What makes envy sometimes so unappeasable (leaving us so inconsolable) that, long afterward, we remain intolerant of all other differences on which our envy chances to fasten?*

This question takes note of the fact that, in the state of mind of envy, when we compare ourselves with others, we do not merely make distinctions; we make distinctions with a difference. *Something is bound to be preferable to something else.* Since what we deem to be preferable is not always or alone a sensual experience describable in terms of homeostasis or libidinal gratification (as noted, the infant, for example, can feel torn as to whether the pleasures of receiving succor and love are worth more than the possibilities of "owning" the breast), there can only be another aesthetic involved. The aesthetic would be meaningless without two counterparts: *a disposition for choosiness, and a bent for making selections.* This, not that. But such a trope toward selectivity would be incomplete if it didn't have a reciprocal: *I want this not that because this is what others prefer and select.* Given the earliness at which envy comes into being, the terms of what is preferred or disdained must precede sociocultural indices of value and worth, important as these in time become. *Choosiness, preference, selectivity must all adhere to preconception.* This would explain why envy can be present before the eureka of realization.

Psychoanalysis, as a therapy, as a theory, and as an ever-expanding set of clinical observations, is a work in progress. (That is why it continues to exist even while alternative approaches have risen and fallen around it.) It can readily be seen that answering the question posed by envy along the lines I have propounded requires some reformulation of psychoanalytic theory as it now stands (though whether this reworking will stand as progress, only time will tell). In that reworking two other of my writings, *Passions of the Mind* and *Sleights of Mind* (Boris 1993, 1994), are with the present one all of a piece constituting a kind of trilogy. The work you are reading both follows from and advances the reformulation of classical and neoclassical psychoanalytic theory presented in my other two works. Some of its chapters lead up to the reformulation, some present it, others follow from it.

I begin where I began, with the problem of hope. In this first chapter I take a step beyond hope considered as an affect, as in hopefulness and hopelessness, to the structural basis for hope and despair. I find this to be a natural system, the function of which is to control or moderate desire. I do not go as far as to suggest, as I do in Chapter 4, that a metapsychological principle must underlie the expectations to which hope is attached, but I do draw the reader's attention to the universal quality of expectation (or something like it) that variously inhibits desire or impels it.

In Chapter 2, "Tolerating Nothing," I move on to consider the absence of realizations for expectations. Following Bion, I observe that these absences of what is expected are not merely absences or nothings, but no-things that have a presence as objects that menace the borning self. The capacity of a person to tolerate the possibility that no-things are nothings, are merely absences to be mourned, represents a shift of no little significance. Under such circumstances greed can be converted to appetite, hope synthesized with desire.

Chapter 3, "Identification with a Vengeance," deals with people's uses of identification as a means of coping with no-things, insofar as their intolerance of nothing remains in force. The particular form of identification I describe here is motivated by spite and revenge of the sort the have-nots characteristically feel toward the haves. I do not quite advance the thesis that vengeful identifications misuse the natural activity of identifying with others, as I shall later on, but I lay the groundwork for considering identification and object-love as two quite different activities motivated by two different sets of forces.

It is in Chapter 4, "Black Milk," that I begin to broach the idea that the have-not feeling of envy arises very early in life out of the infant's feelings of the dread that he or she is not meant to be. Later on I attach this state of mind to something akin to the Darwinian idea of natural selection, which I argue has psychological representation in the primitive mind. The elaboration of that thesis is taken up in *Passions of the Mind*. For the moment I am directing my investigation to the roots of who's who and what differentiates them.

Thus in Chapter 5, "More of the Same," I consider the implications of the discovery of differences in kind, that largely unalterable set of distinctions, which are, however, so pregnant with hope and possibility—and therefore with envy. Picking up the theme of Chapter 3 and of identification, I describe one common "solution" to the problem of being different: that of converting differences in kind to those of degree. Such conversions lead to agglomeration—more and more and *more*—and thus at once serve greed's insensate nature and keep hope alive. But at the metapsychological level that same agglomerative impulse accumulates accretions of the very likenesses of which PAIRS and GROUPS and species are formed. When we see others as very like us—as, that is, more of the same, we can the more readily form identifications and groups based on those identifications. The "deconversion" of more-of-the-same leads to the discovery or rediscovery of differences, opening wide the possibilities for intercourse based on differences with a distinction. These include barter and nonincestuous sexual intercourse.

With these sets of distinctions, of difference and commonality, of hope and desire, of identification and object relations based on differences in kind, all subject to the disposition of the self and to how the ego pays attention, the next avenues for exploration are inevitably the unautonomous ego (on the inside) and dispositions of the Other. Chapters 6 and 7, "The Equalizing Eye" and "The Self Too Seen," use the actuality of vision and the metaphor of sight to explore both questions. In Latin, the word for envy is nonsight or *invidia*. Dante represented the envious as plodding in coats of lead, their eyes sewn shut with leaden wire. We choose, but no less are we chosen. *We* select: by a blink of the eye we can see now this, now that, now figure, now ground, issues earlier set out in "Black Milk." But even the eye with which we look has been and continues to be *selected for us* by our experiences working on our genetic possibilities. Just as the foreign invader "selects" our immunity to the disease it embodies, so what we see forms our eye (actually the nerve cells of the ocular bundle: cf. Edelman 1987, 1992).

Is there a contest as between what the eye wishes to see and what it is shaped to see? If, as I think, the answer is yes, the eye as organ and metaphor for the "I" replicates the paradoxes (of difference and commonality, hope and desire, of identification and object relations based on differences in kind) previously mentioned. It is becoming clear that these are not so much psychodynamic tensions, arising only in particular contexts at certain points in life-historical time, but features of a selection process in which the individual has one stake and a role and the group (represented in the state-of-mind PAIR) another.

Before such a generic source for envy can be established, however, the question of time has to be addressed. In Chapter 8, "About Time," the mutual influences of time and envy are explored, in particular why, if time is the great healer, it is often precluded by envy from healing. Many of the qualities (size, shape, strength, prerogative) of which the child is envious, are in due time appeased by the child's own development. Other characteristics initially devalued by their owners turn out to be valued by others as contributory to the COUPLE, the PAIR, or both. Thus gender envy succumbs to sexual gratification and the ability to generate children; one, the other, or both.

But time runs on two sets of clocks—the ontogenic and the phylogenic. We are at once creatures who live our own egoistic lives in our own private lifetimes and, as social animals, live a life encumbered with the needs of our (as any) species to propagate and survive. Each incumbency is by the other moderated in the direction of merger. Out of contest comes harmony. This is represented in those states of mind that feature the lineage of a quest that then has attainments of epiphany. Man as individual and man as subject and object of identifications, that is man as a member of a COUPLE and man as a member of a PAIR, live on separate clocks. The PAIR contain Mr. and Ms. Right. Hope teaches them what's right, envy goads them toward attaining it. The COUPLE live on the pleasure principle, on desire; its cohorts are Mr. and Ms. Right-now. Desire drives the COUPLE toward novelty, choice and consummation.

As *objects* of identifications, we are selected to be members of the PAIR and through it the GROUP. If we identify in turn, it is one for all and all for one. But the GROUP may soon be done with us, either because we have served its purposes or because we have been deemed unfit to do so. The chilling realization may reach us: You are redundant, supernumerary, not quite or no longer the right stuff—stand to one side! Make yourself scarce, for that now is the only way to make yourself useful. With such injunctions we must comply: we have identified with the PAIR and GROUP: they have given us our identity; we are they; they are the embodiment of all our hopes. How *can* we but envy them—those who gave us our psychological lives! How can we not obey?

In Chapter 9, "Toward a Natural History of Envy," I draw together what I believe to be the biologically functional values of envy. The aesthetic impulse, of which envy is a by-product, is necessary for differences among objects to be laden with preference. Choosiness could not work on behalf of a selection principle were there not experiences of which some were more or less beautiful, elegant, attractive, and meaningful than others. The selection principle presupposes good guessing. It presupposes that what is now pleasing will later also prove to aid survival. People as we are now constituted may survive air-conditioning, but will we survive global warming!

As an incentive toward being selected, certain objects inspire gratitude and admiration, and are polar opposites of objects that excite envy, as Klein (1957) pointed out. At encounters with such objects, people cry or ecstatically shout. In our culture, the roly-poly characteristics of our young and those of other species appear "cute," and, like beautiful brides and handsome grooms (who make lovely couples), are imbued with such characteristics. The deeper movement from envy and the quarrel over attributes to jealousy and disputes over people is at the same time a movement from the PAIR to the COUPLE. Such movement is necessary for the consummation which produces the progeny on which the selection principle is founded.

To free-associate out loud, the basis for therapy of psychoanalysis, the patient is asked to put aside such criteria for selection as relevance, importance, interest, and coherence. He is asked to be unselective, to report *every*thing. This is, of course, impossible because ideation and feeling flow far more quickly than does speech, indeed more swiftly than consciousness itself.

Nevertheless it is necessary. And so with this paradoxical beginning, the course of psychoanalysis gets underway!

As a result, the tensions the patient feels about selection are displayed in vivid detail, offering the analyst the opportunity to take note of process as well as content. Since the pain of envy is often such as to be very nearly unbearable, it is not likely to appear in content for some time. But by the same token it is there in the activity of analysis from the beginningmost assay at free-association. Unless the patient's unconscious envy is dealt with early and often, it can only intensify. This is because a powerful defense against envy is the breaking of the link between the feeling and the person who stimulates the feeling. "You!? You've got to be kidding! *Just who* do you think *you* are?" As the analysis becomes more and more useful to the patient, the deniability contained in the preceding statement begins, of course, to erode. This means that the patient has either to break off treatment or render it innocuous. (Foresightful "patients" cunningly never do become patients.) The most efficient way to render the analysis innocuous is to reverse the arrow of the transference. Samuel Beckett observed that the "quantum of wantum" could not truly be renegotiated; nevertheless if the patient can experience the analyst as the source of want and himself as the absence of it, the arrow will appear to him to be reversed. From a sniff to a sneeze, everything the analyst does will be selectively perceived as betokening his need of the patient. Such a field of forces foretells the final farrago: What when the patient offers altogether to break off the analysis and go to pot instead?

In the last chapter, "Envy in the Psychoanalytic Process," I consider such issues. Without insisting on the worth of that quality, psychoanalysis has something unique to it. It is perhaps the only relationship in which, without being indifferent to him, one person (save for money for his time) forbears to want anything for or from another. What, if anything, the patient does with the encounter is entirely his or her own affair. That this is the case arises out of the analyst's self-possession; at least for the time he is with his patient, the analyst's life is complete. As such, he can retract himself, leaving many degrees of freedom for his patient to use. When his patient can make use of that freedom, this proves a very nice state of affairs. But before he can, it feels perilous. Every reason for escape from freedom of which Fromm wrote, and then some, comes into play. And it excites envy. What *is* this wherewithal the analyst has that produces such composure?

If psychoanalysis "works" at all, it works by bringing into experience experiences distorted, forgotten or never before fully experienced. The more fully the experience comes into being, the more helpfully the encounter can be realized or re-realized. Why should a patient who finds his envy unbearable submit to experiencing it more fully? Part of the answer lies in the dimension full experience affords. Mental pain, as Bion observed, decreases in the measure it is suffered. Reconstructions that are able to take the patient back into the birth of his envy turn out to have alleviative power. Reconstructions of states of mind apprehensive of or consequent to being or not being *selected* in the PAIR (—*not* of not being "chosen," viz. the COUPLE) provide interpretive relief not previously available on a systematic basis in psychoanalytic work.

HOPE

If one searches the standard psychoanalytic literature (I have in mind, for instance Freud, A. Freud, Fenichel, Fairbairn, H. Segal) one is apt to find little in the index between "homosexuality" and "hysteria," save "hunger." "Hope" itself is nowhere to be seen.

This is no accident. Psychoanalysis is primarily a theory concerning desire and its vicissitudes. And contrary to its popular usage, hope is, as I shall attempt to show, something quite different.

The relatively scant attention paid to hope by the psychoanalyst[1] leads the would-be student of the subject to the poets, who do not overlook its significance in the affairs of mankind. Even so, one comes away from a rereading of the poets with the sense of hope's ineffability. Consider, for example, the two versions of the lovely story of Pandora (as commented upon by Bulfinch 1855).

> The first woman was named Pandora. She was made in heaven, every god contributing something to perfect her. . . . Thus equipped, she was conveyed to earth and presented to Epimetheus, who gladly accepted her,

---

[1] Erikson is one exception. He (Erikson 1964, p. 115) defines hope as the "enduring belief in the attainability of fervent wishes, in spite of the dark urges and rages which mark the beginning of existence."

though cautioned by his brother to beware of Jupiter and his gifts. Epimetheus had in his house a jar, in which were kept certain noxious articles. . . . One day [Pandora] slipped off the cover and looked in. Forthwith there escaped a multitude of plagues for hapless man, — such as gout, rheumatism and colic for his body, and envy, spite and revenge for his mind[2] — scattered themselves far and wide. Pandora hastened to replace the lid! but, alas! the whole contents had escaped, one thing only excepted, which lay at the bottom and that was *hope*.

"So," remarks Bulfinch, "we see at this day whatever evils were abroad, hope never entirely leaves us; and while we have that no amount of other ills can make us completely wretched."

There is, however, the other version of the myth:

Pandora was sent in good faith by Jupiter to bless man; she was furnished with a box containing her marriage presents, into which every god had put some blessing. She opened the box incautiously, and the blessings all escaped, *hope* only excepted.

Bulfinch comments: "This story seems more probable than the former; for how could *hope*, so precious a jewel as it is, have been kept in a jar full of all manner of evils, as in the former statement?" (Bulfinch 1855, pp. 16–17).

How indeed, unless hope is not the blessing Bulfinch takes it to be.

But whatever the case, hope has *some* role to play in human events and as such it promises to repay serious study.

The way I shall proceed is to precipitate out desire, with which, thanks to psychoanalytic theory, we are more familiar and, having subtracted the role of desire from various situations, see what may be left.

THE NATURE OF HOPE

Hope vs. Desire

Here are three possible instances:

1. A hungry child sits glumly refusing to eat his bowl of cereal. His
   mother thereupon dips into the cereal, tastes it and elaborately pats

---

[2]The particular aptness of these three qualities, "envy, spite, and revenge," will be taken up later. Professor David Belmont (personal communication) of Washington University supports Bulfinch's translation of these words from Hesiod's version of the myth.

her stomach, saying, "Mmm . . ., good". The child then eats the cereal hungrily.

2. A patient, who for various reasons is feeling quite overwhelmed at a new job, believes that the people she overhears in the corridor outside her office are trying to tell her something. Precisely what they are attempting to communicate is difficult for her to tell. She demands of me whether I believe that these conversations need not be random or coincidental or whether (here she becomes very angry) I believe her to suffer from paranoid delusions.

3. A young woman feels fat and flabby, though she is only several pounds overweight. She feels unfit to be interested in a sexual relationship with a man, though she experiences sexual frustration. She wonders if the trouble she takes to keep herself fat is not a way of avoiding men. Her life is going by; soon she will be beyond childbearing age. This is a source of great misery.

In each of these instances one will find, I believe, something more or other than desire at issue. Desire itself, as we know from Freud, adheres to the pleasure principle. It wants gratification, and it wants gratification now. Although desire will come to accept moderation to the reality principle in order that pain may be evaded or eased, its acceptance of delay and modification is reluctant and, at root, time is only a fair-weather friend to desire. Desire, moreover, wants a real object and real fulfilment. In its headlong coursing towards real fulfilment it will take the path of least resistance: if it's not near the girl it loves, it will love the girl it's near. When near, it will accommodate, going from active to passive or from one sensual modality to another, adventitiously. When still frustrated, desire will fissure from its aggressive component and dissolve into rage and frequently into jealously. In the end, however, if desire continues to be thwarted, the object of that desire will be replaced with another object more available to it, as Freud (1917b) observed.

Goethe epitomized desire in Faust who, meeting Mephistopheles, wagered that he would never be caught experiencing desire:

> Let that day be the last for me!
> When thus I hail the Moment flying:
> Ah, stay Moment—thou art so fair
> Then bind me in thy bounds undying,
> My final ruin then declare! [My translation]

Contrast Faust's situation with those represented in the three instances to which I have previously alluded.

In the first, the mother appears to have surmised that hungry as the child was, he nevertheless hoped for something better. Her elaborate pantomime said: This cereal is not only what you desire, it is all one could hope for.

In the second, that concerning the young woman who felt that the conversations she overheard were not random or coincidental, the patient is suggesting a view that two theories, hers and my own, appeared to her to be competing for facts on which to feed and grow strong. Indeed, each theory, if it could not acquire the good facts for itself, might be driven to spoil those facts lest the other theory profit from them. In her view, my hopes would be served by the idea that she had paranoid delusions: her hope was that she need not resort to the necessity of experiencing mistakes and going through the slow drudgery of learning from them. To serve the theory based on her hopes, it helped her to believe that the events in question were not random but rather were suffused with meaning and significance. Indeed, so ardent was her hope that she preferred remaining unable to decipher the import of these overheard conversations to making the possible discovery that they were empty of meaning.

The third instance shares with the second the preference for a degree of ambiguity. The patient fears that if it is not fat that is wrong with her body, it will turn out to be something else, about which there is a great deal less she can do. She hopes that it is flab and fat that is the matter and is prepared to enslave her desires to the ascendancy of that hope. Her feeling fat is thus considered a defect akin to a fault. The patient takes pains to keep this defect, for not only does it conceal the real defect, it preserves the ambiguity. I do not realize my hopes, she seems to say, because something is wrong with me and not because my hopes are unfulfilable.

In these comments I have already used the term *hope* to speak of what I do not believe to be desire. Desire, I have suggested, is epitomized in Goethe's "stay, Moment." Hope, let me now propose, is epitomized by Dante, who placed at the gateway to the Inferno the sign: "Abandon all hope, ye who enter here."

Hope resides in time and it is lost, therefore, both to the timelessness of eternity and the instantaneousness of the moment.

These twin check-reins upon hope — eternity and the moment — reveal its paradoxical nature: hope is potential, and potentiality is lost both to actualization and to finality. As Bion (1961) puts it, "Only by remaining a hope does hope persist" (pp. 151–152).

The stayed moment, the static situation, the constant object — these are the conditions propitious for desire. But for hope they are too finite, too unambiguous. Hope flourishes in change, uncertainty, and flux. Clinically, for example, one notices that when people begin to feel quite hopeless, they commonly begin to change almost everything that is not nailed down in their lives — job, spouse, locale, and even health (cf. Jaques 1965).

Such hopelessness is, of course, not the loss of hope itself. It is the losing of hope for one's hopes. The hopes remain, and it is the purpose of this hypomanic activity to rekindle hope for one's hopes. Should these bouts of change and flux fail to accomplish this, people may freeze into paralysis — depressive psychosis, autism, and catatonia are instances of this — as if, by stopping themselves, they can stop unchanging time, which has now become the dreadful foe of hope.

An example of this is provided by Searles, one of whose patients responded to the various shifts in his demeanor or posture by experiencing 200 or 300 therapists in her room during any given session — "as if," Searles remarks, "in watching a motion picture, one saw it not as continuous motion, but as broken into a series of stills; the stills," he continues, "remained on the scene and accumulated." One can surmise that this patient's hatred of time induced her to convert motion, which, of course, takes place through time, into "stills" which she could instead distribute into space and so deny time's passage. Searles adds: "She let me know also on another occasion that whenever I changed posture she identified me as some different person from her past" (Searles 1965, p. 307).

When a hope is genuinely abandoned, its renunciation is followed not by despair but by the burgeoning of desire; the child of my first instance, having let loose his hope of a superior sort of feeding, felt not hopeless but hungry.

This fundamental antagonism between hope and desire is crucial. Freud, I think, was searching for this in *Beyond the Pleasure Principle* (Freud 1920) but came up awry by supposing that the antagonist to Eros, or what I have been calling desire, was a death instinct. Freud (1937) developed further his clinical conviction that something beyond the sources of the usual resistances ran counter to the lively, lusty emergence of the libido. Was not the time-limit he imposed upon the Wolf Man that death-knell for time which itself fueled the hope that kept desire at bay?

But it was earlier, in "Mourning and Melancholia" (Freud 1917b), that Freud drew the antagonism most sharply. In the face of loss, desire will take the path of least resistance and find a more accommodating substitute object. But, as we know, this does not always or even frequently happen. Instead, people elect to imagine that the object is within themselves, either as a part of the self, endowing them with various attributes, or as a somewhat separate figure remarking, cruelly or kindly, on their attributes — parts, that is, of the ego-ideal or superego respectively.

In this latter choice (internalization, introjection) I think we also see hope's hand at work, for where desire's aim is the giving and getting of pleasure, hope longs to have and possess.

But to make these and other distinctions between hope and desire plainer, I have to suggest something of the sources and origins of hope.

The Genesis of Hope

In attempting this I shall necessarily have to be very speculative indeed, taking facts from here, notions from there, and assembling them all with an aura of coherence that belies the highly speculative nature of what I am about to say.

Piaget reports (Piers 1972) the following findings from an experiment. Seven-year-olds are shown two balls of plasticene clay of the same size. The children examine them and agree that they are of the same size. The experimenter then rolls one of the spheres of clay into an elongated snake shape. The children watch this operation. But when asked which shape has more clay, they say the cylinder does. When the cylindrical shape is patted back into a sphere, they say that now both are equal again.

Similarly, children feel that a full narrow glass holds more water than a short squat glass, even when these vessels have been filled from an ordinary glass and poured back again so the children can see that the same volume of water has gone into the wide and narrow glasses.

To my mind, these experiments (among others) suggest that people have ideas about things which are powerful enough to induce them to disregard both empirical experience and their own good powers of inference. That is, they have a sense of how things *should* be and this sense of the seemliness or fitness of things prevails over actual experience.

Kant and Bion are among the relatively few who have dealt with this phenomenon. Kant (1781) suggested that people have what he called "empty thoughts" to which experiences with real events are more or less approximate. Bion (1963) holds that people have preconceptions for which experience more or less provides realizations. Such so-called "structuralists" as Lévi-Strauss, the anthropologist, and Chomsky, the linguist, also find it logically necessary to infer that people have inherent ideas about experience. These ideas they call "deep" or "metastructures," and they view these structures as giving a shape to experience prior to, sometimes independent of, the influences of actual private or cultural experiences. (Chomsky 1972, Gardner 1973, Leach 1970, Lévi-Strauss 1966, 1973, Lyons 1970, Piaget 1973, and Piers 1972.)

These metastructures, empty ideas, or preconceptions are like flexible containers into which experience, when poured, gives shape and substance. But they are not without their own shape, as Piaget's experiments show. Ethologists, for example, report countless instances along the following lines.

An experiment was done to investigate what qualities of the female attract the grayling butterfly (Tinbergen 1958, 1965). Mock-ups, models, were made in which every conceivable variable — size, shape, color, flying speed, flying pattern, and so on — could be systematically altered singly and in patterns in order to learn which ingredients proved to be the critical ones.

Color, as it happened, proved to be of vast interest: the darker the color of the female mock-ups, the greater the number of males that would fly from their roosting tree in far-ranging pursuit. A jet-black color had the greatest arousal value. But that color does not exist in nature. It is as if the grayling butterfly has an idea of what the female of the species should look like, and the closer the actual female approximates to that "platonic ideal," the more satisfactory she is.

The room left over in the preconception after actual experience has contributed shape and substance appears to exercise a frustration no less painful, perhaps indeed even more redolent of danger, than the frustration of desire. As Piaget's experiments reveal, children, at least for some years, deny the teachings of experience in order to cling to a view of the world based on how things should be. Surely this same tendency was in evidence in the people represented by the instances I have given earlier.

If we take this idea of hopeful preconception as something inherent, we are able to put it side by side with traditional libido theory.

That theory begins with the infant and the breast. The infant is hungry and, more, he wants to suckle. Then there is, or is not, the breast. If there is, things go fairly well. If there is not, the infant has to cope with pain or terror, frustration and rage.

But now let us introduce into this situation the notion that the baby has an idea of what the breast should be like. If the idea is that it should be there and full and calm and it is, the actuality will exactly match the idea, the hope will be congruent with the desire, and as such, the hope will be, as it were, quite invisible. So let us suppose instead that the breast is full and there, but instead of being calm, as the baby we are imagining hopes, it is active.[3] Now the infant faces a conflict. His desires for milk and suckling are fulfillable enough, but his hopes will be somewhat thwarted. It is easy to see from this very early situation how the relationships between hope and desire can be antagonistic, with hope going to the *quality* of the experience and desire to issues of satiation. But we can equally see that there exists not one but two sources of frustration. The one is the familiar frustration of desire. The other is the frustration of hope. Indeed, there are circumstances in which one frustration cannot be eased without at least in part incurring the other. An example familiar in psychoanalytic theory is this:

Another of baby's ideas for the breast — his hope — is that it is a breast that is his. His desire for the breast is that it feeds and nurtures him. When it occurs to baby that the breast, though provident and regularly nurturant, is nevertheless not his, a crisis — the so-called anaclitic depression — takes place.

---

[3]Films or direct observations of infants feeding will not fail to illustrate sensitively such differences among mothers.

It is, however, a mistake to regard the crisis as one of desire, as weaning is. The crisis is one of hope; hence the depression. Patients are usually obliging enough to reveal that the depression, the emptiness, is precisely where on them the breast was supposed to be: the depression being literally that concave configuration left from where the breast was supposed to be, but is not. Baby is outraged not because his desires for nurturance and suckling are frustrated but because mother has a breast and he has not.

I am so far speaking of phenomena Freud and others have dealt with in terms of primary and secondary narcissism. But it will be clear that in thinking in terms of hope I am re-sorting matters such that hopes have not primarily to do with the self and only by projection or projective identification (Klein 1957, Kohut 1968) with others, but with what I think are more basic, or metastructural, antitheses.

That is, the realization that mother has a breast may fulfill the infant's oral desire, providing him with pleasure and gratitude. But at the same time it fulfills his preconception that he should have a something-or-other of his own with evidentiary substance: the something-or-other now turns out to be a breast. This bite, as it were, of the apple of knowledge produces an "Aha, so that's what I should have" and then a state of acute envy.

Later, the same sort of preconceptions will hold sway in the Oedipus complex. There will be not only desire for sensual satisfactions from the mother, but also hope for satisfactions at least the equal of those which father is presumed to enjoy. Similarly, women who find satisfaction from their lovemaking with men may nevertheless feel depressed (again the concavity) by the presence of a penis which, however well it fills their desires, does not fulfill their preconceptions. The patient I mentioned who keeps herself overweight frequently keeps herself from intercourse and almost always from orgasm. She is fearful that the gratification of her desires will undermine her hopes.[4] It is possible to speculate whether the stage of latency is similarly motivated more strongly by hopes, capitulating only when desires, rejuvenated by the wellsprings of puberty, grow too strong for it.

The persistence of the attraction to the oedipal parent is, as we know, awesome indeed. Is this a function simply of desire? Or is it that the parent fits the preconceived hope? It is so frequent clinically as almost to beggar mention to find such attitudes as "if I can't have my parent, I don't want anyone" or "whomever I can have can't be the right person because, by definition, the right person is the person I can't have."

But lest we suspect "imprinting," it is important to note that people maintain something akin to a lifelong shopping list of hopes, for which they

---

[4]I believe this fear that their desires will erode the strength of their hopes to be crucial in understanding the schizophrenic.

collect "evidence." Surely any psychotherapist who has heard other therapists and other methods extolled by patients who feel their hopes languishing as a result of the therapy will be familiar with the pastiche patients form to feed and fortify their hopes.

In summary, hope arises from preconceptions of how things and experiences should be. These preconceptions at once structure and are shaped by their encounters with actuality. Insofar as they are matched by actual experience, hope and desire can coexist and become coterminous. But where preconceptions and actuality are too far apart, hope comes into being as separate from desire and in fact serves as a restraint upon desires more fundamental, in my view, than anxiety, the defenses or other structures of the mind.

Biological, Social, and Cultural Considerations

To make this point concerning the function of hope in restraining of desire clearer, it may be useful to view matters against the background of man's biological evolutionary heritage. Present biological thought continues to offer strong ethological and experimental support for Darwin's thesis that species are not merely passively selected by the exigencies of their ecology. They also select among themselves, and this too determines which genes survive to be passed down the generations.

For such active selectivity, such as that of mating partners, to occur, two factors must be present. There must be characteristics that distinguish members of a species not only from members of other species but also from one another. And there must be a predilection to choose from amongst this varied array. Without such morphological characteristics as size, color, age, shape or such acquired discriminates as territory or dominance position in a social hierarchy to choose from, the predilection for choosiness would be meaningless. But equally, were there not choosiness, were choice random or governed by such chance factors as proximity or propinquity, the significance and function of the characteristics to choose from (indeed, in all likelihood the characteristics themselves) would ebb away into the mists of time. Something to choose from and a predilection *to* choose are both, therefore, essentials.

As Mayr (1972) observes:

> It is well known that the mating drive in the males of many species is so strong that they display not only to females of their own species, but also to females of related species. If the females were equally lacking in discrimi-nation, an enormous amount of hybridization among closely related species would take place. Since hybrids are ordinarily of considerably lower fitness, natural selection will favor two developments: First, any genetic change that

would make the females more discriminating, and second, any characteristics in the males that would reduce the probability that they be confused
with the males of another species. Such characteristics are designated
isolating mechanisms. [p. 98]

Mayr notes that earlier, in 1942, he had "called attention to the fact that
the conspicuous male characteristics sometimes were lost in island birds when
there were not other closely related species on the same island. The loss of
these characters was apparently due to a relaxation of selection for the
distinctive isolating mechanisms" (p. 98).

The inhibition of the procreative drive pending the approximation of the
object to the "preconception" paradoxically facilitates the release of the drive.
That is, the readier and more assured the capacity not to choose *A,* the easier
and quicker the capacity to choose *B.* Though sexual selectivity involves this
procedure, so too do feeding and parenting, eliminatory and aggressive
actions and interactions. In all of these, inhibition until the "right" conditions
are present makes for greater ease of release once the "right" conditions are
present.

How far animal preconception represents a variation on what I have
been supposing to be human preconception is subject to the same uncertain-
ties as the resolution of how far animal drives are variants of human drives,
or what I have been calling desire. For myself, I find it reasonable to put
forth, not as a substantive analogy but as a hypothetical construct, that
preconception in humans may be a residue of Darwinian processes of natural
selection such that hope's effect upon desire can be viewed as having a
species-specific survival value in carrying out nature's blueprints for humanity. Hope holds desire from taking its any old course of least resistance and it
keeps desire from static satiety by calling it to finer possibilities.

In proposing such a construct I do not intend in any way to minimize the
role of man's social universe; man is born into a social order, the values,
ideals, and sanctions of which importantly shape his hopes, aspirations, and
expectations. But neither should it be forgotten that the social universe was no
less born of man: he shapes and reshapes it, even while it does him.

By regarding man as the shaper of his social universe and not exclusively
as its product, one is in turn able to see beyond the unique differences among
particular societies to what all social systems were endowed with by humankind.

No known culture, for example, is without a system governing the
relations of kin and hence of nonkinship groups. And none is without a
religion. The explanations for these facts are so complex as to be by no means
in hand. But hope, as I have been regarding it, permits at least certain
hypotheses to unfold.

When hope attains ascendancy over desire, future time takes on a correspondingly magnified importance. If hope is to be maintained against the erosions of hopelessness and desire, time needs to be conserved and preserved — the more so since the pleasures attendant upon the gratification of desire are not present to console or compensate for the loss of hope. Nor will they be until hope is renounced and desire given its head. The burgeoning importance of the future escalates the horror and fear of death[5], clinically so central to the suicide (and illustrated so aptly by a patient who, even while seriously attempting to kill herself, was giving up smoking). As antidote to such fear, a future beyond death's limits upon hope must be devised, and maintained free of jeopardy.

The social order — family, group, tribe, and nation — has, to this effort, a considerable contribution to make. The removal of personal hopes to the group — the sense, fantasied or real, of being part of something (or it of one) larger, stronger, and more enduring than one's self — offers a powerful ameliorative to the incursions of mortality. But in return for the opportunity of vesting his hopes in the social unit, the individual must relinquish his desires of it: he eschews cannibalizing it; neither may he plunder or foul it: and he is constrained to follow its rules of exogamy and incest (Boris 1970, Boris et al. 1975).

Religion, too, is ordinarily organized to afford reprieve from the fatal limits of real time through construction of an afterlife or one or another form of deathlessness. Although religion competes with the secular group for its use as a source of hope, as the story of Abraham and Isaac suggests, accommodations ("Render unto Caesar . . .") between the two are generally to be found.

Religion's offer of reincarnation or other versions of transubstantiation, like the group's offer of investiture, is not without its price: desires must be abdicated or taken only in symbolic form; but in return there is the proffer that hope may be realized without being lost to fulfillment. Indeed, lest hope be lost on the way towards the hereafter, certain remedies are available. Perhaps chief among these is the endeavor by the mystic to reassimilate hopes, with their specific preconceptions, into a global hope that has no preconception other than the direct and consummate apprehension of God (see in the list of references: St. John of the Cross [1957]; also St. Augustine [1952] on the relation between hope and faith). Specific hopes are more vulnerable to

---

[5]I use the words "horror and fear" of death to refer specifically to the state of mind that obtains when hope is regnant over desire and hopes are propelled into the future. When desire is paramount, fear of losing the means and opportunity of taking pleasure in the object, e.g., the castration–death transformation, is preeminent. When hope is vested in the group or afterlife, the horror and fear are proportionately diminished and people, as in war, often face death with docility and relative equanimity.

fulfillment and renunciation; hope itself is more easily retained. Time, too, is transfigurable through altered states of consciousness induced by drugs or other means, so that time may be made more elastic while people await the ultimate. Finally there are more worldly measures, ceremonies and rituals, employed to restore flagging hope.

Still, hopes and hope require other sources of nourishment, and these are built into other parts of culture. If, as Weisman (1965) observes, "The most comprehensive antithesis of a meaningless existence is to believe that whatever happens has significance," (p. 235) science (and, indeed, madness) shares with religion the task of rejuvenating hope with infusions of meaning.

But it is not alone the contents, the reassuring news that the universe is lawful and fathomable, that restores hope. As in art, form (e.g., the elegance of the scientific solution) has its contributions to make.[6] Both, in the Aristotelian proposition, imitate but improve on nature. Aesthetic pleasure, that sense of exhilaration and admiration, reflects this. In what is aesthetically pleasing, that-which-is has been brought into closer identity with preconception. That is, there has been an "improvement" in the sense of ownership of that-which-is and there has been a "refinement" of its quality, for both ownership and quality appear to be intrinsic to the preconception of what is seemly and fit, and both, accordingly, inspire and sustain hope.

THE PSYCHOTHERAPY[7] OF HOPE

When life becomes nearly unbearable, and a being can change neither of those twin prongs of his nature—his hopes or his desires—any further, and yet the events, conditions, and people on whom he depends for the fulfillment of his hopes or his desires are also not to be changed, he ordinarily takes that one further, fateful option open to him: unable to change his experience, he changes what he experiences of what he experiences.

Much of psychoanalytic theory, as indeed much of everyday psychotherapeutic practice, is taken up with these alterations of the experience of what one experiences. These involve people's use of the mechanisms of defense. Perhaps the simplest way to review these for purposes of discussing the psychotherapy of hope is to recall Aesop's fable of the fox and the sour grapes.

In that fable, it will be recalled, the fox was unable to reach the good, sweet grapes. To relieve his intense feelings of frustration—the frustration of

---

[6]Greenacre's (1953) observation that the middle part of a three-part dream will always refer to the genitals is an example of the preconscious use of form as a source of hope.

[7]I use the term psychotherapy in its generic sense to include psychoanalysis primarily but not to exclude psychoanalytically oriented modifications.

his desire and the frustrations of the hope he had that he was a fox who could reach grapes — he modified the terms of the experience. The original terms were something like this: I, a hungry fox, want to reach sweet, good grapes. The fox changed these in the simplest way possible. He used denial; the terms of condition then read: I, a hungry fox, cannot reach bad, sour grapes.

If that change were one that did not offer him the relief from his twin frustrations, the fox had still other options for changing the terms of the experience. He might, for example, have changed the idea that grapes themselves were involved. Or he might have changed the idea that he was hungry. Or, for that matter, he might have been driven to change the idea that he was a fox.

The use of denial, a subtractive procedure, is, however, not the only one open to beings. Indeed, it is often all too weak a solution to the pressing pain of frustrated desire or the anguish of thwarted hope. Accordingly, the fox may have used, in addition, the introduction of terms that might buttress his attempt to alter what he experienced of the experience. That is to say, in addition to denial, he might have constructed a cover story. He might, for example have said: I, a bad fox, cannot reach good, sweet grapes because I am bad. This is the sort of procedure that the patient in the third of the instances I previously presented employed by keeping herself somewhat overweight. She was saying, it is the palpable presence of my flab that is what is wrong. One can see from this the great value of elements taken into the superego and kept there as manic defenses against the depressing realization that life may be simply what it is.

But whatever the precise fantasies employed to transform and transfigure the original experience into something more tolerable, the fateful results are inevitably the same: in exchange for his relative freedom from the pain of frustration or humbling of hope, the individual becomes prey to anxiety and insecurity.

If, however, as Homer observed, happiness consists in being able to make use of whatever the gods toss our way, the task for the psychotherapist is obvious. It is to enable our patients to experience — really reexperience — the original experience, to tolerate it, to learn from it, and thus be free to take such other experiences as they can fashion together with life and to derive benefit from these.

This is as true for the psychotherapy of hope as for that of desire. But having said that, one is close to exhausting the likenesses. Desire will be shy of frustration; it will be surrounded by an array of defensive maneuvers and security operations, and will come screened and transfigured. But its nature is appetitive and urgent; if it takes time, it hates the time it takes. So sooner or later, via the transference, desire and its crises will unfold for therapist and patient to know about.

Hope, as we have seen, having a different sort of nature, does not ordinarily come to the fore. It is vested — for example, in the very outcome of the therapy, months or years away — and, being vested, follows an almost Parkinsonian law: it spreads, elongates, permeates to fill the space and time and possibility available to it. As such, special measures are required if the analysis of hope is not to be left to that scant period of time between the establishing of the date for termination and termination itself.

I shall address myself to these measures, but I want first to set the backdrop in terms of which various approaches or procedures can be viewed. The ideal datum, the condition from which both patient and therapist can best work, is present when the patient is experiencing a crisis of hope in the here-and-now of a given session and will talk of it fully precisely as it occurs. This means that the crisis has to do with the therapy, the therapist, and the patient in the instant. That is the ideal, and it is seldom realized. For one thing, when the patient is feeling hopeless, he is ordinarily not inclined to cooperate by communicating his experience; but he will convey it and, by certain procedures to which I will come presently, conveyance will cumulatively develop into communication.

Much stands in the way of this happening, however, and these impediments must be pared away as best one can.

First of all, as I have already implied, there is the very fact of therapy itself, which functions as a powerful source of hope. About this there is nothing one can do; but it is of no conceivable use to the patient to aid and abet his hopeful attitude towards therapy. Therapy is a basic research project, not unlike any in molecular biology or nuclear physics. Two — or more people when a group is involved — join forces to make "a systematic investigation of self-deceptions and their motivations" (Hartmann 1959, p. 20). As in all such endeavors in basic research, one may learn something, but whether it will result in breakthroughs or indeed have applications is uncertain. I do not know what the figures are for successes in those other fields (if a word like *success* is applicable), but outcome studies of psychotherapy certainly would not engender general optimism in any save the sort of people who regularly buy the Brooklyn Bridge. No therapist has reason to "sell" therapy — or even to recommend it. The only thing he can do is offer to share the attempt at research and discovery and, along with his patient, see what they shall see.

Of course this stance can be assumed only by that therapist whose own hopes are not dependent on the progress of his patients. Therapists also invest therapy with hope; as a supervisor, one frequently hears reports of progress or, alternatively, of stasis in terms that cause one to wonder how distinguishable the patient's hopes are from the therapist's. Perhaps the kinship of therapy to the religious systems of the preliterate peoples of the world, reported by anthropologists (Erikson 1963, Mitchell, personal communication) needs closer attention. But psychotherapy is not a substitute for religion or, for that matter, for education or socialization, as people sometimes think. It has its own function. And as in the psychotherapy of desire the therapist ordinarily learns through his own analysis and supervision to become free of making his patients the object of his desire—his voyeurism, rescue impulses, and the like; so in the psychotherapy of hope the therapist must recognize the force and play of what he hopes for, for or from his patients.

One way of doing so is for him to notice the verbs he uses in speaking of his work. If in making a therapeutic alliance he hopes to convert the patient to a psychodynamic viewpoint or if in making an interpretation he hopes to shed light, he is performing a religious function. Socialization functions will reveal themselves in hopes to instill or inculcate or to provide corrective experiences. Offering support to a patient or a faction in a patient is a socio-political activity, better left to affairs of state. Winnicott (1965) observed that he could tell when his doing of therapy slipped over into educating by his use of phrases beginning with "moreover." The function of sage or guru is in evidence when the therapist proposes a view of life: "What did you expect?" or "Do you think you're the only one?" or "Who promised you a rose garden?" Schafer (1970) has identified several of these life-views. But the point to be made here is that the therapist's vicarious hopes for his patients or his need for daily rejuvenation of hopes of his own soon find him doing something other than psychotherapy. An interpretation given to get a patient to stop doing, thinking, or feeling one way and get on to something else instead is not an interpretation; it is a legal brief. Bion (1970) has remarked that it is important not only to understand a patient's communication, but the use to which it is being put. Much the same holds true for the therapist in regarding his own communications (Boris 1991).

These divestitures of hope in therapy itself help the patient to become self-conscious of his own investments of hope in therapy and able then to deal with them when he is so inclined. But ordinarily before he will do so, he will shift his hope from his preconceptions of therapy to the person of the therapist himself. Flattering as this is, the fact remains that hope vested precludes crises of hope from being reexperienced. Once again, though the therapist can not (nor should) do anything to repudiate this investiture directly, it will be important for him to determine whether he shares this charismatic view of himself. Some therapists do. They have a touching faith in their teachers, their reading, their ideas, and for them therapy is a process whereby they await the opportunity to make revelations based on these. Whether or not the revelation is correct is not at issue here. What is at issue is that such a procedure orients the patient to the therapist as the font of insights and thus hope. Neither patient nor therapist are much interested in learning from the experiences they jointly have. The therapist has already learned all he wants to know from elsewhere and is impatiently (or even patiently) awaiting the opportunity to deliver himself of some portion of it. The patient, far from attending to himself and what he is experiencing, is behaving like a contestant in a quiz show — say the magic word and you receive the revelation. Therapists who can forget their preconceptions — and obviously this is tremendously difficult; one has after all invested so much hope in studying, learning, gaining wide experience — but, therapists who *can* forget their preconceptions *must* learn from each given patient.

However, even clearing away the therapist's hopes from and for therapy and in and of himself will not by itself bring crises of hope to the fore. The patient for whom hope is the matter will have his hopes deeply invested in activity. It is as if no sooner does he begin to experience crises of hope than he swings into actions designed to forestall these. And once he does that he cannot speak of his hopes because in the realer sense he does not experience them.

A patient tells of a fight with a girlfriend: he may be hoping — Now do you see what you mean to me?

A patient is silent: he may be hoping — Now do you see how bankrupt your methods are?

A patient tells a dream. What we should consider is not so much the meaning of the dream but what it is that induces this patient, having an experience, to express it in images and convey it in that form to us.

Similarly, here is a patient.

She struggles for hope. She is "afraid to close any door." She tries desperately "to keep her options open." She is afraid of closed spaces, of elevators and airplanes particularly. The elevator will get stuck, the plane can crash. Even seeing a plane disappear behind a cloud fills her with panic. She imagines the people as shrinking to the proportion of the dwindled size of the departing plane — until "they are small creatures inside this long tubular thing." When she has to fly, she thinks to take tranquilizers or a drink or two. But then, once she has swallowed these, they are in her for good and there is no reversing the process. Thus both entering and being entered are torments of irrevocable finality.

The material here, a few minutes from a single session, is rich with symbols and unconscious equivalencies; knowing the patient, one could interpret it with relative ease. But the material is narrative; its substance, so far, takes place outside the session. If one interpreted the penis-breast equivalencies, the castration fears or the fantasies about intercourse, conception, and birth, the patient would gain insight but something of great momentum, not yet evolved, would escape the session. In fact, interpretation under the circumstances would probably serve to bind and make coherent something not yet experienced in all its incongruity and incoherence. In other words, interpretation would serve as a defense. Like the narrative of the patient, the interpretation would talk about an experience not present in the session.

Narration is spurious. It gives an order and meaning to experience that the experience is unlikely to possess. When Plato was pondering who should rule the Republic, he decided against the artist on precisely these grounds. The artist, he felt, gives a verisimilitude to nature that is meretricious. As Trilling (1971) says:

> It is the nature of narrative to explain, it cannot help telling how things are and even why they are. . . . But a beginning implies an end, with something in the middle to connect them. The beginning is not merely the first of a series of events; it is the event that originates those that follow. And the end is not merely the ultimate event, the cessation of happening; it is a significance or at least the promise, dark or bright, of a significance.

Narration, then, is the language of action; it presents not an experience but a semblance of an experience; it is told for effect. And while being told, it may hold such thrall for the therapist that he may become more taken with what is being told him than with how and why. Since, however, the object of the psychotherapy is to divorce hope from its various vestments and activations so that it can become an experience capable of being experienced, the therapist will do better to wonder to what purpose this is being told him than to succumb to the temptations of searching out the contents of the story and replying to these with an interpretation that, after all, is likely to be a narrative of his own.

So far I have suggested a series of renunciations — of hope in therapy, in one's prior knowledge, in one's person — followed by a series of restraints: from engaging with the meaning instead of the purpose of what patients communicate, of attending to narrated rather than currently experienced events. This is no easy prescription, partly because we are better trained in the psychotherapy of problems around desire. But if one recalls the peculiarly paradoxical nature of hope, namely, that it fears fulfillment as much as frustration, for both produce hopelessness, one can see that fairly special measures are required.

Let me now assume that the therapist has managed all of this and that crises of hope have begun to evolve. As these crises of hope evolve, they must be worked with minutely. The aim now is not their emergence but their reconstruction. But little help can be expected from the patient, who is likely to have become outraged or spiteful, depressed or apathetic, mute or as changeless as he can be. It will be for the therapist to put things into words.

Even so, the patient should be expected to adopt towards the therapist's words the aloof, haughty attitude of the suicide, a prospect which, of course, is never far distant. The therapist will accordingly need always to be mindful of how persecuting the patient finds his interpretations. For example, with the patient whose session I have excerpted, I need to acknowledge that an exceedingly frightening part of periodic sessions is that out of envy I will ruin her enjoyment of her penis. Or, equally, that she will do so to mine and so will no longer have someone to acquire a less defective penis from.

The point to bear in mind is that when the patient has got past attempting to activate his hopes and has let the crisis evolve, the resulting experience is so immediate, so "now" as to be veritably real. Interpretations, accordingly, need no longer be tutorial or explanatory: they need simply describe the experience that once, and now again, derived from the preconception involved, but which, to protect the hope, became transfigured out of recognition and recall.

When the total experience — the preconception, the experience, and the untransfigured experience of the experience — is available to the patient, that portion of the therapy is complete: the research has been done, in vivo, as it were, and the discovery made. In time, the task of the therapy will become the more familiar analysis of problems with desire.

SUMMARY

I do *not* split hope into good and bad hopes, normal hope or delusional hope, necessary hope or dispensable hope. To my mind, that would be like saying that hope is better than desire or desire better than hope or stars better than molecules. Stars are: hope is.

The preconceptions out of which hope arises concern the following:

> the quality of the breast; the ownership of the breast;
> the quality of the mouth; and the ownership of the mouth;
> the quality of the feces; and the ownership of the feces (or sphincters);
> the quality of the genitals (often their size); and the ownership of the genitals;
> the qualities of the parents; and the ownership of those qualities;
> the qualities of one's group; and the ownership by one's group;
> the quality of life; and the ownership of life.

Though several of these preconceptions conjoin with the familiar developmental orientations of desire, desire and hope are different. Desire is sensual; hope is not. Desire arises from the cyclic, appetitive passions of the body; hope appears to arise from preconceptions of how things should be. Desire seeks gratification and surcease—it is kinetic; hope is possessive and potential. Desire likes the here-and-now, the definite, the actual; hope likes the yet-to-be, the changeable, the ambiguous. When thwarted, desire tends to retreat, we call it "regress," to its last best success, while hope goes forward, beyond even a lifetime or outward beyond the confines of probability. Desire, frustrated, gives rise to rage and jealousy; hope—to outrage, and to envy and spite and revenge. When renounced, each, however, gives over to sadness; but desire changes its object while hope changes over to desire.

It follows that in the treatment situation, the therapist need neither a painter nor sculptor be: he need neither infuse hope (or desire) nor pare it away. But by revoking his own hopes, he will make it possible for his patient's hopes to move from being vested to being experienced and thus to being subject to analysis and reconstruction.

2

TOLERATING
NOTHING

A poem Carson McCullers read to (wrote for?) her psychiatrist upon her hospitalization in Payne Whitney:

What the No-thing Isn't

When we are lost what image tells?
Nothing resembles nothing. Yet nothing
Is not blank. It is configured Hell:
Of noticed clocks on winter afternoons, malignant stars,
Demanding furniture. All unrelated
And with air between.
The terror. Is it of Space, of Time?
Or the joined trickery of both conceptions?
To the lost, transfixed among the self-inflicted ruins,
All that is non-air (if this indeed is not deception)
Is agony immobilized. While Time
The endless idiot, runs screaming round the world.

There are some people for whom there is no such thing as nothing. In their psychic calculus, zero does not exist. Inside the zero, where there might otherwise be an absence, there is instead a presence of an absence. One patient, later, when he could afford to be whimsical, described the no-thing inside the zero as a breast sticking its tongue out. What follows are some of the ways I have come to think about this intolerance of nothing.

One way of thinking about it and the way it has mostly been thought about is that what is discovered in the nothing is what has been put or projected there: the self's sadism or beneficence is evacuated into the object and "discovered" there. I have no difficulty with this formulation. I think there are circumstances in which the aggression induced by frustration or explosions of desire is simply too much, and some form of decompression needs to take place. But this is a temporary affair.

Then there are circumstances in which this frustration induced by the absent or otherwise unsatisfactory object is evacuated not into it, but into an internal representation of it, which also represents the self. This representation precurses the superego and requires of the self that the self locate the remaining affection and disaffections elsewhere. This is the motive for the projection that Freud described when considering the homosexual fundament of paranoia. In Kleinian terms, it is a version of projective identification when the object takes on valued but troublesome aspects of attributes of the self. But this also is not quite what I think is involved.

Rather, I think there is something in some human natures that abhors a vacuum. "I see what you are saying," says one patient, "but as you know it makes no sense to me. When the pain is so steady and so continuous, how can I not believe she is doing it to me. When she was away last weekend, it stopped. I was in peace. I got some work done, for a change; I even cleaned up my apartment. Then around four o'clock on Sunday . . ."

Ψ: The torment resumed. She might have been back.
P.:   Yes. Would she call? Should I call?
Ψ: A steady stream of emissions; an unending current of pain.
P.:   Well, when she's not there, the agony isn't there. I don't say she causes it, just that she does it.

In this patient, like others of his ilk, the concern is not with motives, as it is with patients who are projecting intentions they do not wish to have associated with themselves. Rather, as he is hoping to make clear, his experience is of a malignant, not a malevolent, emanation. He, at other times, complains bitterly of what he has to do for her (and me) to get the malignancy stopped, or at least ameliorated, but he does it all the same. Deeply rooted in his belief system is that there is good in her, if only he can bring it out. He hates any thing in himself that can be understood as implying he overrates his capacity to inflict good or evil. Cause and consequence are blurred, but there is nothing that doesn't contain one or the other.

NOTHING AS A CONTAINER

If there is no such thing as nothing, then what may seem like nothing turns out to be a no-thing containing a some-thing, as the zero was a breast sticking its tongue out.

Regarding that image, children (and older people sometimes, as well) stick their tongues between their lips when they are concentrating—for example, at 4 or 5 years, forming letters on a page. The body language there seems to be, "Don't bother me now; I'm trying to express something; I'm not, at the moment, receptive." This same gesture easily lends itself to defiance and even insult, in the stuck-out tongue: you have nothing to offer me, so there! The breast with the tongue protruding where the nipple might be condenses these images, as if in a dream. The breast says: "You have nothing to offer me, so there!" This breast is a container that has everything.

However, the reciprocal to that sort of breast, namely the infant, needs the breast in two ways. It needs to take nurture and succor and pleasure out and it needs to put overstimulation in. It is the latter function that the breast with the protruding tongue seems particularly to blockade. The breast may express well enough, but it is unreceptive.

The expressive function of part—and later, perhaps, whole—objects is so obvious and so well known that I shall set it aside and consider the breast that contains so much that it is unreceptive. Is it that unreceptivity that constitutes the malignant thing that is the no-thing in nothing?

THE CURE FOR DYING

Some infants, more than others, may have an idea that they ought to die, if not now, soon, if not acutely, chronically. I think the idea comes with the genes; it is part of the Darwinian scheme of things, a scheme that I think is more potent in infancy than later, simply because infants have to go on lots of inherited reflexes and such until they can learn things from the family and culture. But as analysis shows, primal programmatic urgencies continue throughout life, showing through like pentimenti when people have setbacks and losses.

In the Darwinian scheme of things, some flourish, some falter. Choosiness is built into the system, such that the fittest display characteristics that assure them (and theirs) advantage in sending their genes into the generational gene pool. Big territory, big tail, big talons and talent are rewarded by being chosen.

But of course this process is not at all fang and claw. Contests for advantage are intense, but brief. The winner shows mercy, the loser deference. This too is programmed in. Some survive, some give way; some dominate, some defer. This process is in effect in territorial disputes, mating contests, and, of course, concerning the pick of the litter.

I think some babies need to ask the breast about their fate. I can't prove this, of course; even the children in my child practice have grown out of infancy by the time I encounter them, and the transference waters are by no means transparent. But I think so all the same, and I tell the children and grown-ups who can tolerate nothing so.

That is, I think the infant who has a dread, a premonition, that it must die puts that sense of impending doom into the breast and awaits the results with bated breath. What I think it wants to hear is: There, there, it's all right, you'll do, not to worry. This is different from a feeding, however munificent, and it has to be personal, not general.

I referred to an idea or premonition. I don't think it an idea in a sophisticated sense or a premonition of a defined fate. Nameless dread or intimation of a terrifying imperative might describe it. When I imagine I encounter it later, in the consulting room, it has a psychosomatic quality — not in the sense of a particular illness, with its acquired symbolic meanings, but in the sense that the dread makes the respiratory and alimentary and vascular systems all awry.

The cure needs to be a personal, not a general, reassurance. By this I mean the baby needs to be sure that it is known; otherwise it will suffer all life long from the idea it is an imposter and in danger of being horribly unmasked. I think there is a way some mothers know their babies and other mothers can't see the baby for the preconception. Preconceived babies have a difficult time getting emotionally conceived, let alone born. As the baby goes about trying to get some idea of who and what he is, he will naturally hope that what he discovers directly about himself enjoys some congruence with what Mother and Father know — even if the knowledge does not reflect well on him. There is a narcissism that is a consolation prize, involving being made much of; but the mirroring that stimulates growth requires fidelity, not flattery.

MEMENTO MORI

The imperative to give over and die feels like one were under orders.[1] Of course, if the mother hates the infant, only a very kind fate can rescue it. But we are here concerned with a baby that is trying not to internalize that hate and is therefore looking to a breast to denature it — to rob death of its sting. Must I die? NO: some babies must die, but not you, not yet. For babies, I think this is what being and feeling loved is all about — and, it may be, for others, too.

I am now ready, like the infant itself, to put the two ideas together. The presence of the absence, the malign force, is the conjunction of the breast and the imperative. The breast has refused in its receptive function either to take

---

[1] Readers of Iris Murdoch's novels will be particularly familiar with this experience, for she articulates it with precision and moment.

the threat into it — to take it in as a matter of the utmost seriousness — or to return from its container function as experience of exemption. This, as it were, implicates the breast, which is now experienced as radiating death. The infant leaves a vacuum — hoping, as it were, that the jury is still out — but what it gets back is nothing. It is left to its fate. And given that fate, there can be nothing worse than nothing.

The primary persecution — the unbearable absence of the absent — I have been describing (and attempting to distinguish from projections of motive or intentions) means that the people so plagued grow up with unusual reserves of stubbornness and a feeling that they must continually infuse the other with something the other will accept and use and eventually give back in the form of an exculpation or exemption. At the same time there is at work a vengeful and vindictive spirit, all the more virulent since the blood-price has already been paid. That price is considered paid by virtue — by virtue of the self having been obliged to live under a perpetual sentence of death.

In the consulting room this presents a sometimes puzzling picture of temerity and passivity, of self-sacrifice and vengefulness, of guilt without contrition and of hatred without anger. Perhaps most oddly of all, such people appear to feel of all things "entitled," as if they were free to demand anything and to give nothing. But this, of course, is the condemned man's last meal. (I shall return to this point later.)

"FORT — DA"

It will not have escaped many readers that we may be back on the road to Thanatos, upon which so many analysts wish Freud had never set foot. But it is with a difference. Freud follows out a particular thread. He is baby-sitting. His grandchild is hurling a wooden spool from its crib. "Fort — da," it orders, and its grandfather dutifully returns the spool to its young master, who, of course, hurls it forth once again. Repetition — symbol — ritual — omnipotence. Then: repetition — compulsion, the trauma dream, the exception to the Pleasure Principle. Then Duality, the zest for life and the arcing return, the great parabola, toward nirvana, death, and inorganicity. The cell reproduces itself a limited number of times — period! In its DNA there is a stopping point, beyond which. . . .

I am saying something other than this. I am saying that in what for some people is an absence, a void, an echo, there is for others a presence, a menace, and a pain beyond measure. Nothing doesn't feel like merely nothing, but as a no-thing filled with malign and dreadful implication. These people, despite the evident fact that they were conceived, gestated, and born, have not come fully into possession of their lives.

There is a story regarding Samuel Beckett, the Nobel laureate, for the authenticity of which I cannot vouch. But to my ear it has a ring of truth to it, so I will relay it. Beckett was in therapy with Wilfred Bion. This was in the 1930s, well before Bion had qualified as psychoanalyst. The therapy was limping along. There were periods of communication and understanding, alternating with periods in which Beckett was ill and mute and hardly there. At these latter times Beckett would begin to muse about going home to Ireland and his mother. Bion would remind him of how disastrous and debilitating those visits always were, and Beckett would nod and leave for Ireland. At length Bion saw that whatever was in this cycle was still inchoate to both himself and his patient, and so he made no efforts to dissuade Beckett from ending the therapy. Instead, he invited Beckett to a farewell dinner, after which they strolled over to the Tavistock, where Jung was lecturing.[2]

Jung's lecture concerned a young girl he had seen, one of whose dreams foretold her early death. But what impressed Beckett was the interpretation of this condition. Jung put it that the girl had been born before she had had a chance of coming fully and securely to life. So that although she had had her nine months in the womb and was presumably of normal health, she was psychically frail and hung to life by a thread.

This, Beckett felt, described himself to a T; this was the interpretation he had been looking for; this is what drove him again and again to his mother and away again feeling deader than ever. Beckett made this the theme of more than one of his novels — *Malloy Malone Dies*, and particularly *Murphy*, which he wrote not in his mother tongue but in French.[3]

The spool of Freud's grandchild was interpreted by Freud to represent the absent mother and the "Fort — da" the magical control of the absent object. An alternative view of the spool might have been that it represented not the mother but the child itself, who felt flung away and needed to be regathered and restored. Otherwise why follow the thread to the looming presence of Death when an object relations view would have been the more obvious and parsimonious one?

---

[2]Jung was, of course, a great one for inherited archetypes, the racial unconscious and that sort of thing; and Freud was at great pains to put and maintain distance between them. Alix and James Strachey's correspondence during the 1920s on their translation of Freud's writings shows their care in finding words that didn't "Jungize" Freud's ideas. But in the ongoing questions of Nature vs. Nurture, Freud continued to move to "Nature," nowhere more so than in *Beyond the Pleasure Principle* of 1925. His critics argue that his choices between the nature of the psyche and the nurture of the child followed what he could believe of his own life history. Thus one could note that in the early '20s he was analyzing Anna, whose life history he may have felt he had reason to know!

[3]I am indebted to Margery Sabin of Wellesley College for calling my attention to Bair's (1971) biography of Beckett, from which I recount this story.

COMING FULLY TO LIFE

People for whom there is no such thing as nothing cannot, in Gertrude Stein's elegant phrase, believe "there is no there there." They have perforce to describe *some*thing and what they describe is an experience tantamount to a kind of pure paranoia. In life-historical terms they describe the usual instances of visited pain—bad parents doing bad things. But in these recitations the effect on the analyst they strive for is not sympathy or an alliance of anger or even to have their suffered disappointment made up to them. Rather it is a search for validation: Yes, it did happen; yes, it was terrible. Given any other response, such people feel profoundly misunderstood, even trashed. During particularly long and arduous seiges when the patient simply sees no further use in talking and I am given to feel that my own lack of receptivity is deadening if not veritably deadly, the worse because I am taken to know what is needed and my density is only apparent, not real, I wonder why the patient doesn't leap up from the couch and go to a therapist who can sympathize.

The answer, I think, is that the patient knows something about the doubts that propel these urgent needs for affirmation and validation. That is, the patient senses (later, knows) that the events he or she is narrating are emblematic and factitious.

Now there is something in the practice of psychoanalysis that is different from psychotherapy, and that is the analyst's resolute search for meaning. We, in our way, also say there is no such thing as nothing; everything, we say, has meaning; there is always more there than meets the eye.

> What we call "seeing the lawn" is only an effect of our coarse and slapdash senses; a collection exists only because it is formed of discrete elements. There is no point in counting them; what matters is grasping in one glance the individual little plants one by one, in their individualities and differences. And not only seeing them: thinking them. Instead of thinking "lawn," to think of that stalk with two clover leaves, that lanceolate, slightly humped leaf, that delicate corymb. . . .[1985, p. 33]

That is Italo Calvino speaking telescopically through his Mr. Palomar. But, closer to home, here is W. R. Bion.

> To the analytic observer, the material must appear as a number of discrete particles, unrelated and incoherent. The coherence that these facts have in the patient's mind is not relevant to the analyst's problem. His problem—I describe it in stages—is to ignore that coherence so that he is confronted by the incoherence and experiences incomprehension of what is presented to

him. . . . This state must endure until a new comprehension emerges.
[1980, p. 15]

These qualities of thought provide to the patient the mind he needs in order to come fully alive. He will do so not by verbally pouring his heart out but by projecting and reprojecting fragments of himself into the analyst.

SPLITS, FRAGMENTS, AND TWINNING

The experience that threatens to be recapitulated in the transference reinvokes the dread and the fury the patient must originally have experienced if the patient did not continue to use a particular array of protective maneuvers.

Perhaps foremost among these is the use of pain as an anodyne for pain, or more precisely physical pain as an anodyne for mental pain. This surrogation appears to serve dual purposes. In the first instance, it does offer relief, of a sort, from the more diffuse and nameless pain of persecution without villainy. And in the second it brings into the transference ways the patient when infant and child found to exact a concern, even if falsely extracted and falsely given from the parent. It is to be remembered that it was not the provisioning aspect of the breast that was problematic, but its receptive function.

But there is a third purpose, too. The anxiety the infant experienced was so primary as to be almost as much somatic as psychic. Thus in the consulting room as these crises reemerge, the patient is likely to approach states of somatic shock. Blinding headaches, pallor, trembling, dizziness, palpitations, erratic respiration are all likely to occur. But simultaneous with these states, the patient, emotionally, will feel relatively nothing—for a change!

Needless to say, from the beginning the patient will have felt untaken care of. If he or she survives (I put it this way because I think there are likely to be infants and children who don't) it will have been through the development of a certain kind of precosity, one in which the infant prematurely becomes caretaker to itself. The precocious self is, however, hated. It is a false self jerry-built to save the real self from catastrophe. The false self is so enlarged in this dualization of function and image as to jeopardize the continual existence of the real self. In the analysis the precocious self (I prefer that term, for the term false self has, from Winnicott, a somewhat different and yet precise meaning)—the precocious self, then, is very wary of the analyst. If the analyst allies himself even in the slightest degree with the "exact replica," as one of my patients called it, the patient feels his not-yet-fully-alive self is being doomed. Here is a dream that puts all of this quite plainly:

A woman put me in charge of her babies, only they weren't babies, just formless protoplasms, shapeless like amoebas or paramecia, horribly dressed up to look like babies. But they weren't and one was even slipping out of its clothing, bonnets and such, and even out of the carriage or basinet. It was the smaller and more ill-formed of the two, and it was just slipping away, and I was trying to hold onto it. I suppose this is one of those other breast dreams (this is added bitterly) but my mother always said she thought right up till the end that I was twins.

The reference here to the so-called other breast is to an interpretation in which I told this patient that I could imagine an infant held to two entirely ample breasts starving because it could not stand the pain of losing the one upon choosing the other (see Boris 1994). Soon after this interpretation "took," the patient had the first of the twin dreams. In that one the twins were merely heads or headlike things on either end of a rigid tube that made putting both the infants to the breast impossible. The tube was an I.V. tube, also implying a Siamese-twin image. The patient was letting me know that my interpretation was correct, as far as it went, but things were not nearly so simple as that.

The agonizing sense of disparity between the twins is echoed in the following. (The association following the story was to a girlfriend who had a twin sister and how special that must have been.)

There was a story, the worst and most upsetting story, supposedly a children's story, though how anyone could suppose children would not be horrified by the story, I don't know, can't imagine, about a time when the birds and babies understood one another, talked a common language. Then not only did the babies outgrow the language — but this is the awful part — they forgot they ever could talk to the birds. But the birds remembered and they couldn't understand why the babies weren't as upset as they were. I mean, it's one thing not to be able to talk anymore, but for one to forget he ever talked and so never to know what makes the other so sad is just horrible . . . terrible.

I don't want to suggest that the twinships invoked or implied in these communications are merely self-self realizations. The fury at and envy of the no-thing and what it contains or could contain is such that it is the target of desperate attacks designed to demobilize and demolish its powers of frustration and torment. In his paper on the Imaginary Twin, Bion emphasizes — may I say it — the twin attacks: One splits the breast, the other the self and, indeed, the ego. These splits are then resymbolized along the lines of the Prince and the Pauper, Dr. Jekyl and Mr. Hyde, true self and false self, good breast and bad. This is the position on matters that Melanie Klein called the paranoid-schizoid position. As Bion (1950) puts it: "Only when I had been able to demonstrate how bad I was at all levels of his mind did it become possible for him first to recognize his mechanisms of splitting and personification and then to employ them, as it were, in reverse, to establish the contact they had been designed to brook" (p. 19).

Bion's model in this paper and its cohorts (e.g., "Attacks on Linking," 1959) is of the perception of a pair who are enjoying and flourishing in an intimacy from which the developing infant feels excluded. Its hatred of the emotions these realizations generate, and "therefore, by short extention, of life itself," stimulates the "murderous attack on that which links the pair, on the pair itself and on the object generated by the pair."

I am plainly placing my emphasis on the "by a short extension life itself," which quickly complicates the experience no end.

SURVIVING

Even a cursory reading of the material from the patient I have cited will reveal the poignancy of the guilt experienced by the survivor. One will live and one will die; one will grow and the other will be forgotten: and it is too unbearable.

In this regard, tolerating nothing takes on a second meaning. The patient now *must* tolerate nothing. Any degree of flourishing, any hedonic pleasures, any development toward well-being, and the fragile connection is severed and the Other dies. Perhaps, needless to say, this means that the patient is not allowed to use analysis to get well in. If development is to take place it has to be on the analyst's head that the implacable blame will fall. This contributes to the patient's need to communicate through projective identification.

A word, therefore, on projective identification. The refusal, as it seems, of the breast to take in the infant's idea that it may have to give way and die seems (if recapitulation in the transference is any guide) like a perverse and deadly mirror that merely refracts and sends back what has been brought to it. Lacan justly uses the mirror motif as an explanation, within his system, of the terrible otherness of the Other. This cool refraction drives the baby toward greater and greater attempts at penetration, mobilizing its native sadism and what it increasingly comes to regard as the sadism of the refraction. When these, as it seems, are then again merely refracted they begin to further endanger the infant, who then can only slow and muffle its attempts to extract what it needs. The precocious self develops and sees to it that the protoplasmic self (to use my patient's image) is not endangered from the emission of refractions.[4] The ruthlessness of the self in respect to the Other—the Other being now the proto self and the breast—is tempered severely by the murderous and envious wishes for the demise of the Other.

---

[4] For the relationship of this dynamic to anorexia nervosa and bulemia, see Boris (1994), *Sleights of Mind*.

Then comes a point when the precocious self can no longer ask. It must dawn on the other to give. Of the patients I have been considering in preparing this communication, one was almost totally silent over the two and a half years of therapy, one speaks but is mostly inaudible, and a third speaks as if reporting someone else's experiences. If anything is to be known it is through my getting the idea. A fourth has yet to make any of the usual commitments to analysis. Each session is de novo. These seem to be conditions for survival. Yet, paradoxically perhaps, the very diffidence of such individuals is extraordinarily entitled and taxes one's empathy to the limit. One has daily to experience and cope with a powerful wish for their death; nothing less.

GETTING THE IDEA

By far, then, the largest part of what patients of the sort I have been discussing communicate is in the form of projective identification—which is to say they project and the analyst identifies. This is a special sort of relationship.

The transference relationship, it could be said, deals with the expressive function of the object—the breast, penis, and vagina as provisioners, the parents as lovers and rivals, the anus and its productions as coins unto the bargain. Lust and love, envy and jealousy, hatred and rivalry are the states of mind that pertain to this state of affairs.

The people I have been describing bring these interplays into the transference of course, and the tensions and alleviations that characterize the libido and its vicissitudes are dynamic. The projective identificatory relationship, in contrast, is static—fixed.

Since "projective identificatory relationship" is a piece of jargon of a particularly awkward sort, I shall now abandon it and replace it with the expression: getting the idea. People in this disposition resolutely work at invoking and evoking until the analyst gets the idea. The plan is that the analyst has to get the idea and give it back. The patient experiences great anxiety lest he is the first to get the idea. Verbal communication of the sort I am at the moment doing, in which I have an idea or two that I would like you to consider, is not at all their method of operation. Because they cannot tolerate the experience about which it might be possible to have an idea, the moment they have an inkling of the experience, they project it. If they are lucky, they can project it before the idea dawns or even the experience is experienced as anything more than a premonitory tremor. Such projections have, however, to be received and assimilated. The paranoid personality, especially the psychotic personality, who deals in projecting characteristics and intents, can also distort and disfigure the receiver, who is then perceived as harboring what is projected. But when the projection is meant to be received intact in the hope that the receiver will detoxify, sanitize, moderate, or clarify it, the intent of the projection is not to defile or ravage the receiver.

The problem then is: How can the patient give the analyst to know something the patient cannot stand to know and therefore has no words to tell it in? I am contrasting this with projections in which the patient doesn't want to know something is true of him but instead wants to believe it is true of the analyst. These disfiguring projections also occur, so it is important clinically and conceptually to know the difference.

This pattern of communication, of course, echoes preverbal communication. It does so because the issue at stake—whether or not one must give way and die—is preverbal, though it is not merely preverbal; for instance, it is reraised with the conception and birth of every successive sibling. But it echoes the preverbal state also because the danger of the question is such as to have successfully caused the question to be refused a conjunction with a verbal idea. The person grows up but the experience stays young—which is why I use part-object terms like breast rather than words like mother.

In the consulting room, then, the analyst must get the idea that these often verbally very sophisticated patients cannot communicate anything of significance in words. Indeed they do not value words except as things by which to evoke the emotional states within the analyst. These patients do not give information; they speak, or as often do not speak, for effect.

From their fruits, so shall ye know them . . . might be the principle these patients follow. The emissions they could not originally put into the breast are now insinuated into the analyst for him to metabolize, detoxify, or gestate as the case may be: and then to return them alive and well. Of course, there is an element belonging to the transference in this, but the essence of the activity is to get the age-old question answered. Its thrust is to achieve a secure birth.

3

IDENTIFICATION WITH A VENGEANCE

One person identifies with another out of a variety of motives. One is to share in qualities that elicit love; another is to express admiration; a third is to augment the self or the other ("I wish to associate myself with the Honorable Gentleman"), a fourth is to gain mastery and competence, a fifth is to acquire or assure identity. Then there are identifications made in a spirit of envy. These are not merely acquisitive; they are also designed to deprive their owner of the attributes in question. Indeed, as in the joke, "I'll never forget what's his name!" the idea that the once-owner of the characteristics around which the identification is made ever owned them is banished from recollection.

The process required to achieve this is somewhat intricate:

In effecting an identification of a more kindly sort, it is the very resemblance between the two people that is the prize.

A youngster is playing at being a batsman. Home run after home run soars over the distant, imaginary wall. Presently the game changes. He now displays to his onlooker the various special characteristics of a number of all-star players, naming each in turn. He is pleased with how well he has "captured" these stars. Now the game changes once more. This time it is he who is at bat, but incorporated into his stance and swing are some of the very stylistic variations he had just displayed. It is plain that he is no longer like his admired heroes: he *is* them.

This is a shift from simile to metaphor. The likeness that links the child and his heroes has been erased. When this is noted for him, he smiles and says, "Like [Senator Joseph] Biden, huh?" In the response is another expression of identity, but the likeness is not only acknowledged but also necessary to express the affiliation.

In their extreme form, identifications driven by envy obliterate the likenesses between the twosome. The process employed is as follows. The original element is analogized, and to its analogy is linked a third analogy. The first analogy is severed, leaving only the latter two. Hence: Mother's fecund and marvelous reproductive capacity is no different from having a creative and productive mind. I have a fertile and productive mind. Therefore I have nothing to be envious of, for were there something, what could it be?

Identification is, of course, a fantasy given substance by mimetic activity. The likeness a youngster might wish to advertise in respect to his father or sports hero is, as the example illustrates, achieved through emulation in costume, manner, style, and deed. The more the likeness is faithful to the original, the better the fantasy is served. When envy enters the picture, however, the likeness is intended to disparage the original. The intervening analogy—the ability to conceive and bear children is equivalent to the ability to think or write—does some disservice to the mother, indeed to women more generally. The effort to express likeness contains the damaged equivalence: since I think and write, what is so special about Mother? Indeed, what has she that I don't have? But this is not a question; it is a scream of outrage. The answer, lest it arrive, is necessarily but resolutely seconded to oblivion: the breast is to the mouth as the thumb is to the mouth. The breast is a thumb, as, therefore, the thumb is a thumb. The thumb is therefore to the mouth. Teddy is to me as Mommy is to me. Teddy is to me as I am to me. Teddy is a Mommy which is a me. Ergo: what breast? what Mommy?

The logical scheme for these Wonderland feats is based on the destruction of the linkages ordinarily found in the analogy (see Bion 1959, 1970). The nonanswers to the unasked questions once established need urgently and passionately to be maintained; entire lives are spent with scarcely more object in view than assuring the absence both of query and reply. However, since the question and its implied answer threaten to come, explosively or chronically, to the fore in the transference, leading either to the abrupt termination or the ongoing nullification of the analysis, the issue is of more than theoretical interest.

In developing my lines of thought, I begin with a consideration of the nature of envy and go on to a brief exposition of the selective deployments of attention by which links and analogies are forged or undone. I shall particularly consider the analogic relation between mental acts and emotional or relational connections. Particular mental representations are, of course, used to portray object relationships in the way one wishes to experience them. But the *way* in which one thinks about others (broadly, specifically, piecemeal, disjunctively, and so on) is also used to effect and represent actions one wishes to impose on others. A severed mental link is used to reorganize the relationships one otherwise encounters. Splitting, condensation, displacement, repression, projection, and of course identification are all analogic to actual actions. Their analogic relationship can be so forgotten as to yield the impression that they are not analogies but veritable equivalents. Helplessly envious people feel their envy is served by such assertions of equivalence.

ON ENVY

In some people the greed we are all born with does not evolve securely into appetite. Even what appears to be quite adequate maternal care, for example, somehow cannot persuade the infant — as Mr. R. put it (see below) — to rent the breast instead of forlornly and furiously requiring to own it outright and wholesale. On the contrary, the more desirable the breast, the more disenfranchised the baby feels.

But even an undesirable breast excites greed and therefore envy. The undesirable but nevertheless coveted breast, moreover, cannot, in its absence(s) or its otherwise unsatisfactory nature, provide the consolation that the infant gains when it accepts what the good breast may ultimately have to offer. Thus the bad breast remains the object of greed and of envy longer and more intensely than the more desirable and admirable one. In this manner the infant is hindered in its efforts to let go of its greedy wishes to own and control the breast, while making do with the consolations of receiving. Remaining, as it does, an object to be attended to and contended with, the bad breast is more difficult for the infant to become oblivious of than is the good breast. This gives the breast an obtrusive quality, for while the baby won't take it, neither can he leave it alone. This is soon experienced as if it were the breast that does not leave the infant alone, for the good breast, *because* it satisfies, can be both remembered *and* forgotten. It seems therefore to surrender to the infant's sense of rhythm, timing, and interval. The unforgettability of the bad breast endows it with a persecuting element more potent than the infant's own will to become oblivious of (so to obliterate) it. This of course further stimulates the infant's envy.

Upon contemplating this state of affairs, many writers — Winnicott (1960), Bion (1962), Green (1983) among them — have come to see that in addition to having a provisioning, libidinal function the "good enough" mother must have a receptive one. She must "take in" the baby's dilemma and help the baby to go through its grief and grow out of its greed. For if it does not develop appetite, it only has its grievances as things upon which to nurse and gnaw. Without such assistance in mourning, the frustration of its intentions to possess the breast and not merely receive from it is all too likely to feel so unendurable that for the infant to take at all (more accurately, to *know* that it is taking) is to feel the loss of possibility as a pain too deep to be borne.

Such infants may be gratified in the sense of being provisioned. But for the baby to develop it is not enough for him to be gratified: he must also know that he is *being* gratified. This knowledge is a necessary precursor of knowing that there is a person there who is providing the gratification. Only with that realization — or acknowledgment — can gratitude become linked with what previously stimulated only envy. And only then can admiration grow up to become a reason for identification. Such identifications, in contrast with those motivated by envy, preserve for both parties the characteristics and qualities that previously were in such bitter contention. Without such assistance, however, without the secure evolution of appetite, the spirit of contentious-ness follows people throughout life: every choice is wracked with the pain of the unmade choices, "roads not taken." Thus every choice — the path to take in regard to work time or free time; whom to choose between one person and the next; when to do something, now or later; even what to feel and about what (see in this regard Deutsch's [1942] luminous paper on the "as-if" personality) — represents a source of pain. Nothing ventured is for such people nothing lost. They show up clinically as suffering not only from depression, but also from obsessive and schizoid personality structures, unable to choose without hating the choice they make. For them, hope continues only so long as possibility is not potentiated; the loss of hope to choice is thought by them to lead to hopelessness and despair and not, as with the more resigned soul, who has become capable of appetite, to a release and burgeoning of desire.

It is, thus, in the state of greed — the acquisitive expectation to have and control the object of one's desires, if by no other means than by controlling its very desirability — that envy arises to do its work. The urge to take charge of the envied object has several components to it. First, of course, is the denuding (an idea) and disparagement (an emotion) of the inherent value of the original. This makes possible what follows, namely the idea that the "knock-off" (the "as-if") is in every way the equal of the real thing. Simulation, facsimile, verisimilitude are considered faithful representations: hence the possibility of analogic replication. The hostility expressed in the generation of these fantasies and feelings — for mental activities are also considered tanta-mount to actual acts — is potentially a source of great guilt. That guilt, however, is contingent on the original object having or gaining any sort of worth. This is especially the case where the original gains or regains worth, at the same time that envy is still rife. For the guilt under those circumstances is a guilt still devoid of remorse or contrition. The imminence of such revaluation and guilt is defended against by a paranoid view of the object as one not only empty of worth but filled with menace. (In the case of Mr. T., below, the discovery of the mother as a person capable of stimulating longing is "stopped dead" by a departure of the patient from analysis for a while.) At the same time envious activity is stepped up. The individual at these times feels he simply cannot do enough of whatever it is that he considers the analogic equivalent of the original object's desirable and valuable quality. Repetition and quantity are used to counterfeit fineness of quality. To assure that the original's quality cannot be remembered, it is obliterated again and again. The goodness of the self is contrasted vengefully with the worthlessness and menace of the Other, producing a degree of entitlement that then off-sets the dawning of guilt. Since the Other is a victim of all these machinations of mind, which are thought to be the counterpart of a "hostile takeover," the Other is imagined to be additionally degraded—and so the source of additional talion terrors. One such terror is the feeling that the Other can read one's mind; it is linked with the fantasy that one's mental acts are the more powerful in that the Other doesn't know that he, she, or it is their victim.

The mother, as I have suggested, can help soothe the raw and ravaging envy by allowing the infant the illusion of owning the breast until such time as it can mourn and so grow to tolerate the fact that the breast does not belong to him. And at this point an identification with the breast as a benign and providing function becomes possible for the infant as a way of resolving through illusion the bitter loss and emptiness, the depression and rage, that otherwise might follow. Such illusions show up in mimetic activity—Mother gets fed, baby feeds itself with thumb or blanket, dolly and Teddy get fed and so sometimes does the new baby. The infant is throwing his or her lot in with the mother, as later it will do towards the rival parent in the spirit of resolving the tensions implicit in the Oedipus complex.

That there are, however, elements of vengeance even in such relatively benign identifications should be clear: the infant does not abandon its wish for ownership and control lightly. Thus even while an identification is taking place, and the infant or child is duly—and perhaps dutifully—enacting its likeness to the parent or his or her parts, it has not given up wishing to maintain the differences—of mouth, for example, from breast—and while maintaining them, continuing to enact his hegemony over the frustrating breast. There is a fantasy of control expressed in being able to be the same-as; it says: What is there to this? Anyone, can do or have or be it! Yet the "it" is preserved—the breast-mother or the penis-father survives the identification.

As in the example given above, the baseball stars are preserved. Their prowess is—to a degree slyly—employed to "smack" and "slaughter" the ball-breast and the balls-testes.

The relative benignity of this sort of identification needs to be noted, even, or especially, when its enactment appears to inflict hostile consequences upon the Other. I have in mind the two canonical instances of our field—the child practicing medicine or dentistry upon the doll and perhaps later the lover; and the Good Nazi syndrome (also observed in the Patricia Hearst hostage situations), in which the emotions aroused by being the victim give rise not to hatred and rebellion, but to emulation and identification. It is, I think, true to say that a good deal of hatred is repressed in the figuring forth of these identifications. Helpless passivity is converted into aggressive activity and the sexual fantasies stirred by being victimized are banished by repression, which repression is then further secured by the subsequent acting out of the victimizer role: but these, I think, however important, are not the primary impulse. Although vengeance is expressed in the stealing of the vanquisher's thunder, the identification represents a furtive admiration for the powers and gall of the oppressor. As identifications do, this identification with the aggressor ameliorates the helpless, guilty, and abject loving of him or her as a differentiated object. When this occurs in the training analyses of candidates, it is clear that a transference is being hidden under the identification— although *replaced by it* might be the better expression.

The conversion of greed into appetite is an event of the first importance. Appetite, as I have noted, is susceptible to satisfaction. Greed is not. In greed, which is a state of mind and of feeling—though urge might be the apter term— *any further gratification only further stimulates the greed*. In turn, this inaugurates a retreat from appetitive desire to greed and to attempts, rather, to identify with the object out of possessiveness. Yet these attempts are defeated by resurgences of desire, setting up a further round of failures that serve only to increase envy. Only when the baby can endure merely being fed does the experience become and remain tolerable.

Without the cessation of the torment (taunt, tantalization, and teasing) which the object seems to exercise upon the Self, hatred mounts and with it spite and a lust for vengeance. Poe (1927) had hold of this in his story "The Cask of Amontillado." I had remembered the particular horror of the story, but it was not until Mr. R. (see below) remembered his childhood fear of the basement in his parental house that I reread the story to see what I had forgotten of it. Poe writes:

> The thousand injuries of Fortunato I had borne as best I could but when
> he ventured upon insult I vowed revenge. You, who know so well the nature
> of my soul, would not suppose, however, that I gave utterance to a threat.

> *At length* I would be avenged; this was a point definitively settled—but the
> very definitiveness with which it was resolved precluded the idea of risk. I
> must not only punish, but punish with impunity. A wrong is redressed when
> retribution overtakes its redresser. It is equally unredressed when the
> avenger makes himself felt as such to him who has done the wrong. [p. 205]

This profound sense of insult is, of course, what makes envy so
peculiarly difficult for people who, without being able to tolerate it, nevertheless experience it—and also for those who are envied. When what the
Other has, good or bad, can only inspire envy, the Other must either be kept
from offering it or punished for being *able* to offer it. There is, in this
condition, no escaping the vengeful quid pro quo so vividly described by Poe.

The method of obliteration for the young and helpless cannot, however,
immediately be revenge. Unlike Poe's protagonist, they are too young and weak
for revenge: they cannot sack Rome or lay siege to Babylon, much less
immolate Fortune. Nor can they as yet "waste" others, not even themselves.
But if spite is the only means open, it is at least a port in the storm. To refuse
to take, to refuse to know one is taking, and to refuse to know there is aught
to take are felt to constitute safe harbors until revenge becomes possible
(Boris, 1984 a, b, 1988). As the latter two of these refusals has obliviousness
as its métier, to the matter of oblivion I shall turn.

But one other feature of the Poe story deserves to be noted, by way of
prologue to a consideration of oblivion. It is encompassed in the words *"At
length* I would be avenged; this was definitively settled. . . ." The reference to
time here refers to the difficulty the infant has in forgetting the bad breast;
how obtrusive it seems to him to be, and how obdurate about slipping away
as satiety sweetly issues forth. The "length" of time involved is hated and
becomes precisely part of the revenge. The protagonist will not make himself
known to Fortunato, who may therefore think, as time passed, he has been
forgotten. But what could not once be forgotten now will never be forgotten.
For Fortunato, too, there will be no such thing as "over."

OBLIVION

The innate capacity to pay attention selectively enables people of every age to
have some say in what they experience. Without such an ability, what we
experience would simply be imposed. With it the ego can interpose itself upon
the outcomes of the ongoing attempts to mate inner wish and outer
circumstance. Indeed (Poe's image may serve further as a metaphor here), it
is not too much to say that the very boundaries of inner and outer are
contrived by and from this selectivity in attending. Were it not possible first

to notice and then not to notice there would be no reprieve, no interposition of will and choice — of self and ego — between the raw data of sensory and cognitive experience and consciousness. Much depends on this. Without being able to weed out *this* in order the better to attend to *that*, both the construction and the destruction of experience would be impossible. This procedure is so simple that an infant can manage, and of course that is precisely its value: infants *can* do it — and do, as easily as they fall asleep and waken, look now at this, now at that. By the simple expedient of switching their attention from *this* to *that*, they can behold *that* and become oblivious to *this*. The elegance of this procedure is of course, twofold. It permits some portion of experience to gain the amplification of attention that it requires, while, at the same stroke, some other portion of experience is sent firmly off to nearer or further darkness. Needless to say, this ability is not absolute. Certain portions of experience cannot be dealt with so summarily. A gunshot will be heard willy-nilly. Moreover, experience that comes at once from perception and from memory has a double claim on attention. Desire when experienced in the presence of the object of that desire is unlikely to go unnoticed.

Yet the very simplicity of the process, the mere oscillations of attention, steered as if the wheel of an automobile, can do much to create and protect particular experiences and versions of a world. Paradoxically, however, it is the very simplicity of that process in which its vulnerability lies. For if one *notices* that one is creating one's world through the *legerdemain* of selective attention, that world will then seem no more substantial than a dream. The elusive elements of that creation would thus be ever open to self-discovery. To protect against what would otherwise be the transparency of self-deception, one must not only not notice something but not notice one is deliberately not noticing it.

The concept of the screen was of course at the very heart of Freud's metapsychology. It was the instead-of, the something else, the memory, perception of interpretation of events that reliably substituted a *this* for a *that*, an *either* for *or*.

Because since the screen — that self-created, subjective, solipsistic world — cannot seem to be what it is but rather must seem to be the one and the only true world, it is not secure from dissonant information coming from all sides unless the means by which it is created are also screened. For they too must seem true and measured and in all respects a faithful process of representing exactly and only what is so. The simple act of selectively paying attention must seem to be something different from what it actually is.

The screens by which acts of attention are given to seem more or other than simply what they are exist both in the collective life of theory and in the fantasy life of individuals. In theory they are given substantiality by being termed one or another of the mechanisms of defense—projection, for example, or the mote-beam maneuver. This reification provides a certain discreet veiling of the notion that one is blinding one's self to one's own motives or intentions by discovering them elsewhere. Yet note that even this choice of words—veiling, blinding, discovering—echo the eye motif of the reification, and help hide (!) the idea that we are simply talking about a deployment of attention.

In the fantasy of individuals, the particular deployment that we call projection is an act that cleanses the self while despoiling the other, and has attached to it ideas about exit places, transmittal characteristics, and entry points; often, indeed, involving looking. Such fantasies provide the necessary illusion that one is doing something other and more determinative than simply paying attention in a selective fashion. And because they do so, the acts they simulate become sources of anxiety or guilt. How one imagines one thinks is as much suspect to reactive feelings as any other act or deed. A patient who felt himself to be a "plagiarist" feared being stolen from or, more accurately, being stolen back from. To protect himself he wore wristlets that took the form of decorative string or bead bracelets or sweat bands (in bad times, both). These augmented his wristwatch, for in his fantasy, among what he was stealing was time. Later he was to pronounce: "There is no difference between adults and children, except size. Adults invent differences to give themselves power and prestige and to try and intimidate children." (For a detailed examination of this phenomenon, by which differences in kind are converted into differences only in degree and amount, see Chapter 5.)

But though overdetermined for each person's life history, some general items lend themselves to particular use as a screen. Mr. R., to be presented in some detail below, used anality as his model. He wished to maintain that what he could produce was no worse than, indeed no different from, what his mother produced—for example, in the way of babies and the food for babies. Once established, that analogy prevailed: not only was he the very model of a productive child—timely, organized, filled with material, diligent—he also regarded his cognitive processes as if they were means of production. This led to a stutter when thought, speech, and fantasies of evacuation became cognate. Inevitably, overwhelming despair attached to the possibility that his products and methods were not so impressive as to obscure any hint that women had something different to offer. His life, accordingly, could be characterized by the ascription, "He could not do enough." It was his most ardent claim and his deepest fear.

Anal analogies come relatively later; they are used because they are powerfully persuasive. For in fact the Mother often *does* want from the child activity and output that is easy enough for the child to confuse with his wishes for mothering from her. But before that analogy gets established, there are two others that serve. One is hallucination; the other, the use of other parts of the body-ego to represent the mother's parts and functions.

Freud wrote of the hallucination of the breast as the infant's attempt to provide for himself in the absence of the actual breast. This was later elaborated in the understanding of dreams as a whole as wish-fulfilling experiences by which absence, frustration, and defeats were set right. The use, however, of the hallucination or dream as the equal of the actual object or person, indeed the use of hallucinosis as a process superior to any discovery and encounter of the other, is another story. The former is meant to gain sweet oblivion, and then to compensate and console; the latter is intended to obliterate the real thing and to substitute an impostor for it. The case of Mr. T., detailed below, illustrates the occurrence of hallucinations when a gap would, if left for a moment, usher in realizations of the breast and mother.

The thumb and the transitional object can be used in the same two ways: to provide solace during those times when the real thing is absent — or, so to rival the real thing that the latter is cast into an oblivion that will be unmourned and unmarked. The thumb or Teddy can be like the breast or either can be as good as the breast; or either can be the breast in such a way that the breast is no longer. The process by which the substitution is made, when it is also screened to seem as if something other than a sleight of memory or perception, secures these surrogations. This is, of course, the function of the good analogy: it has a so-ness to it that makes one not disposed to look further. The Teddy, the dream-symbol, the good simile or metaphor are arresting; they seem like attention's true destination, journey's end. The idea that they conceal something further is shocking; it inspires, rather, disbelief. More-over, the idea that this has been contrived seems impossible, for how would it have been contrived? One has simply been paying attention to what *is!*

The ego must reconcile inner wish and outer possibility and sort through the analogues that it makes and discovers in the direction of increasing the goodness of fit. It is as important that the ways in which Teddy is *not* mother be understood as the ways in which Teddy is. This accomplished, the child can rest awhile with its illusions before going back to elaborating and discovering better approximations of the real thing.

When the ego is bound to regard the analogue as if it were real-er than real, so-er than so, and when it is further bound both to forget and influence others to forget the original article, it is seriously compromised. To that burden on the ego is added the ignorance of how it processes the vast and awful and wonderful potentiate of experiences it might be having were it not succeeding in having only those it has selected. That ignorance contributes to its helplessness. Add then feelings of guilt engendered by false analogizing — which is a kind of bearing of false witness, and it is easy to see how debilitated a person can become. People ordinarily try therefore to remain oblivious, at least of the guilt.

The ego can remain oblivious of that guilt, but only as long as the original object being maligned is not "discovered." But once the object — the breast or mother — is linked up again, the guilt becomes almost unbearable. It is defended against by a one-two punch of projection into the object of envious and otherwise malevolent intentions toward the self and thus arise both the rationale and the need for a spate of further attacks on the object. Yet as love and regard for the object threaten to return and, with these, tender feelings — a desire to protect the Other — the sock gets turned inside out, and the self becomes the target of its own hatred and envy and its own unexpiated guilt.

For people who have premised their entire lives on simulation and analogic replication, the idea that they are in analysis is mystifying. They more or less know where they are and with whom, but the question of what they are doing there is a puzzle. The easiest answer is that they are there because for some reason, perversely undisclosed, the analyst wants something of them — perhaps a cure of some sort, though of what that purported cure could consist is probably more a contrivance of the analyst's envy than something for the patient's well-being. The more the analyst disabuses such patients of this notion, the more apt they are to conclude that their idea, though true, is not at all popular with the analyst and had better not be brought up again. But the belief that the analyst is out to expose the patient to what in the world of business is called a hostile takeover, though it makes for a poor spirit in the working relationship, assures the patient that he need not discover a goodness that will first inspire such wishes in himself only then to encounter the guilt consequent upon such inhumane intentions.

As I shall try to show in citing the case illustrations that follow, the difficulty is that envy and longing tend to converge into greed or gluttony. This leads to a use of the Other as a parasite uses its host. It does not matter that this use is not actual; the way the Other is used in fantasy and in the way it is used, for example, as a recipient of repression and projections (without so much as a by-your-leave) is enough.

SOME CASE-BY-CASE ILLUSTRATIONS

Mr. T. came for analysis in his twenties, upon discharge from a military hospital where he had been placed owing to the onset of a psychotic state that had left him confused and disoriented. He had hallucinations. He saw the penis of whatever man he was looking at and felt the thrust of that or other, unvisualized penises, upon the surfaces of his body. He was penultimately to describe the latter as being like the thrust of a dog's muzzle, but, at the outset, the description he gave was of an effect akin to the buzz of those gimmicks concealed in the hand in order to startle the other party to the handshake.

As the analysis proceeded, where one might most expect references to his mother, there were silences akin to mutism; these were accompanied by increased bursts of hallucinatory activity. He attributed the silences to the preoccupying effect of his hallucinations, but I began to think it was rather the other way around. Periodically Mr. T. would return nostalgically to a treasured daydream. In this he was a sniper high in a tree in the depths of the darkest of nights, everything quiet around him, the other men asleep, the terrain still. The stillness and quiet, so much in contrast with the agitation of the hallucinations, put me in mind of the Wolf Man's dream and its undoing of the primal scene (Freud 1918). But in my initial approximations I was more general: I would interpret this as him being a parental presence awake as the little ones slept. In time, however, I interpreted the fantasy as holding in abeyance Mr. T.'s own wish for a mother awake at his bedside. The patient flew into a rage and left the consulting room, not to return for several days. Upon his return he instructed me never to say one word more about his mother — ever. "Even the time it takes to say her word costs me two bits," he said furiously. Manifestly the "two bits" referred to a quarter of a dollar, but I thought it encompassed a reference to the mother's nipples, which it might cost him great pain to remember and think about; they were positioned to bite him, so to speak. But now the combination of silence and hallucinatory activity threatened to drive him mad, so incessant was it, so impinging.

I interpreted this increased activity as the by-product of his effort to keep Mother out of mind. The mother was what Freud called the "negative" hallucination: "An attempt to explain an hallucination ought not to attack the positive hallucination but rather the negative" (Freud 1917, p. 232 n. 3). This interpretation was, of course, staunchly resisted by the patient, but gradually the following story emerged.

At the age of 5 the patient had been sent to overnight camp, where he had been desperately homesick and frightened, particularly at night. To ward off the dangers of the darkness and to keep from wetting his bed (there was more than a suggestion that this embodied weeping as well), he became insomniac. By morning he could scarcely function. (I felt fairly certain that this was a psychotic state, forerunner to his subsequent breakdowns at college and then in the service.) The camp authorities finally decided to allow him to stay with a man who raised dogs. (Inferentially, there is a question of whether at this time the mother was capable of having the child at home or was not herself too depressed.)

This proved a salvation of sorts. The dogs, Siberian huskies, proved an ideal receptacle for his own warded-off urgencies. He could project into and identify with them, both at once. (Here was where, in the analysis, the muzzle thrusts became linked up with the tactile portion of the hallucinations.) And in caring for them, he could identify with the good bits of his mother. The problem arose when camp was over and he had to return home. He pleaded to be allowed to take home with him a puppy the kennel man had offered him. But his recollection was that mother would have none of it. He began to cry (unusual for him) and, in his tears, said something he could never quite remember. His mother's reply, however, he recalled only too well. "Oh, dry up! Who asked *you* to put *your* two cents in?" Telling this, the patient was, for the first time in the analysis, moved to tears, which he attempted quite literally to punch away.

It was at that time after camp that he took his revenge. Where in his care for the dogs he had maintained an identity with her, now (as with Fortunato) she disappeared — out of the links of the analogy. He replaced her, sui generis, with himself. First it was she, her breasts and nipples, who wanted him, and not he who wanted her. Next her breast was excised and replaced with the puppies' muzzles and Daddy's penis. These then nuzzled him — and not her. But he envied those penis-muzzles, and as soon as he could, began to try and acquire them: he began to exercise and lift weights as soon as puberty arrived. Soon he became a football player who "did not merely run over people, but ran through them." It was his failure to make first-string running back at the university, to which he had been generously recruited, that occasioned the first episode of hallucinations. Not only did he feel a return of the old camp loneliness, but he felt defeated in his effort to obliterate mother. Sitting around one day, watching baseball, the pitcher's fly appeared to open and out came . . . his penis. At least it wasn't her breast. But if Mr. T. didn't have the penis aspect of the breast, what did he have and who was he? And if he had the rest of what it took — whatever *that* was (he could not know this without knowing what mother had to offer), why was he being so sadly neglected? He joined the Marine Corps to regain the lost penis and so to live out the sniper-in-the-tree fantasy, which was to replace his earlier "three, two, one . . . He scores!" hero-of-the-game dream; but it took too long, and he needed to break down and make a fresh start.

Mr. R. was "allergic" to his mother from the start (probably he had a lactose metabolism problem). Starved for what also made him ill, condemned to spit up and out what he longed to have and to hold, he contrived to find a way of undiscovering his need of her by discovering hers for him. Straight away in the transference he did with me what it was his practice to do with others: he set out to help me to the point where he became my slave. Where others might complain of too little coming their way from myself, he was uncomplaining. To this there was one exception, and it was, of course, noteworthy. He complained bitterly that the fifty-minute session was all wrong. He wanted marathon sessions, for that was the only way anything valuable could get done.

This conception of matters was a masterpiece of ambiguity. He could state his complaint without having (in the words of the limerick) to notice who was to do what and with which and for whom. He insisted only that he could not work in arbitrary units: he was not "built that way."

Mr. R. was a little under a year old when a brother was born 2 months prematurely; a sister was born when he was 7. There seems no question that the mother encouraged each of her children to grow up quickly, but the brunt of this fell upon Mr. R. He, of course had his own reasons to try and outgrow his mother, so that in his case at least she was soon preaching to the converted. By the age of 9, much of this began to get elaborated in the fantasy that he was from an advanced era of time—à la Twain's (1889) *A Connecticut Yankee at King Arthur's Court*—and had merely used his mother as a vehicle by which to get to present-time earth. With his birth, her function in his life was complete. Later, when he was to look through Dr. Spock's baby books, he felt amazed that breasts were conducive of milk (Spock 1945).

A quiet, well-behaved child, he was frequently to be found at work making constructions of various sorts, one of the most absorbing of which was to draw and otherwise represent optical illusions.

Periodically he would emerge from these projects, take a microphone and tape-recorder and describe and interview his mother: "Let's move over to the kitchen now, folks, where Mrs. R. is, yes! cooking potatoes for the family. Could we have a word with you, busy as you must be?" His memory of his father centered on standing about holding the end of wood pieces that the father sawed or joined in his workshop.

He fairly boycotted his brother, putting as much distance between them as possible; but enacted for his brother's benefit a special relationship with their sister. This, among other activities, involved getting undressed and watching television, laughing uproariously at jokes he didn't understand. He was surprised to learn my "view" that this mimicked relations between his parents, in part because he remembered them as either always being out or entertaining at home or separately busy: for these memories he had one or two emblematic recollections. He remembered nothing of their sexual life, save a few remarks he could construe as meaning there wasn't much doing; this despite the fact that for a while he shared the parental bedroom.

He was terrified of that part of the family room where the "bodies" were "buried." These buried bodies were to turn out to represent the unborn babies that he had stifled or killed to protect his illusion that his mother, since she did not reproduce, had nothing on him.

As with Mr. T., there were breakthroughs of desire that kept the identification from evolving manifestly into homosexuality or transvestitism. These occurred during latency, when with various electronic devices he invented, he managed to keep himself awake until his parents returned from wherever they had gone or had come up to bed. It was his mother's custom to look in upon the children before she herself retired. Seeing that he was awake—he pretended to awaken only upon hearing her enter his room—she would sit on the side of his bed chatting a while before going off to bed. Her proximity brought him to paroxysms of desire. He would, in the guise of stretching, rub himself against the sheets experiencing as much frustration as pleasure, and at the same time an absolute conviction that despite his attempts at disguise, she knew very well what he was doing—what, more to the point, she was doing to him. This pretended innocence he found unforgivable, and it was therefore later to become an important part of his own makeup.

Never would he make an overture to a girl or woman. Rather he would insinuate himself, or allow himself to be put into proximity with the woman, affecting the same sort of know-nothing qualities he espied in his mother—not even looking when the woman preened or displayed, though seeing her very well—until the woman veritably forced the issue. Once he found a woman who tied him (loosely) while she looked at him and masturbated herself; this was just the ticket. (However, this same woman's practice of resting her forearms on a table and leaning her breasts upon them infuriated him to the point that on those occasions he would have nothing sexually to do with her.)

When otherwise involved sexually with women, he would go to great lengths to "satisfy" them, almost always via cunnilingus; as for himself, he would go home where he had a large collection of movies and magazines, find a picture that approximated the woman he had been with, and masturbate while looking at it. This not only deprived the woman of his excitement over her, but enabled him to replicate her, reestablishing an illusion of ownership. If engaged in intercourse, he would abstract the woman involved, until she became diagrammatic: the illustration in Tampax packets was the first edition of such an abstraction; later they became more detailed. But the idea of abstracting, in the sense of to remove and steal, was the same.

Mr. R.'s envy was resoundingly unconscious; he remembered his mother vividly, could describe her in great detail, would animadvert on her poor qualities with enthusiasm, and blamed her copiously for her betrayal of him. This consisted in all he had done for her and the zero, in the end, she did for him. He thought often of killing himself in front of her to show her what she had done to him. He was too intact not to notice the many ways in which he was like her, but he blamed her for those, after which the question of envy could not arise.

So too, the dominant feature of the transference was for a long and determined time a degree of puzzlement concerning what he was doing in analysis. That I wanted him to be there was clear: I had upped the sessions from the initial one or two to five; had him lie on the couch; and so on. My technique (unlike that of the woman who loosely tied him to take her pleasure of him) of course forbade me acknowledging my intentions, even from acting as if I had them (save for indicators like frequency of meetings), and it apparently didn't allow me to say what I had in mind in the way of outcome. However, from time to time I made interpretations, which though they might seem random and cryptic conveyed purpose or intent—or why would I say anything? Initially those periods in which I left him to his own devices worried him. Could it be that I needed nothing for him, let alone from him? (Later these periods of quiet "inactivity" allowed him to encounter his envy without at the same time feeling more envious than he could bear.)

There were, to be sure, other disturbing moments: dreams in which we sat by the fire: one or two where we kissed; one where we sat side by side on the couch and the others were gradually pushed off—a variant of musical chairs came into being. It was in this context that the memory of the fearsome basement family room first surfaced.

The degree of jealousy that developed in concert with these suggested the additional value of a position in which envy dominates. The father, as a whole person, becomes subsumed into an extension of Mother, namely her penis. The penis becomes, thereby, just another one of the attributes initially to be envious of, then to acquire through the identification. This is the more valuable since the identification with Mother's other attributes, if it is lock, stock, and barrel, to succeed, weakens the value of the penis. (Mr. T.'s need, after his failure to be the first-string running back, to restore the penis to himself in the form of a gun barrel, illustrates this concretely.) Indeed the penis is to a degree an obstacle to a vengefully obliterating identification. To have what Mother has decreases the value of the penis and increases the interest in castration. Hence anxieties over castration increase proportionately. From this position, to take on the father as an oedipal rival is just too frightening: better to subordinate him to the status of Mother's penis. This also serves envy's need to disparage and denude. Each evolution of Father/me as a beloved object was accordingly fought back.

With jealousy receding when envy acceded, Mr. R. could regain his rivalry with the mother over which of them had the better and which the poorer qualities. It became increasingly evident how little admiration had to do with his envy, for it was only after rudimentary sorts of gratitude developed that he could find her admirable at all. The progression went from an acknowledgment of his guilt to a sense that he mayn't have been an easy child for her to raise, to a realization that she coped with him in her fashion, to a dawning sense of gratitude and thence to furtive bits of admiration. By then he was no longer comparing her on an axis that consisted of which of them was better at the same sorts of things, to a double axis involving how they were different.

The last case in point is of a brief encounter with a 4-year-old at a lakeside after dinner. The older children were occupying the time between stories and sleep with a row out upon the twilight lake, but Jenny was deemed too young to go. As the boat pulled out of earshot, Jenny leaned over to me and remarked with a conspiratorial air:

"My name is Galen."

"I see," I replied. "Then that is not Galen out there in the boat?"

"No, that is Jenny."

Presently the boat turned back, and the other children's voices could be heard.

"I am Jenny again."

"Ah."

"Don't tell Galen."

"That for a while you were Galen?"

"People don't like to have their names stolen."

"Or their places in the boat?"

"Someday I'll be older."

"A consoling thought," I replied, feeling my age.

Discussion

Neither Mr. T. nor Mr. R. wanted to know any more than they had to about what they wished to receive from their mothers. More, they didn't want to know that their mothers had anything much of value to offer. They both established the belief that being like was as good as being the same as. With this in mind, they were able to find analogues for whatever of value their mothers might have had. These equivalencies, however, could not recall the original; if they did, the associative trail would be reestablished and not, as it was meant to be, severed. One thing was *not* to lead to another.

The analogues were in each case different, though the function was the same. In Mr. T.'s case, hallucinosis itself was deemed to be the counterpart of encounter and discovery. Muzzles (of rifle and dog) were analogized, and these were then used to represent the penis which was itself used to represent, occlusively, (or misrepresent) the breast and, especially, the "two bits," "two cents," or nipples. Thus could a story be told: I know nothing about mother. My rifle-penis-punishing body is what there is. Little children and big men muzzle me. It is very annoying, but what can I do?

Mr. R. also had a story. It also began with a know-nothing statement, for the provenance of the analogue is to be and remain unknown. Of course this introduces an air of mystification into a life. As a youngster, Mr. R. took care of it with the fantasy of being from another space-time like the (1972) Roeg film about a man from another planet who benignly travels to Earth but is malignly forced to remain here — *The Man Who Fell to Earth*. Mr. R's story was: there are amazing and wonderful qualities of mind and character, and to whomever possesses them all good things accrue. What puzzled him was that when good things did accrue, their value lay only in the support they gave the premise of his story. He could not fathom what he wanted because he could not bear to know. So long as the mystery remained, he had of necessity to substitute quantitative for qualitative sins of being good, better, and best. However, since he felt his mother used quantitative measures for herself, he had to use quantitative measures of qualitative things. Thus he was less materialistic than she, more subtle, tasteful, and loving. His diligence in "satisfying" women arose as a reproof of his mother for not satisfying him. But almost always he found women who would not reciprocate his concern for giving sexual pleasure, or at least not so sensitively and with such care and imagination; in this way, he prevailed.

His concern for having enough time was, of course, multideterminate. Since he believed there weren't enviable differences between him and his mother, those he discovered had to be put down to something, and like Jenny and Mr. T. he put them down to a matter of time. This was to explain why he could not "do" sessions with me: I refused to allot him the necessary time. This turned the qualitative situation into a quantitative one. But time in the space-time continuum is used to obliterate realizations concerning space — such as closeness, as in his dreams of being on the couch, sitting before the fire, or kissing. Such a use of time is dangerous. Jenny was momentarily intent on leapfrogging her years, but not so intent as to be unable to wait:

"Someday I'll be older." But Mr. T. ran out of time: and his psychosis effluoresced. His time-is-money attitude toward the mention of his mother also reflected the hurry-hurry-hurry position he felt himself in. Mr. R. was periodically suicidal, for when he ran out of time as an explanation, it was of no further use to him — and what else was there? The time in childhood to be *come* is not available to those whose need, so urgently, is to be. Neither of these patients saw much value to playing in their sessions.

Moving now further to the general from the particulars, it was difficult for each of these people to have to be on the receiving end of things. Only a very good set of experiences could, I think, have consoled or compensated them for so being. Were these forthcoming, the owner of the supplies received, the other, might have been admired and forgiven for having them to offer. Part of the "goodness" of supplies may be actual and consist in the care the mother or Other is able to offer. Certainly that care includes what the Other literally provides — his or her presence and constancy, and the nurturance and its abundance that follows. It will also include the receptivity of the Other to what the self experiences: the empathy, imagination, and "capacity for reverie" (Bion's term: 1962, pp. 36–37) that the other can make available, particularly as this related to the greed of the baby, its envy, and its difficulty in knowing and wanting to know who owns what.

This is so for the psychoanalytic encounter as well. Aside from whatever narcissistic gratification patients garner from being attended to so minutely and with such regularity by the analyst, the latter's ability to take the patient in, so to speak, must surely be a minor portion of the "psychoactive ingredient" in analysis. For we do not gratify our patient's libidinal urges; rather the reverse: those satisfactions we trust the patient will look for and, with luck, find elsewhere as the analysis proceeds. But the receptive function is as central to our work as it is to what infant and child care requires of the mother in the first place. The patient who does not come to feel essential for the analysis, but who rightly or wrongly feels that the interpretations would flow no matter what his or her contribution to the process, has a tutorial, not an analysis; and as a result, may learn much but will grow little. Deficiencies in being able to make one's self felt (not just heard) make it almost unbearable for the self to be on the receiving end without there being a danger of feeling it all spoiled by envy. Even when the getting is good, but especially when it is impoverished, the wish, otherwise consolable, to own or replace the source gets magnified beyond measure.

But shall it be left at that? Shall we say, well, this is what happens when the Other — for example, Mr. T.'s or Mr. R.'s mother (or Mr. X's analyst) is not quite good enough?

Or, shall we ask: to what extent is goodness (like beauty) in the eye of the beholder? When is good enough good enough? Are there preconceptions to which actual experience fits—or does not fit?

We do not assume *tabula rasa* any more; the concept of human nature as having not only impulses, but aims and objects, even if these are unconsciously elaborated, was an important part of Freud's contribution. Yet these are better known as part of the impulse life than as precursive ideations or hopes. Can we, indeed, stomach a thought that infants have ideas that are not learned? Can it be said that the goodness or badness of mothering, for example, has to do with the goodness of fit between a preconception and a realization? Can we say that the preconception—the hope—is the source of the greed? And that only painful resignation, in these instances, can be conducive to appetite despite the otherness of the Other (cf. Bion 1970; Boris 1976, 1986)?

For in both the cases I have related, I think there was a badness of fit: in Mr. R.'s case between his powerfully charged preconceptions and the mother and others he encountered; and in Mr. T.'s, not only between the mother he expected and hoped for and the one he found, but also between the infant and child his mother expected and the youngster she encountered. If this identity of mutual antagonism were the case, I would suppose it to be the rock on which they built his psychosis.

Mr. R., too, had an idea of how things should be, and he found what he encountered toxic. I feel virtually certain that in his fantasies Mr. R. expressed his experience of being an infant born with preconceptions of what a Mother should be—that he had arrived from another, later civilization, one more advanced than that of his family's. Later editions of that fantasy (for example, of being *The Manchurian Candidate* of the [1962] Axelrod & Frankenheimer film, in which a man is brainwashed, his identity taken from him, another superimposed) reflected a view of analysis and of me that further expressed his sense that his specifications for who and what his people ought to be were utterly other than what he encountered. What are we to make of this? One must see this view of the world as a projection of his own covetous intentions, his own thievery of identity. And certainly this is how I put it to him. But there was a model he provided for himself: "When I first entered analysis, I thought I was allergic to the world. I have come to see that this allergy is as much as anything due to the overabundance of my own histamines."

Who then judges what constitutes the good-enough mother, the good breast, the beautiful painting? I think we must say the beholder (allowing of course for the fact that other beholders may not agree). But surely Mr. T. and Mr. R. could not find sufficient goodness in the earliest experiences with the breast to go on to experience anything like pleasure, ebullient appetite, the discovery of an whole-object mother beyond the part-object breast and so further on to experiences of gratitude and ultimately, admiration. Unable to take her, neither could they leave her alone.

To find one's self in a no-exit situation with an immutably actual mother who does not begin to approximate to one's preconceived specifications feels unspeakably dangerous. I think something akin to an immunologically phagic reaction sets in. What is offered is attacked because it feels toxic and lethal. At the same time, a rapacious greed for what is absent sets in. This is not mere ruthlessness, it is the predatory attitude the parasite might bear for the host. But what if what that greed encounters feels wrong and false, as if by some dire substitution, a pretender were in place? In this circumstance the infant cannot but feel that the "role" of Mother is wasted on the mother who occupies it. Why then should they not occupy it themselves, and oust the usurper? (There is something of this in *Hamlet* in respect both to Claudius and Gertrude. Hamlet thinks it is so of Polonius and Ophelia, too.) Since such infants cannot take from the mothers they have, there has to be a way out. It is the classic purple cow dilemma: is it not sometimes better to be than to see one?

In summary, identifications motivated by envy, in contrast to those based on admiration — a desire for affiliation or augmentation of the self — attempt to wreak vengeance on the object by denying it as a source. Instead of expressing the identity between subject and object, these identifications analogize to it, and then destroy the link. Envy is based on greed. Greed, unlike appetite, is insatiable. The ongoing desirability of the object makes it appear powerful and unforgettable — hence an object of ongoing envy. The question of what makes people unable to develop appetite is considered both from the point of view of the object and the possible innate unsatisfiability of the subject.

4

BLACK MILK

Envy, as a state of mind, is of no particular bother when one feels able to acquire something just like or just as good as what is envied. The trouble arises when one feels that one cannot, because what rouses the envy is beyond one's hope of acquisition. At such a juncture, one must either give up the wish and one's hope for it, or create a scenario in which acquiring what one envies will be possible under a given set of circumstances. Thus of penis envy Freud wrote that the little girl may hope either later to acquire the penis (it may grow inside out from within) or symbolize it such that it can be *represented* by a baby or something else. The little boy may tell himself that the problem is but a matter of time and that some day he may acquire a penis the equal of his father's—and then his mother will succumb to his ardor and his charms. And in fact under favorable circumstances these scenarios may get the children through long enough for them to value that which they do possess. The woman the little girl grows up to be may be so delighted with her baby that its symbolic function is shed off; and so far as the penis is concerned, it is very nice when it is pointing in, thanks all the same. The little boy may, to his surprise, so fall in love with a woman other than his mother, that her pleasure in his penis gives him the pleasure he has been waiting for.

Such happy outcomes, however, depend on a number of factors. The first is probably the nature of the relationship in which the initial envy takes place. A second is the help the child is able to receive when attempting to give up enough of the wish and hope in the present tense to make the use of future possible. A third is the capacity for symbolization available to the child as he or she tries to establish the scenario. A fourth is the scenario itself—its value as a plan by which the desired achievement can be brought to pass. (The fifth is, as usual, purblind luck.) I shall take these one by one, beginning with this and going on to other parts of these notes.

The infant who covets the breast does so in the context of a relationship, just as the child who covets the "better" genital does. The happier the baby is with what it receives from the breast, the more he is consoled for not possessing it himself. The less copious the satisfaction on the receiving end, the less the sense of consolation—or compensation.

"If you want to understand me, you have to understand one thing and understand it good: Comp-pen-sa-tion" said a nine year old to me. "I li-i-ive for comp-pen-sa-tion, I live for *getting my own back*" (my italics).

But, as is so often the case, matters are not quite so simple. The discovery of the world of objects takes place not prior to but after the discovery of relationships between objects. Things exist only incidentally until the pattern for them is established. The pattern, the relationship, is inborn; it is configured innately; it is as merciless to what might have been experienced as is the morphology of the retina or the range of what is perceptible itself. We can see a spider's web, but insects, with their ability to see ultraviolet light, see flowers woven in the web, with the spider as a kind of alluring centerpiece, and, they favor that sight by 50 percent over webs stripped of that stage lighting by the experimenter. Things seen are *as* seen. Human beings have a kind of *black-light* to their spectrum of experience. For us there is no such thing as nothing, only a no-thing where a something should have been. And there is no such thing as a no-space, only a hole or a blank or a piece of darkness where a something should have been. Black milk, where milk was to be.[1] Black holes where time should have been. These blacklighted so-nesses forever recur, in the ambiguous undulations of life, as dark encroachments of the original catastrophe, chaos in motion and not in motion, desire without an object of desire: the nothing that cannot peacefully be there because the no-thing is always there in its place.

Expectations are in the affirmative; as Freud showed in his (1925) essay

---

[1]The phrase "black milk" is from Paul Celan: *Schwartze Milch der Fruhe wir trinken sie abends/wir trinken sie mittags und morgens/wir trinken sie nachts/ wir trinken und trinken*. Celan (*"Todestuge"* ["Death fugue"] in *Poems*. Persea [1989] uses the phrase to describe what the Nazis "gave" the Jews and Gypsies in the holocaust. It is so poignant in its connection that one hesitates using it to express what a person "gives" himself. And yet so precisely does it describe what one seems to be having when envy is being the leading state of mind that I do use it. I know of none better.

on Negation, disappointments are also in the affirmative. The object that is absent in time or space is a no-object; it suppurates no-ness. Bion (1965), Grotstein (1990a, b), and Michael Eigen (1986) have each given clinical realization and theoretical elaboration of this presence of the absence.

But neither is anything truly present *only* in its no-ness. Beyond the warp, beyond the moonmath, it exists as someone else's affirmative: when the no-thing is my portion, the yes-thing is yours. If I see that the yes-thing is yours, while the no-thing is mine, I feel both envious and jealous. If I manage not to see that the yes-thing is your portion while mine is the no, the not, and the never, I feel merely envious. But always there is the dependence of opposites, for of these, day and night, earth and air, chill and heat, neither can exist without the defining force of the other. A "two-position" relationship consists of me and you, and which of us has It. But then it may occur to us that another beyond you or me is having It, and that then there are three of us. At this point a triangular event comes into being. If we are a COUPLE, that third may become part of one another's Oedipus complex. However, if we are a PAIR, that person might become part of our GROUP. If, as is usually the case, we are at one and the same time a COUPLE and a PAIR, that person will ambiguously be either or both — wife and mother, father and would-be slayer; half-things, like Tiresias, who was both man and woman, and the sphinx, part woman, part creature. We must prepare for paradox.

The better and more abundant the breast, the more it is worth and the more enviable it is. But the less abundant the breast, the greater its ability to affect the infant, and the greater that affecting power is, the more enviable the infant finds the breast.

This leads to the other function of the breast — its capacity to reciprocate. A breast that can affect and be affected is less enviable than one that can only do the former. The breast is thus host — it offers and it receives . . . or does not, or does both unequally or erratically.

The provisioning function is by now well known as both an event of succor and as a psychosexual experience rooted in the pleasure principle in which emotional gratification and the psychological sense of well-being are almost commensurate with the satiety of the wishes to mouth and suck and eat one's fill. But the "almost" in the thesis is of the utmost importance. The subjective experience of an event does not necessarily accord with the event looked at from an alternate viewpoint, as any baby and mother will attest. Another way of putting the same thing is to say there is an experience and an experiencer that are by no means necessarily congruent. An important example of this is that a good feeding of an envious baby may be worse than a poor feeding of a grateful one. (The same may hold true of a psychotherapeutic session.)

The receptive function is also well known. But it is a function that the breast cannot itself provide, except in the infant's phantasy. A mother or other person is required, and she, he, or they must be present and ready to become attuned to whatever transmissions may come their way. (Some astronomers and others are setting up such stations on earth for any extraterrestrials who may want to reach us.) As many writers have noted, one of the more urgent of the communications has to do with the infant's sometimes overwhelming fear that it may die. On the basis of my own experience with a number of patients, I have to go further than this: I have to think that some infants at least feel that they should die, and when this is the case they very badly need to be reassured, even convinced, that they need not. For such infants, about whom more in a moment, the provisioning experience seems wildly wrong, even jeopardizing. They need to be helped not to tempt fate by flourishing and feeling gratified.

ON THE ORIGINS OF ENVY

Originology is a perilous pursuit. Yet it is endemic to psychoanalytic methodology. We say, so-and-so is acting (feeling, thinking, dreaming) as if X must be the case. This yields our interpretations. We then further say that so-and-so is acting as if Y must have *been* the case. This yields our constructions. We then say for such-and such to have been the case for both so-and-so and so-and-so, X and Y must be true of people or of the children they were. These hypotheses are as undemonstrable as hypotheses that there is a mind, a personality, or any other nonsensuous intangible — like anxiety or love. To "operationalize" hypotheses does not help very much. We cannot say, "When I speak of anxiety I mean a feeling of excitement accompanied by adrenal rushes, trembling, and a temporary color, flush or pallor" — for this can describe the feeling of being in love. Even if we add a subjective feeling of being endangered, we are no better off, for who but a fool could not fear falling in love? In any case, many of us suspect that often "anxious" means "eager" in the Unconscious (another problem area) whatever the consciously subjective feelings may be. Indeed, some of us might say that when we feel frightened it is not always of the Other, but often for him — and he, counting on that, is not feeling it himself.

   This series of methodological difficulties is somewhat escapable by saying we, like our patients (from whom we learn much of this) are dealing not with facts but with representations of facts. They represent their experience one way, we another. They say anxious, we may say eager; they say eager, we may say frightened — or counterphobic. They say therefore, we say because; they say coming at, we say coming from. For some people this sometimes appears helpful to identify portions of experience that hitherto did not square with other portions of experience. But this is by the by; it does not verify our hypotheses any more than the "Dianetics" or the astrologic story does. We are still left with a process of inference ontologically or originologically, as the case may be.

I make a point of this because I am about to propose a piece of originology called the selection principle and attribute to it the status of being the proximal "cause" of envy. This proposal will present some of the same difficulties as Plato's ideas regarding the Ideal and Kantian concepts of the noumenon. And since my proposal is based on Darwinian concepts of natural selection and the survival of the species, it will pose those difficulties as well. And of course it will re-pose all the difficulties that Freud posed in speaking of a pleasure principle, derived from the soma, but represented psychically as a set of drives and urges that demand and imbue attention.

Plato's thinking concerned a hypothesis of an Ideal to which all things really were only approximations. The Ideal was at rest; there was nowhere further it need go; it was fully evolved. The real, being only an approximation of this ideal, was in need ceaselessly of change; as it changed it became more true, more beautiful, and more enduring. Kant's noumenon is also unapprehendable; it is a category that phenomena more or less adequately fill out and realize. Interestingly, Darwin's survival principle has much in common with both Plato's ideal and Kant's noumenon. Species are supposed to realize their term of being alive and, in that sense, actual, by perpetuating themselves unto future generations. Their "destiny" is to change and adapt selectively so that primarily the very best of their genes are sent forward into the gene pools of the generations to come. Though Darwin of course does not say so, it is as if there will come to be an evolved condition so perfect as to endure forever. This may be thought of as an Edenesque version of an eternal after life:

> Ah, happy, happy boughs that cannot shed
> Your leaves, nor ever bid the Spring adieu;
> And happy melodist, unwearied,
> For ever piping songs for ever new . . .
> "Beauty is truth, truth beauty"—that is all
> Ye know on earth and all ye need to know.
> (John Keats, *Ode on a Grecian Urn*)

Meanwhile, through selection and selectivity, each species further refines itself for its work of penultimate survival. "Heard melodies are sweet, but those unheard are sweeter."

Freud spoke of himself as among those revolutionaries who, like Copernicus and Darwin, took mankind from being at the epicenter of the universe and made him but one more of all the creatures. He did this by attributing to man the Id, that boiling cauldron of atavistic pleasure and pain-driven instinct, urge, or drive. If man did not actually behave like this, it was due to self-preservative needs acquired by and lodged in the ego and adhering to the social and empirical facts of the reality principle. There was also posited the censor and later the superego, an internal representation of the persons important to the growing child, and their particular culture and values. Later there was the ego-ideal, an agent asking consonance with the admired qualities and traits of the governing subculture. Both the superego and the ego-ideal were internalized when the id gave up on an object as suitable or possible for the pleasure principle and used it instead as a source of internal relationships and identifications. Freud's famous assertion that the superego is heir to the Oedipus complex put this clearly. The child gave up one parent as an object of his longings and lusts and the other as his deadly and dreadful rival, and instead identified himself with the position of the once-rival, that his or her claims were prior and superior, by looking elsewhere for his or her id-ish pleasures. Melanie Klein disputed this only insofar as she felt the rivalry began earlier and over the breast (Klein (1961).

But the attribution of the bestial id, and with it a libidinal and psychosexual life starting at birth, was basically the only way in which Freud took humanity to be but one among the species. The rest of the energies that made up his dynamic and his economic tensions, conflicts, and modifiers were all ultimately derived from the id, neutralized in some fashion and then turned back upon itself. Freud was himself dissatisfied with this formulation, and in 1920 or so began to think out a formulation he was to call *Todestriels* (death drive or instinct) or the Thanatos principle. This instinct provided him with another wellspring for the great duality he needed for his conflict theories; it explained certain exceptions to the wish-fulfillment theory of dreams; and it brought into play the repetition compulsion as a force of its own. Essentially the death instinct is an entropic force, set against the high, questing arc of the more, more, and yet more of the pleasure principle. Presently, however, Freud abandoned this hypothesis — so far that its retention by Klein and her group was to become and remain a source of controversy between Freudians and Kleinians.

This then left the pleasure principle with its urgent wants for the most and the soonest and to the devil with him or her who stands athwart — and only superego anxiety and the fears specifically attendant on self-preservation to moderate its heedless, impulsive nature. The pleasure principle seeks satiety and its quest is for Miss Right Now.

Suppose, however, that something of what Darwin thought to be true of other creatures were true also of mankind? This would install selectivity alongside egoistic hedonism. Miss Right Now would become Miss Right,[2] and the need to select and to be selected would moderate propinquity, randomness, and opportunism. We have of course versions of this in psychoanalytic theories. Some come from the interpersonal school led by Sullivan, some from those, like Kohut, who have focused on narcissism. Indeed, Freud too spoke of narcissism, saying (1914): "Love of self knows only one boundary, love of others."

But I wish to put forth the idea that group or species "narcissism" is an imperious requirement, no less in the germ plasm than the pleasure–pain principle, and no less disinclined to make itself known and felt than the desire for pleasure and gratification. The two principles are subject to coalescence, conflict, and compromise, but are in continual dynamic tension. If it weren't for the urgency of the pleasure principle, one might wait forever, studying the menu of choices but never choosing. And if it weren't for the choosiness of the selection principle, egoistic lust and fear and nothing else would drive the engine of action. This is to be thought of as a dialectic.

Desire and the feeling of satiety represent the pleasure end of the pleasure principle, and frustration and deprivation, the pain. These experiences are sensual and make themselves known as such to each individual, though either desire or frustration may be so painful that steps are taken to unknow the fact or the feeling of them. The selection principle makes itself manifest in feelings of hope or despair, in ideas of idealism or of meaninglessness. They are existential experiences or crises, surely less sensuous, perhaps purely mental, in which the pleasures of being contrast or comport with the needs and feelings about becoming. The gratification of getting "it" any which way and how — the polymorphic quest for release, relief, and then satiety — plays in a key entirely different from the push to wait for better — for other, or more, the despair, the emptiness, the blankness, the exhilaration, the euphoria, the sense of being at-one with the right and the good and part of the whole. Good or, in Winnicott's language, "good enough," represents a compromise between hope and desire, a bonding made jittery and tenuous if any tilt in the balance of the two constituents to the compact should take place.

The need to choose is half of the selection principle, the other half being the need to be chosen. It is the latter that is easily mistaken for narcissism, though that appellation is often assigned people who are thought to be too choosy. The fulfillment of the need to be chosen can come out of mutant qualities, which is to say the quality of being different and distinctive — or it can come out of being the best of the quality preferred by the centrist group.

---

[2]I take these words "Miss Right" and "Miss Right Now" from Robin Williams (1989), the comedian.

Or both: a study of Greyling butterflies measured that attractiveness and selective advantage in mating of various colors of grey. Mock-ups of jet black roused the greatest pursuit from the tree-roosting males. This color, however, does not appear in nature; it may be thought to combine both distinctiveness and competitive ultimacy. It may also be said to represent the triggering of desire when as yet unrealized hopes are given shape and form.

The array of characteristics available for choice indicates both the degree of the choosiness and the competition for being chosen. But these characteristics are of little use unless they are regarded as holding possibility for the destiny of the species. Thus there is a great gulf between distinctiveness and deviancy and choosiness on the part of the would-be chosen and snootiness on the part of the potential chooser. In the face of such drift in both parameters, some species have the choices pre-programmed. But this leaves them inflexible when time to accommodate to different environmental conditions comes along. To be sure, further selection will presumably rectify that inflexibility, especially if there is the Joker of the mutant gene in the pack. But mankind has bred in itself predispositions rather than explicit imperatives. Its categorical nature is such that the categories are but half full, awaiting experience and socialization to fill them to the brim. That we don't know what will be advantageous for the species is a powerful irony; we barely even know how selective evolution takes place (though see footnote 5). Feathers, for example, are thought to have been given impetus from their first mutant appearance as a thermal-control device. One day some thermally conserved creature flapped its warm ensnuggled forelimbs . . . and birds were launched!

Our preferences as to particulars await discovery; but the predilections arrive perinatally with the germ plasm.

That this may shape our fantasy and affective life is indicated by many experiments of which the following is an instance: Children under age 8 appear to favor long and tall over short and squat. Shown a given amount of water and then of clay, they feel that that water when in a tall, thin glass is more than the same amount in a short, squat one, and they repeat this assessment when viewing clay rolled into a snake shape as compared with a sphere. Piaget, who conducted these studies, attributes the findings to cognitive development; I suggest they reflect propensities that only gradually give way to the adoption of empiricism — itself a preference (Boris 1989). On the other side of the equation are those many experiments in which individuals "see" lines as longer or shorter one way when alone, another when told of the contrary decisions of "others." Stanley Milgram's studies of the effect of peer influence upon social behavior — subjects ordered by the experimenter to administer what they were told were progressively stronger electrical shocks to other "subjects" (actually confederates) did so, even at lethal levels, when assured it was necessary for their well-being, despite the bloodcurdling sounds of those whose well-being was being cared for — may also be looked at as suggestive (Milgram 1974).

In the face of the array of the variables and the complexity involved in ordering them for purposes of choosing or being chosen, there appear to be two somewhat paradoxical trends. One is that like seeks like. The other is that like seeks unlike. The categories we use have to do with the biggest and the best — but this can be penis or bust or clay size. And it can range, analogically, perhaps, to the "size" of money, territory, rank and influence, and the like. I have termed the first predilection the COUPLE status and the second the PAIR.

In the former, unlike is subsumed by *vive la différence!* In the latter it is accommodated by superiority — by *having more of the same.* The couple may be said to express itself in the preference for the heterogeneous as in heterosexuality. Homophobia would represent the extreme of the drift toward the attraction of likeness for likeness — which at its opposite extreme involves a sort of xenophobia. The former would lean toward acceptance of the mutant (or mystic).[3]

So far I have dealt with what might be called active efforts at selection — self-perfection in the service of being among the chosen, selection of the best and most beautiful to enhance self and species. But there is a passive side to selection, too — what might be encapsulated in the term salvation. Each species is prey to another — including itself, at those times when subspeciation takes place. The enduring tensions over birth control, abortion, and infanticide reflect the power of this arbitrary drawing of limits and boundaries in regard to individuals being permitted life itself by the doyens of the species.[4] Then comes the matter of protection from outside the dyad — of child abuse or sexual misuse or castration or defeminization. Finally comes the matter of protection from intraspecies tensions — of what has sometimes been called Social Darwinism, where some are used at the convenience of, or to enhance the survival of, others. This is far from specialization, where some till and some teach, each according to their abilities and the needs of the group. Specialization is indeed a species-enhancing procedure. But taken too far this process of commensurate activities for commensurate gain disintegrates into parasitism, where the value of the one is merely to keep the other alive and flourishing, no matter the former's fate. These are the seedlings that are thinned, the branches that are pruned, the lives shadowed by the heights of other lives — the COUPLE aspect. Insofar as one may not have one's own life, one must have some thing. And that something is a life lived vicariously — that

---

[3]Bion (1970) remarks on this in his chapter, "The Mystic and the Group." Freud, of course, believed that bisexuality was endemic to us as a species.

[4]It should not be forgotten the Oedipus was himself a near victim of parents who were pro-choice, and that Laius was prepared to kill him at the crossroads when next they met.

is, allowing someone to take the place of the self, and living through him surrogately, the option provided us by the PAIR aspect of the selection principle.

To fail to put one's self in the other's shoes means that one is not a species creature. All one is fit for is aggressive or sensual coupling. Such persons can become the leaders of a species group, however, for the wish of groups to couple with other groups is benefited by persons who cannot see commonalities, only differences. After all, what all groups have in common are their differences, and the discernment of even minor differences makes more and more Others available for purposes of coupling, even as, by comparison and contrast, it appears to highlight the commonalities that enable the members of each group to feel more like one another. (How boring, complained Oscar Wilde, that all people seem to be able to talk of are their similarities when it is their differences that are so interesting!)

It is no accident that when I becomes We there comes about a great, deep guilt about individual survival and the ruthlessness that propels it. In many psychoanalytical writings this is discussed as the result of a dawning awareness that the mother is not simply an assembly-kit of objects for the infant's delectation or wrath; rather she is a person quite like he or she is, and so subject to gratitude, protection, and admiration. This is said to mark the arrival of the so-called depressive position. The point I wish to emphasize, however, is that the possession of a category into which to assimilate the realization "another-like-me" is endemic. The species must know Like from Other; I may eat Other, but I must not eat Like. Subspeciation—the term given when like finds differences from the nigger, geek, wog, cunt, etc. that are sufficient to dis-include them from being among the "brothers"—is an agreement that exempts each and every one of the subspecies from keeping a lock on all the inhibitions pertaining to the membership in the species taken as a whole—including whom to protect from cannibalism, incest, waste-disposal, rape, slavery, death, and the like. People who for various reasons are unsure of the operative distinctions often have to look quite far afield—they may have to marry (or propagate) well outside of their own nationality, gender, race or religion—in order to be sure of having discerned the X's from the O's. Lines and borders obviously are blurred, since where they are placed has, in Sullivan's phrase, to be consensually validated by the group that might or might not turn out to be subject to or exempt from predations of this sort.[5] Within the group there are "outs" and "ins," and divisions based on special-

---

[5]The sad affair of Panama illustrates this; the USA killed many civilians, who are Us, but did so to keep the soldiers safe, who are even more Us, and to rescue our ally, Panama, from Noriega, who was Us, but isn't anymore; but our Pentagon may lie to Us about this because it doesn't want Us to be against it, especially on the matter of civilian casualties.

ization, which further complicate the matter of where one makes one's identity and where one takes one's pleasures. Distinctions are also context-sensitive: some boys become girls when at public schools, and boys when on vacations after graduation. When is an X not an X, but an O, when is an O an X in a specialized function? Are the patient and analyst equal, or do their differences in function make one an X, the other an O?

SIGNS AND SIGNALS

Because of the vast and multidimensional ambiguities involved, features of the Whole are elevated into signs and signals, only some of which are conscious. Conscious ones involve, for example, the use of colored handker-chiefs and the pockets they peep out of by homosexuals to signal what their particular pleasures are. The size of a man's penis or woman's breasts, or the length of her legs, may not simply be titillating; they may also serve, unconsciously, as "releasers" — that is, triggering signals that copulation may take place, for he or she is not of one's own kind. As signs (or signals) the information, when felt to be reliable, immediately releases whatever lust or bloodlust that has been held in abeyance pending the information ("We have an X here. Negative on O — this one's a definite X!"). When matters are obscure, as during adolescence in Western industrialized societies, kids are veritably ablaze with paraphernalia from hair to toe, indicating who is and who's not who. Special lingo also helps them (as it does psychoanalysts) to make fine distinctions among subgroups. But O! for the twosome when first they try to kiss or touch: are they subgroups, like sisters and brothers, or a couple, like mother and father?

Yet there is bound to be a We as there is an I; and, to that We, I must proffer and require in his turn some degree of deference. The We, once recognized (or taught), becomes the species to whom the individual must act moderately so far as individual pleasures are concerned. The rules for the preservation of the species are quite intricate, but, in the abbreviated version, concern who and what may be put to immediate use as an object of the pleasure principle and who must be preserved for purposes of selective advantage.

The other side of this blueprint of deference is equally true: certain figures among us are spun-off to sets of rights and privileges that the rest of us not only do not ourselves enjoy, but which we do not envy or begrudge those figures. To the contrary, we live through them vicariously. They are said to have charisma: these figures are our shamans, our self-ideals, our leaders and tastemakers, our mystics, our demi-gods. But the grace we give them is not perduring. Towering Trump totters. When someone like

Ceausescu falls, the outrage over his riches and hoardings is immense — so great, indeed, as to shade any sorrow or hate over the murders, imprisonments, and abominations of which (from the COUPLE point of view) they have been equally guilty. It is understood that from the PAIRING point of view, each of us has to give way to others at any and each time in the life cycle, and, moreover, must do so peaceably and with envy suppressed, so as not to jeopardize the fitness of those to whom one does give way; that deference is for the greater good, and it is not meant to be exploited. The rituals employed in lieu of outright competition of fang and claw may involve any other sort of display; size, strength, territory, rank, family, acquisitions — such as the magnificence of the bower bird's bower. But whatever it is, two elements restrain. These are an inherent choosiness and an availability of choice. (Restraining that restraint, of course, is the urge toward pleasures, eagerly and impatiently pushing toward the making of the choices.)

In this movement between the force of any one set of forces and any other, there is a dynamic: stasis/crisis/stasis. The concept of regression provides a poor model, since it implies movements that are more and less fit; regression/progression is a point of view deriving from the generationally oriented time schema of the PAIR: the COUPLE do not know forward and backward, only back and forth. Relation ↔ ships at rest tend to stay at rest, in movement to stay in motion — until a crux (as in crucible, crucial, and crossroads) is reached, whereupon a shift takes place or not at all. It is a matter of the selfsame persisting, until BOOM! it shifts over to other. The word for this model might be crisis.

The initially expected relationship, moreover, not only remains in effect, but also provides the template for other relationships, which are then, accordingly, perceived as analogous to the preconceived archetypical relationships — of which one obtains to the species, the other to the individual organism. One simple instance of this, already mentioned, is that the presence of a third party makes a triangle in the COUPLING mode and a group in the PAIRING mode, and internalized, a superego in the COUPLE mode and an ego-ideal in the PAIRING mode, producing guilt in the former status and shame in the other.

Another example is that there is a ready capacity innately to divide by two — to split one into two or by two again into four, eight, and n objects. (Bion [1970] called a result that approached n "bizarre" objects.) The reverse of this process is agglutination: it is the extrapolation of one to infinity, such that one is not merely one, but the forerunner, symbol representative or incarnation of all, ever and everything. "God" has this quality. So, sometimes, does "We." Distinctions are not seen to betray differences: rather, they cumulate into an ever greater wholeness, through successive identifications of each with others. This is the modality of group formation, whereby the very differences and distinctions that interest those intent on coupling go unnoticed in the interests of agglutination. The shifts which take place between the one "model" and the other are akin to shifts in the perception of figure–ground relationships. But in the PAIRING mode what is generally called identification undoes divisibility and distinction by reaching for more and more and more of the same.

THE DUALITY OF THE COUPLE AND THE PAIR

In previous communications, I have mistakenly described what I thought to be an evolution of greed into appetite (Boris 1986, 1987, 1988). Further clinical experience shows rather a devolutionary process between the two, with greed, in the sense of agglutination, belonging in the PAIR dimension and appetite or desire to the COUPLE. Each represents a loss of a relationship so far as the other is concerned, and since objects do not exist, psychologically, outside of a relationship, each loss is tantamount to an object loss.

The appetitive breast is a loss so far as the wish to possess it is concerned, as is the breast gained by identification a loss so far as the appetites are concerned. If $\sigma \leftrightarrow \varphi$ stands for the providing breast and $\sigma \leftrightarrow \bigcirc$ for the owned breast, each is lost when the other is chosen. (The breasts are defined by the relationship.) They are the same save that,

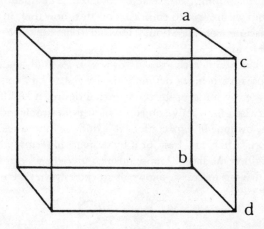

as in the hollow (or Necker) cube, a-b is recessive when c-d is dominant, thus each is "other" to the other (see "The 'Other' Breast," Boris 1986). The breast is selected in the sense that it is selectively perceived or remembered or imagined as either $\bigcirc$ or φ (or $\bigcirc$ or σ) at any given moment: in that way, if the infant has control of its mentation, he controls the breast. But does he have control of his mental processes? This is a problem concerning consciousness and will.

Of what use is consciousness to survival in the Darwinian sense? Such relatively primitive experiences of consciousness as pain, pleasure, hunger, thirst, and satiety may seem to facilitate survival behavior but are by no means necessary for it. Aversive reflexes without a corresponding conscious sensation of pain perform adequately (it would seem) for organisms not thought to enjoy a brain, much less consciousness. Attraction responses, like avoidant or aversive ones, also do not require awareness.

Humans being social animals, it is clearly in one's interest to know something of how others feel, to put oneself in their shoes. Thus a capacity for identifying with the experience of others and relating it to self experience would be valuable for social aspects of survival. But even this does not require consciousness, or self-consciousness; it requires merely a capacity to pick up signs and signals; no attribution of meaning, no interpretation, is required. Nothing need check in at the front desk.

But a moment's reflection indicates that the value of consciousness is precisely that it can, in given circumstances, short-circuit the aversion–attraction reflexes, and the signal function of social stimuli, and thereby go on to provide the possibility of contra-reflexive behavior. Thus when I know that the flame hurts my hand, I can nevertheless save my endangered child; I can anticipate an end to pain, or its diminution: I can plan: I can choose. "Human mensura requires staffing," as Beckett remarked. The quantity of consciousness is fixed, but we are free to embrace now this, now that, in the very special regard of conscious consideration. However, one can't *not* choose and one can't choose nothing.

An experience either chooses us or we it. A loud, sudden report, for example, chooses us: it has a demand quality not to be gainsaid. Driven, in the couple mode, by hunger, thirst, or sexual desire, it is difficult not to see mirages; otherwise unattractive objects look very desirable indeed. Driven, in the pair mode, by hope or expectation, it is difficult not to see events in terms other than good, better, and best; or if by despair, in terms of bad, worse, and worst; features become flaws. Consciousness gives leeway to the demandingness of these driving forces: it allows us to choose what we experience.

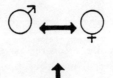

might express the relations between thinking and thoughts or knowing and experiences before choice is made, while

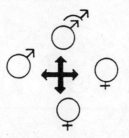

might represent matters after choice is made. Certain choices in thinking or knowing become objects themselves, nearly congruent with the objects they represent. In the vernacular, one can think about men and woman in a masculine sort of way, a feminine sort of way, or not at all. One can think of the breast as if one were its owner, as if one were a renter, or as if it didn't exist. One can think of the relations between objects as if they paired or as if they coupled by thinking of them in a pairing sort of way or in a coupling sort of way. The process of mentation comes to represent the relationship between objects, and thoughts and percepts become (as if) objects in the sense that things are objects.

From the Consulting Room

P.:   Were you anxious to be rid of me Tuesday? I thought you turned away quickly. I felt spitted or spit out — whichever it is. Which is it? You're not going to tell me. Why won't you tell me? Can't you tell me? Were you mad at me? Why did you spit me out?

Ψ: *Such* a spate. . . .

P.:   Yes. What had you said?

Ψ: You spat it out.

P.:   I said, "At least in a nothing life like mine there can't be any emergencies." And you said, "You're saying a mouthful." Is that what you said? Did you say that? Is that you? Did you say that? Am I imagining that? Tell me. Why won't you tell me?

Ψ: You have the idea that in a no-thing nothing devastating can happen anymore, since it already happened. You need to keep your no-thing safe from becoming something. You are spitting up what could stay and happen.

In the manner of the words lies the action. The analogies in mental activity to other relationships become persuasive. Two and two make four: is this the Primal scene? Penetrating thoughts, encompassing perceptions, long memory, soft ideas, hard data, openness to ideas, hard-assed attitudes—are these merely figures of speech? Why is certainty so frightening to those who feel "uneasy lies the head that wears the crown"?

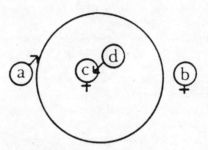

In this diagram, c & d are having intercourse inside the psyche to the dismay of a & b, who are excluded from this primal event. If a or b were a psychiatrist, he or she might be asking, "Are you hearing something—some voice other than my own?" If the intercourse is not satisfactory, presently the partners to the coupling, c or d, might find him- or herself drifting like an errant schoolchild in the hot flybuzz of springtime, to thoughts of a or b. But if c does this, d might be jealous and make such a headache for c that he or she might be unable to even concentrate! O, has a woman scorned a fury greater even than that of a superego spurned?[6]

P.:   [Heavily ironic] Today I felt so bad that I could scarcely get out of bed. I don't know how I made it to the session.

Ψ: It is difficult to know what you mean, *if* you mean.

P.:   Yes, well, words are a debased currency. Linear bits, two dimensional. My irony is intended to be three dimensional—but you, you never get it. I put together a multi-media event—or would, except your technique allows only words. When I hear what you hear of what I say, it makes me despair of talking altogether, and now you're complaining of my irony.

Ψ: If I understand, your irony is intended to add a dimension, to at least season the degraded words on which I insist. . . .

P.:   Words, mere words. Suppose people dealt in other dimensions?

Ψ: Suppose people wanted lingus, not language.

P.:   I am trying to convey more than that, but words don't serve, and you insist on words.

Ψ: Using words, I *think* it as if you wish to convey a lovely three-dimensioned behind, and when it is reconstituted by me from your transmission, it is shit.

P.:   Yes! Do *you* understand that? [This appears to sound odd to P.] I mean, does that make sense to you? [Silence]

---

[6]See my "Torment of the Object" (1988) for a study of a bulimic's relations with her internal objects.

Ψ: [Silence]

P.: Anyway . . .

Ψ: Private thoughts no use to speak—language, not lingus.

P.: [Tells thoughts. These concern a friend who has offered to return a borrowed chair, which P declined to have returned.]

Ψ: And when you were thinking that, I was thinking this: "No, you want to convey more than the behind or the breast, you want to inseminate: to bring into me a baby. But there is some question as to who should have the baby and who make it? [This now appears to me to represent a fairly shameless appeal in behalf of the value of language.]

P.: [Weeps, broken-heartedly] There is a space where good times were, a space and it can only be conveyed as a space. It is architectural. It is a space where *things* were—and people try to fill it with words. But the space is *the space*, it doesn't close around words and get filled.

Ψ: It is the space where the breast was and isn't and where the baby was meant to be and wasn't. And rather than have it filled with words, you want it saved. As virgin woods or as a memoriam to what wasn't.

P.: It is difficult for me to let your words sink in, but I think what you say is so.

Ψ: Words should not be allowed to occupy the space left for the breast or the baby?

P.: Yes, yes, yes, yes, yes. Shit!

Ψ: And this is what happened to you in me, when you hear yourself back: no breast, no new baby, shit. That's all I have made of your insemination.

P.: My mother's [Weeping afresh, a "line" now of further associations, in words . . . But later] It is no good. The point is, things were there even when people left. The chair bears witness. She sat in it, and it was there even after she left. The, the architecture, the *build*ing contains the events. Words are just bits and streams: they are nothing. Why should I expect you to understand? I have to talk to you in words, but *I think in images*. [Silence]

Ψ: I have already said about milk turned into urine, the breast and the penis as semen, but since these are words they are of no use. Worse, they are all you get from me, yet again. My talk will seem as if I have failed to feel bad at your reproaches, and you will yearn for something bigger and more dimensional than language to make me take your idea. Maybe that's why you did not tell me your images, but were silent instead.

P.: Is one ever-doomed to be a helpless, furious infant?

Ψ: Can making babies now ever be like making them then?

"I have turned into a big glass eye and a big glass ear," says a physician's child, one of whose remembered nightmares is an oscilloscope screen gone wild. "And you are some kind of one-celled creature under a microscope. What if the analysis is ready to end, would you tell me?"

"Whose were my legs over your shoulders?" asks Phillip's wife in Roth's (1990) novel, *Deception*.

Why are you feeding me with my breast?

I am so afraid that if I stop, if I am silent, even for a moment, that I will lose even my *name*—that you—they—will say: Who is she?

Prey to fearing the possibility of being "included out," of being the runt of the litter, the dispensable one, the one left to the wolves—from such a "position," envy of those otherwise chosen can only be immense. It makes for a kind of insensate greed. The greed involves the pain of choosing between receiving and having, accepting and owning, controlling and submitting, the pain being so great that it becomes too intolerable to choose any one for fear of surrendering the other.[7] As appealing and gratifying as receiving nurture and love may be, there remains the bone in the throat regarding those who *own* these life-giving, life-having attributes. Thus the envy of the breast so well known to psychoanalysis. For where there is greed, there is envy.

GREED AND ENVY

There is a rivalry that precedes such other rivalries as that involved in the Oedipal trio (and is displaced from the Oedipal trio to sibs). It is the rivalry of the twosome over whether and to what degree to be a COUPLE or whether and to what degree to be a PAIR.

The infant in a state of mind to COUPLE wants merely the fruits of the mother's manufacture; as a person-in the state of mind of a PAIR it wants to own or share in the control the means of production: to be a partner. To each member of the twosome, the other represents not merely a libidinal object, but the group or species of which it is a member. Thus the relationship between infant and mother is inevitably, and from both sides, at once collaborative and competitive.

It is also competitive and collaborative within each: for example, the parent has to look after the infant, but after him- and herself as well; and the infant has to be gratified, but also to learn this business of becoming a member of the PAIR, group, and species; to choose wisely but not too well; and to be among the chosen ones. If they are someday to be resolved, the inherent tensions within the COUPLE will have to give way to various degrees of PAIRING and the PAIRING to COUPLING. This means the recognition that the two being a PAIR are as such part of the larger group or species. But within that context with its rules governing predation and coupling, the two can take and give (certain) pleasures to and inflict (certain) pains on one another. The so-called socialization of the infant and young child is thus a cache of information

---

[7]For a fuller development of the pain of choice and its contribution to the maintenance of greed and so the virulence of envy, see my "The 'Other' Breast" (1986), in which I deal with the inescapable sense of loss that choice imposes, and the consequences of evading that loss.

concerning rules and attitudes or values for which there are already empty categories innately prepared. In Freudian terms the categories *superego*, belonging to the COUPLE, and *ego-ideal*, belonging to the PAIR, are there to be rescued (to a degree) from atavism by the gradual introduction to the young of the norms and aspirations of the particular PAIR and, presently, group.

So everywhere, of course, there are just such norms and aspirations. These differ from peoples to peoples, but no people are without them. As the saying goes, there is even honor among thieves, which is to say there are rules for deviancy as well as for what is normative. Deviancy also includes mental "illness" of various sorts; some cultures have categories for some illnesses and not others. Our own *DSM-III* is an example of our culture's allowed and unallowed deviant illnesses. As "third-party" payers like insurance companies and the government get more involved in providing mental health care benefits, we can expect the norms and exceptions to change. The issues will, however, most likely continue to revolve around beliefs concerning would and could; if one could, but one won't, one is bad; if one would if one could, one is sick. How closely these determinations reflect changes in norms may be seen in the changing views on homosexuality and alcoholism. How closely these assignments reflect species issues can be seen in reference to the ongoing debates concerning abortion and euthanasia and the death penalty—who has the right to whose life?

Where greed and envy end and appetite and love begin depends, therefore, on the codevelopment of gratitude in the COUPLE and of admiration in the PAIR.

Greed, we can now see, is the natural condition of humankind—its secular original sin. It is the inevitable by-product of the tension between the two principles. Efforts to accommodate greed abound. Splitting the object— dividing it by two—is one of the most appealing and frequently used. Since of course the object cannot be literally sundered (in infancy, at any rate), infants accomplish this aim by being selectively attentive. Where a whole and entire entity could be seen, dreamt, thought, or otherwise surmised, they take two looks instead of one. This act serves more than greed. It provides them a respite from being abjectly dominated by the sheer immensity of the presence of the object. Twin "takes" provide them something toward which to look, away from the abounding immanence of the One. In short, such splitting of the object provides the first opportunity for choice. For when one is not "always one, one alone, and ever more shall be so,"[8] possibilities double (and thence, geometrically, redouble). Thus is greed served, even while respite is gained from painful experiences emanating or seeming to from an inexorably

---

[8]In the words of the song. These referred to the Unity (as opposed to the Trinity) of the godhead.

given time, space, and entity. Later such splitting will assuage envy of the
have-it-alls. Yet of the abounding possibilities created by splitting, and the
accretions that follow from agglutination only some serve sooth, and choice
has ultimately to be made if appetite, and its unique capacity to be satisfied,
is to emerge.

    Socially, this journey is generally orchestrated in terms of when the baby
is allowed how much of what. The parent repeats with the infant what he or
she has experienced in his or her own life and other transferences — or, often,
the opposite of these. These often pivot on when the infant is no longer
considered to be an extension of the mother and when his can-nots turn into
will-nots. These are choices:
    "Oh, leave him be, he's only a baby!"
    "You're old enough now to. . . ."
    "Boy, *my* parents would never have put up with that from me."
    Erikson (1950) has shown how entire cultures seize the opportunity al-
lowed them by the infant's and child's developmental susceptibilities to shape
them into the adults the cultures both want and can stand. For the parent and
the culture two choices have to be made distinguishing woulds from coulds,
before shoulds and shouldn'ts can come into play, and greed and envy must
be resolved there before they can be put to the infant or child to resolve. Often
parents who have not been able to convert their own greed into appetites can
no better make choices for and about their children than they could for and
about themselves. Unmourned regarding the disappointments in their own
lives, they cannot help their children to mourn the loss of everythingness (this
breast and the "other" one as well) that the pleasure and species principles take
them toward. Indeed, what Laing (cf. Laing and Esterson 1970) and also the
so-called systems school of family studies and treatment have shown is that such
parents recruit their children to the ungrieved group, in which anger cements
denial in place, so never is heard a sorrowing word, either from the new
members or the older ones. The family becomes one-for-all; all-for-one in
viewing can'ts as won'ts and bad luck as deliberately imposed pain. As a result
no one may "suffer," to use the word by which Bion (1970) describes the ability
to endure and allow for the inevitability and sometimes randomness of painful
events:

> The patients experience pain, but not suffering . . . the *intensity* of the
> patient's pain contributes to his fear of suffering . . . Suffering pain
> involves respect for the fact of pain . . . Frustration and pain are equated.
> Pain is sexualized; it is therefore inflicted or accepted but it is not
> suffered — except in the view of the analyst or other observer. [p. 19]

In this observation Bion describes the birth of anger, and of course of envy.
The baby has split the world into two: a necessarily-to-be-suffered world, and

an unnecessary, that is to say, willfully imposed world made up of someone else's sexuality.

And now the infant has a choice. He can cut off the breast to spite his life, or he can resign himself to "taking" from the very font of life that torments him with envy. This is a hateful choice. However, when and insofar as he makes it, to say yes will ipso facto yield him appetite. And appetite if sated can, in turn, provide him pleasures perhaps even exceeding the pain imposed by his fear, greed, and spite.

If on the other hand, he does not say yes, but needs to have both the container of the breast and its contents, to continue to be both the manufacturer and the customer, and refuse to "rent" the breast (as a patient once put it), then he is awash with greed with no satisfactions coming in and, for that matter, none allowed. (A patient hated his analytic fees with a particular fury because while paying them he could not at the same time pay off his mortgage and "own absolutely outright" the place he lived.)

What I am describing is an early form of "separation anxiety" in which the mother's provender, namely the breast or the idea of her breast, *separates* rather than conjoins the twosome. Insofar as the breast-or nipple-as-conduit is not employed by the baby for purposes of taking and receiving, he uses it for purposes of evacuating the frustrations imposed by his greed and the venom of his envy. Of course this makes him afraid of retaliation—of the backage of the excreta, and he experiences a paranoia. But his wish would be to have the toxins he excretes through the conduit cleaned and pressed, much as he wants that to happen in respect to those he passes unrethrally and anally. Insofar as the mother or analyst-as-mother is capable of receiving the gorge of the baby's wrath and fear and of "making it better," so far will the baby not choke on his own mental vomit, and so far will his paranoia be eased.

MIRRORINGS

Not all mothers or Others can do this. They lack what Bion called "a capacity for reverie." Not having or not being able to give this kind of sympathetic imagination or empathic intuition, they are like blank mirrors to their infants. He is reflected back, even while she becomes more and more dense and opaque. The breast is more nearly now a sting. It gives "black milk." It mirrors not as Kohut's mirroring is meant to suggest, but as Lacan knew (1949). And as Spitz (1957) and others know regarding psychological "marasmus," it's a killer. I write of the nature of the envy that arises out of this imperviousness as "sent back" or regurgitated through the conduit that finds differences so frustrating as to insist on being and staying a one-way street. The silence, for example, so necessary to the therapy of psychoanalysis, will

Less than

smallness

inescapably appear to some patients as the radiant hostility, indeed the death-doom made incarnate, of the analyst (and his tribe).

This is a distinction with a difference that is not easy to make clear. The impassivity of the Mother or Other excites envy, since it appears so self-assured, self-fed and self-referential (and reverential) that only those chosen, perhaps only god himself, could dare it. This envious response has to do with not bringing coals to New Castle; to such a mother, why should the infant also offer the gift of appreciation and dependence? This is what excites the talion anxiety. But along side of that, often quite at the same time, the infant feels the mother's—the patient, the analyst's—chilled complacency, that blue mirror of indifference in which it sees only its own ugly and deformed depths, its wounds, and insufficiency. That is, so to say, how it knows its own size and shape, and knows, as if from the apple on the tree of Knowledge, its own shame. It sees itself as it feels it is seen, young, grotesque, foolish beyond words. This latter experience is not, however, the imagined return of an intention toward the mother and her qualities and attributes, though later it may merge with that. It is self-sight without the softening of illusion. It is the mirror of pitiless eyes, the *Blaue Engel:* "Ka ka-ka ka-a." Like Adam and Eve, one wants to cover one's nakedness and flee.

Blue mirror of indifference. Promoting Patients

Since this is not projected, the fear of it being sent back through the conduit is not, as the former fear is, a paranoid one. It is a fear of seeing too much too clearly: of having the retina seared by what one sees, of staring into the sun, or at Medusa without the protective shield—not, traumatically, to see her phallicity, but one's own lack; and that without so much as an alas. It is the unbearable so-ness of being alive and in doubt. It is fairly important to make this distinction clinically, because not to make it will seem to the patient the same catastrophe of the living blankness all over again (see also Green 1986). There is reason to believe that the more sensitive the baby, the more this affects him or her.

The envy of that imperviousness and opacity, of that serene-seeming density, will encourage the enduring question: What does he or she have that I don't have? When the answer seems to be "the Breast" or "the Penis," so goes the envy.[9] The greed to possess can only increase in these circumstances, and the lack of whatever it is that is "lacking" becomes identified with the reason one is not chosen—or not going to be chosen. That in turn is so disheartening that some other lack is substituted for it—and if a successful "as if" is substituted—if it obscures and yet stands for the original lack—that new fly in the ointment becomes a pearl beyond price. The original lack, so sharply

---

[9]Klein believed she had seen the answer come back as the Breast with the paternal Penis "in" it (Klein/Richard).

experienced, now becomes mooted and muted by its being turned into a topical depression — a convexed concavity.

But when all else falls, frustration of the pleasure principle gives and (from another point of view) allows impetus to the ongoing press of the selection principle, and attempts to COUPLE give way to attempts to establish a PAIR with the Other. Establishment of a PAIR — a group or a matched and mated species — is however not a simple procedure. Identifying requires commonality and similarity, which means that where there are differences, these differences have to be dissipated. They are "Vive!" experiences so far as coupling is concerned, but equivalently problematic where identifications are involved. Either two (or more) have both (or severally) to lose some portion of their differences, or else the one (or more) has to lose *all* those differences of its own, in an abject capitulation to the Other.

Often psychoanalysis as a psychotherapy is experienced by a patient as involving precisely this — a giving over of all his uniqueness and individuality to an usurpation by the common denomination. Though in a COUPLING vein, this can be understood, for example, as a requirement for emasculation or some other denuding of COUPLING characteristics, in a PAIRING vein it is a question of who has to give up what in order that commonality[10] is reached. The egoism of any one person is likely to be such that the movement toward midway is reluctant and contested. This is, the One wants to instill in the Other an equal valency for movement toward midway — midway, indeed, doubtless as a minimum. (The idea of specialized function amid an equality of everything else does not make sense to such patients. I had once, for a while, to see a young man in my hospital-sited room rather than in my home consulting room because he felt that the odds stacked against him in the latter were annihilating.) People believe this installation to be made possible by ever greater projections, with which then the Other will helplessly identify. Thus in the COUPLING modality, the analyst's efforts to encourage an alliance are experienced as an embrace, if perhaps a suffocating one. But in the PAIRING modality these same efforts are seen as a train of projections sent forcefully into reverse on the same set of tracks.

These projections are as if of genetic material, not in itself hostile in the sense of being inspired by malign hatred of the difference of the Other (until, that is, envy gets involved). The inculcation into the Other of materials of the Self is simply designed first to supplant those qualities that are alienating to mutual identity and then to alter those impediments to such transplantation in

---

[10]In political-economic terms this is a preoccupation of communism and Marxism; in religious terms, it is a question of the rendering unto the Lord, for the sense of compensation is asked in return.

the manner that doctors use such immunosuppressants to enable physical sorts of tissue transplants. "You know."

Installing the genetic material of Self into the Other regularly follows or accompanies the frustrated efforts to inseminate or aviposit the Other in a COUPLING sort of way: "D'ya see? You know?" When envy becomes part of the motivation and the differences of the Other are not merely frustrating but have become hateful and tormenting, this same process is used to sterilize in the Other his or her own contents (e.g., contentment, a good idea, etc.) and to replace these with a parasite through which a hostile takeover is attempted. The medium, in these cases is the message; the message is the replacement or, at least nullification, of the Other's integrity and possessions. When these efforts are active, the Self fears that the very conduit it used to evacuate the materials of Self into the Other will become a two-way street and that the Other may in the end (!) succeed in forcing the flow back from whence it came. Perhaps needless to add, this is a situation reapproaching a kind of primary paranoia.

What is being transposed from Self to Other is, of course, the "genetic programming" with which the Self feels itself endangered. This, in other connections, has been called the archaic superego. These intimations are nascent, but as they begin to dawn, interfering with the easy engagement of Self with the unprincipled pleasures of concupiscence, they begin to become hateful. Either these have to stay and pleasure go, or these have to be evacuated so that pleasuring can remain unimpeded. When projected, the Other becomes the source of all species' injunctions, and becomes problematic and dangerous to the health of the Self's simple pleasures. The Self's effort therefore instead becomes an infusion into the Other of the Self's selfness. The language here is awkward, but the otherness of the Other, so desirable for purposes of COUPLING has, when it becomes useless and frightening, decisively to be modified. The choice appears to be the use either of introjective or projective identifications. In the former case the Self has increasingly to take on the attributes of the Other; in the latter, vice versa. In both cases the object of the exercise is the decrease of all the differences which have become a source of pain, frustration, guilt, or shame. Only the means of closing the distance remain optional.

PAS DE DEUX

The need to close that distance and minimize differences is so great as to make it almost immaterial who takes on whose attributes. The goal is for the COUPLE to become a PAIR and thus each but a cog in the larger unity of the group or species. Perhaps ideally each one would give up some difference and take on some similarity, each gaining thereby a place of being one among the larger many. Thus a good deal of mutual mimicry, say between mother and infant, becomes a vital part of the PAIR exchange. The infant says his gurgle and the mother imitates it, then she says hers, and he imitates it. He nods forward, then she does. In this way, they are establishing not who does what, but that both do whichever.

The important matter is not who is who, but that both are ↔ linked by a reversible set of vectors. Even if, at the worst of times they

argue all night
as to who has the right
to do what and with which
and to whom.

The argument has become the ↔ link. As is well known, when the argument serves as the link, quite soon it hardly matters which side each takes; indeed, twosomes and subgroups frequently reverse positions — simply by accusing one another of (of all things) . . . reversing positions!

The president of a psychoanalytic institute has no taste for controversies that appear increasingly to be occurring. But few members will allow his neutrality. They demand that he make his positions and preferences clear. His idea is that they mean no more neutrality now that you are no longer my analyst! And he suspects his positions and preferences have to do with sexual copulation. But he feels he has no mandate to make such interpretations — that though they occur to him with some force and clarity, he is administratively being rendered impotent from using the thrust of his interpretations. Finally he prepares a statement of his own stand on the issues (these concern the sort of patients candidates should be trained to work with and relations with other institutional bodies). Those previously taking those same positions each now change them. Those previously opposing those positions now embrace them: those standing with him now oppose him. He is asked to make his position clear again.

Whether the identification is made projectively or introjectively matters less than that the identity is established. Similarly, it matters far less whether one's treasures are deposited (as in a safety-deposit box) for safekeeping into the Other, or one's metabolic waste (for self-protection) is thrown out into the Other, the important thing is to keep contents of Self from contaminating or fusion-reacting in one place or container. Which way one keeps the two intact matters less than what either will do to keep each from spoiling or being despoiled by the other. For in the matter of the species the main thing, eugenically, is to keep the strain pure and intact — and forever.

Mentally this appears as a particular hatred of being or feeling "confused." A response to this is found in a patient who:

> sucks up bits of others' identity omnivorously, but out of envy does not recall who or what he has embodied. His mother's "holes" are objects that have become the sources of some of these hostile takeovers. Strange indeed are the reappearance of those holes in himself or his works. They appear as holes in his thinking, his memory, his art-works. As a result, when he approaches a woman's breasts or vagina, he does not know what they are or what they look like. He cannot "take them in." He can only "abstract" them. As he approaches knowledge about what is confusing him, he feels even more confused. His pronouns are the first to go; concrete references follow; abstractions of a high level of generality too wide for anything to be implanted are all that are left.

Whether one is then a receptacle or a depositor, a breast or a mouth, an inseminator or a host in any contemporary metempsychosis is secondary to the preservation of the gene. Compared to that objective, the métier of the species, the division of labor or function within the PAIR or among the group is relatively incidental. But this same latitude is not in effect when the two principles are being compromised within a given person. For there, within the precincts of me or thee, how the fusion between the two aims and objectives is fashioned matters very much indeed.

The mental magic — the sleights of mind by which the fantasies of projection, introjection, and conditions of identity are contrived — is rather rudely measured against a more certain sort of yard-stick — libidinal gratification. The two, the experience of sensuality and the experience of mental ease, must begin to coincide and cohere. For example, the feeling of omnipotence that sustains mental maneuvers doesn't alter the facts. It just alters the person's perception of and regard for facts. For mental pleasure or pain is one thing, but with the pleasure principle, sensuous pleasure and sensual ones are involved. Differences define one another via comparison and contrast — the X's and O's of differences are neither difficult to decry nor too complicated to know what to do with. Pavlov's experiment in which the dog shocked at the square plate (read, X) but fed at the round (or O plate), goes quite mad and begins to bite its own tail as the plates become octagonal, then decagonal, etc. is a tale which might well alert us to the fate of the individual when differences are negated, out of envy or the need to use the Other for purposes of PAIRING. For as he attempts to turn differences into mere distinctions, the ability to COUPLE is put at serious risk.

As you know, I use masturbation to help myself get to sleep. It is not so much sexual as a release of tensions. But I have run out of men to fantasize about. I mustn't use you—you're my analyst, after all. So who? . . . I am considering buying a VCR. They allow one to have a thirty-day trial period. Actually two stores I went to allow this, so I bought two—or rather brought home two. I taped the Olympics—or rather a particular player. Then I transferred him to the tape of the other recorder. Now I have him on both recorders.

The analyst might feel he is hearing of a form of reproduction that falls partway between parthenogenesis and reproduction with a partner, or that he is hearing of a way of controlling the primal scene. But it will not be interpretations of this sort or even one's having to do with this person's anger at being unpartnered by her analyst that will do anything helpful—until the libidinal urge gets precisely identified as something more than nervous tension to be released. When this happens, most of the work is done: the wish for orgasmic fulfillment will reveal the impostors for who and what they are.

THE DIALECTIC

This, then, is the dialectic: there are on the one side those boiling-cauldron needs for the object—to grasp, to hold, to copulate, to consume—and on the other side a quite different set of needs of the object—these to be at one with, to forge identity, to make a PAIR and a group. The first requires the discovery, exploitation, and preservation of reciprocal differences; the second to lose or, at minimum, take captive those very same differences in which copulation exults. These two states of mind coexist, with first one, then the other, becoming dominant and regnant. Each tends to persist until a crux or crisis pushes it into recession.

This creation of objects for use in each state of mind can be done "out of doors," via discovery, in the world of actual Others; or it can be done in the precincts of the mind, mentally, via invention, by acts of selective noticing— either by seeing only differences, or then again only likenesses. Depending on a person's state of mind another X can be a blamed nuisance, an orgasmic encounter—or an ally or a partner in a PAIR. Its differences from the initial X can be used to effect specialization—X can play shortstop. Or it can be the "O," for which X looks when it wants to COUPLE, but, fearfully or enviously, not to couple with a genuine O.

But however infinite the varieties the two X's or two O's can conjure, they cannot do what an X can do with an O or an O with an X. And the realization of the need to find, refine, use *and know one is using hated differences* is the inhering source of envy.

5

MORE OF THE SAME

In this essay I propose to deal with the maneuver by which people try to mitigate their envy by converting differences into similarities, leaving for themselves the far more possible task of merely getting or doing or being more of the same. These are people for whom the expression *Vive la différence!* most decidedly does not apply. For it to apply the differences they encounter must be and have been complementary, reciprocal: the one's hungry mouth — the other's providing breast; the one's excited genital — the other's also excited genital. Such mutuality of reciprocation enables the one to take and give pleasure from, and so in what he or she possesses. Where that complementation does not take place, the longing inverts toward a turn-about. Failing to find pleasure and satisfaction in what one has, one's longings to have what the other has increase proportionately. What is one's own is being wasted, and what the other has is wasted on them. First greed to have both and then envy of the other for having what one has longed to receive from and now longs to own and control comes to the fore. To have a mouth and an appetite for being fed and suckled when there is too little pleasure from leaves one with no great pleasure in. To have the breast thus seems preferable.

This goes for the genitals and, more broadly, the gender as well. Disappointment when having a penis must lead to a change of object, aim, or impulse. The wish one were rid of it contributes to castration anxiety. Although the conscious experience is anxious as in afraid, the unconscious is anxious as in eager. The girl's disappointment from receiving neither the satisfactions her father's penis is imagined to afford her nor the fruits of their intercourse — which might be a baby or some other enhancing quality — leads to a disappointment *in* her genital. Her very specific difference from him, which could so exactly have been the source of their mutual pleasure and creation, is turning out precisely to be the bane of her existence. And the pleasure she might take that her beloved father has just what her conformation and desire would have him have is turning out to be a source of envy. What was to be treasured on both their parts is now wasted on them both. She could do better with what he has than he appears to be doing.

The frustration that arises out of unfulfilled complementation leads then first back to greed — to the wish for both — and then inexorably onward to envy. These introduce new frustrations. The "I want more" of the wishes to be reciprocated in one's differences stays intact. But its aim and object switch. I want more of what is different becomes (greedily) I want more of both and ultimately (enviously) I want more of the same.

With this devolution, such reciprocations of the initial appetite for more of what only you can give recur to pose problems. Nice as they might have been, they now threaten a retreat to the abject longing that the return to greed and the move on to envy previously obscured. Differences in degree replace differences in kind as the only sort tolerated in known experience.

WORLDMAKING

William James began with the "buzzing blooming confusion." Somehow the baby must at once lie afloat this ocean of buzz and blur and bluster and at the same time discover, fashion or fabricate a coherent world. How infants do this is not yet known, but surely it must have something to do with the process of comparison and contrast. This is like That in this way, but unlike That in that way, and thus the Xs are distinguished from the Os. Such a process seems to me not only necessary to distinguish among the Xs and Os and the rest of the alpha-beta of existence, but necessary too so that, starting with the earliest hours of life, we are able to give our selves some choice in respect to the Xs and Os. If we don't have both we are at the mercy of whichever we do have, which may be both as yet undistinguished — an OX that gores and gores and gores some more until we can at least get out on the horns of a dilemma.

If we have time enough, we can examine all the contrasts and each of the ways objects or events compare and painstakingly put them together in gestalts that work — or work at least well enough not to break the mind that fashioned them. A pigeon, for example, can identify the differences among photographs of eight different human facial expressions; but with great respect, I do not think these differences signify; the pigeon is willing to earn its daily bread, but I think it reserves it own powers of comparison and contrast for life and times among the flock: for it, these will not be differences without distinction. The human baby is able to differentiate its mother's voice and image in the earliest days, even hours. How it does that no one knows. The artificial intelligence people are working on this, but they have yet to reconstruct it well enough to program a computer to make the comparisons and contrasts necessary for it to reliably distinguish sounds and images. (Perhaps this is because the baby uses a sense of smell, and having all of us outgrown that sense, we have forgotten how important a valency it has for others.)[1]

But let us consider how difficult it is to tell fish from fowl and from good red herring. What is included in a percept and what excluded out? Chomsky (1972) and others tell us what the Gestaltists told us before him, that we have a preset pattern-recognition facility that helps us sort out and arrange what goes with what and in which way. And once we learn, so to say, that our language is to be English and not Swahili, we can forget all about our Swahili receptors and arrangers. They drop off, the number of brain cells in the speech area shrink, and we are on our way with our native tongue. This idea of preset facility is of course endemic to psychoanalysis as well. Chefs say people eat with their eyes, and decorate the plate accordingly. Freud said babies look with their mouths — at least when the oral stage is lively and at home. Something is guiding recognition; perhaps we should even speak not of readiness to recognize, but to scan — even perhaps, prehensilely to search. There are preconceptions involved: phantasies about what one is in some sense supposed to encounter. And these, Freud maintained, will ever organize experience. Indeed what started off in Freud's theory as a concept of attention as *Besetzung*, or simply attention in the sense of paying attention, became attention cathexis, with its additional meaning of libido-driven cathexis, cathexis as investment in object and part-object choice. Attention thus gained the quality of drive acquiring object, aim, and force. What this means is that the preset facility is not an idle thing, but a questing one: the infant may not know of the breast, but it has a category all ready for its discovery and an appetite to match. (Bion was more than most the person who took up this idea of "appetite to match". He felt that knowledge was especially for brainy creatures a rather basic drive; and of course in his theories it is not impulse or emotion that are altered or nullified, but simply one's knowledge of them.)

---

[1] A 7-year-old in a camplike setting could distinguish whose socks and underwear were whose even after they came back reeking of detergent and bleach from the local laundromat. The idea that he used additional cues dissipated somewhat when his mother came to visit. "How," she asked him, "do you like my hair red this way?"

So the issue is not simply that This is compared with That, in the welter of impressions, but This and That are also compared with a predisposition (Bion also called it a "premonition"). And this puts a rather different complexion on matters. That is, when the baby hears its mother's voice on the playback of a tape recorder, it suckles at a different rate or in a different intensity. Whatever this means, it is likely to mean *some* thing about the experience of hearing a distinguishable or a particular or a special voice. Comparison thus takes on the meaning of goodness of fit, and contrast the freighting of the opposite. But what is this fit, which has a goodness? How does one think about it? Where does one begin?

I have begun with a baby or a fetus needing somehow to sort things out. But I fear that is already too late. So I move backward a bit and begin with a baby or a fetus who has an idea or two about how things should sort out. But if I am to account for those ideas or feelings, I must go even further back and begin with a baby who has been sorted out by eons of selective breeding to have certain ideas and feelings about how things should be sorted out. Or uncertain ideas, but certainly ideas that there are ideas to be had, if only he could discern them from the Jamesian welter of buzz and confusion. I see a head cocked alertly, expectantly awaiting, and I envision a sorting process, probably something in the way of comparison and contrast, just waiting to get its hands on the data.

The idea of selection and survival will ultimately take place as Fate, Destiny, Salvation, Perfection: it will form the undercurrents for the transmutation of Good and the Bad into the beautiful and the ugly. Its singularity, its is-ness, makes it at once desirable and frightening, these comprising awe at once beloved and hateful. People will try to split it into more manageable proportions, and of these, each will find its advocates, but only so when there is the confident, if unconscious, knowledge that the other "lost" versions, the Atlantis, is also safely somewhere, so that devotion is not really lost by making a choice. A patient noticed that on his TV screen the woman's breasts were often undisclosed; the bottom of the screen was too high or just high enough, or the screen image too low, so he bought a new and larger set. Another patient bought a VCR when she wanted to tape an event in which an athlete who resembled her lover appeared. Now there was no danger of missing him: he appeared and reappeared regularly. But something was missing. She bought another VCR, so she could transfer him to it and watch him without risking being unable to tape him on the first VCR should he appear live. Bion used to say that he could tell the real Ella from the Memorex. He also said he stopped his analysis when he could tell which of the many interpretations he and his analyst could dream up was the correct one, and which in contrast were the Memorexes.

Opposites depend on one another to provide the contrasts by which each can be known: to lose one is to lose the definition and dimension of the other. Thus a child horrified by his mother's "castration" takes away her capacity to astound and astonish, but he loses with it the sense by which he is different from her. "How come I looked at everyone funny; I mean how come everything I saw looked so . . . so askew?" asks the no-longer-awed woman into whom such a child has grown.

I saw something like awe in an infant on a television program not long back. An experimenter was moving objects about, and the baby watched alertly until he got the idea, at which point he looked away. When he looked back and saw it was still the same old thing, he looked away again. (I had begun myself to look away, having seen all this before.) But then something new was brought out and he watched intently, hardly moving—hardly *breathing*. And then *I* was hardly breathing. For I was watching a baby watch a ball that moved not around, but seemingly through a solid barrier. And the baby looked long and hard at this. Even after he looked away, he came back to it quickly, and looked long and hard at it again. As he continued to regard it and disregard it, he did so in a way the experimenter, on voice over, said was markedly different from the ways he and other babies look at the other material (for example a ball going over and under a solid object). Did this 3-month-old have an idea that what he was watching was inscrutable? The experimenter thought so, and I thought so too. That is what makes it so difficult to know when the baby begins—when you and I begin and when our patients began.

For example, I have come to think that people, as babies and the children and adults they become, look at someone else, the Other, and they see it in two basic sorts of ways. They see it from the point of view of it and they being a COUPLE, and it and they being or becoming part of a PAIR. When they see it from the point of view of COUPLING, they look toward the differences, particularly the reciprocal differences (like the breast that fits the mouth or the vagina that fits the penis). But when they take the PAIR point of view they look for the similarities, for what it and they have in common. From the point of view of the COUPLE the good and bad differences are based on the pleasure–unpleasure principle: differences that gratify and those that frustrate. From the point of view of the PAIR the bad differences are those that exclude one from whom and what one wants to be like, and the good ones are those that establish a commonality, even a unity of at-one-ness, and which leave someone else out. This point of view is, I think, driven by another principle, the selection principle.

Natural selection has for the most part been thought of as ecology and predation at work by chance or by fortune, selecting out the weaker and less fit of a species. But while this is doubtless true, it is not this aspect that interests me at the moment. I am rather interested in the idea of parents choosing offspring and parents choosing mates. This is a reciprocal process: selection is made to a degree by both when a relationship ensues and is consummated. Choices have to be to the advantage of both and ultimately the species. That is it is incumbent on both parties to a PAIRING (or GROUPING) to choose one another and to be choosable to one another. Otherwise all that choosiness we have, the choosiness that makes us wait for Mr. or Ms. Right to come along, that selfsame choosiness that makes us linger over a menu or wine list while we ignore our partner (though he or she may be glad to take that opportunity to size up the others in the room), the choosiness that makes us ignore the fact that time is passing and we are still obsessing over our choices—all that choosiness would be for nought. We might as well instead have chosen Miss Right Now.

Yet right now is what our children tell us, and we say wait, soon, hold on, don't rush into things, save your appetite. Become someone first. Better is coming.

Is it?

Kafka (in his *Parables*) says it is in the nature of the Messiah not to come when needed, but after—indeed, he is likely first to arrive the day after he arrives. David Rapaport was especially fond of this joke: The old man is dying, his daughter at his bedside. From the kitchen comes the delectable smell of sweetmeats and pastries. "Becky," the old man says, "ask your mother for a little something for me, a little nosh." Becky returns. "Mama says, 'No, it's for after.' "

Plainly both sorts of pressures apply: to wait and select, but not to wait forever. If the selection principle is not nudged by the appetites, it might be unable to select the menu, let alone something from it. On the other hand, if not restrained by the need to fulfill hopes and predilections, one might never heed the call to defer, moderate, compromise, integrate, and make things better for the children.

This duality of principle or pressure enters into how, beginning perhaps even before infancy, people in the deepest sense regard the experiences that unfold around them. But as usual that is already too late: we may not even experience things that are outside the categories or PAIR Stuff or COUPLE Stuff. Just as the physics of optics suggest an absolute continuum of the length of light rays, the psychophysics of perception seem, worldwide, to insist that we see things in the four discrete colors of red, green, yellow, and blue and their combinations and permutations—so it may be that experience can only fall into categories having to do with the COUPLE and the PAIR. Particles or Waves, Mass or Energy—these are questions with which our colleagues in subatomic physics question their phenomena of photons and quarks and all the rest. Some analysts, for example, Grotstein 1990a, b, Green 1986, and others borrow these metaphors for the metaphorical description of psychological phenomena. I like these as metaphors, but I am afraid of them as reifications.

Bion self-reportedly asked Mrs. Klein how she thought the baby knew the Good Breast was good. He might have asked Winnicott the same question about the good-enough mother. But the answer is obvious: It depends on one's point of view — or, as I am trying to add, on which one of one's points of view one is regarding life with, of which points of view, I have been saying, there are basically two. (I note here what will already be known, namely that my division into two is but one such.) Eigen (1993), for example, deals with the dialectic and tensions between what he calls the *distinction–union structure of self*. As, then, the baby sorts the stuff of experience or potential experience, what he encounters is his own question: What about this and what about this? Uhmn, this makes me feel go-od, but which kind of good? Libido good or hope good? Or, this is bad: what kind of bad, sensual bad or mental bad?

The sensualities come with the body: they involve the satisfaction of the drives, appetites, and the copular wishes of the object relationship. Pleasure is what feels good; unpleasure is what feels bad. The other set of pleasures and pains are based on feelings having to do with the species, GROUP, or PAIR. These have to do with mutual selection, that feeling not of rapture but of bliss, not of ecstasy but of exhilaration, when two hearts beat as one. This also involves the relationship between self and other, but here the sorting is based on the degree of how far along the two are toward the perfect at-one-ment, where two together are more than the sum of their parts.

For example the infant may feel that the breast is a very nice thing, but that established, which way should it point? If We, together, have the breast, then We can leave the question be: but if only one of us can have it, in which way shall We have it? Because when the breast is good, it is good in two ways, receiving and owning. But when it is bad, it is not bad in two ways, it is bad in one way: receiving or owning. So in either way there is the greedy wish for both, and in both ways there is envy.

For when I can only receive pleasure, I cannot own the source of it, and however much gratification I get from receiving succor and sustenance, it isn't mine to have or to give, and this is unsatisfying. But when I am not being pleasured by the breast, and I can neither take it nor leave alone, it is owning me, and only owning or spoiling it will do. Thus the chances are pretty good that no matter my sensual fate as a part of the Nursing couple, my fate as a member of the PAIR is unsettled.

Mother is urging me to settle, to eat and sleep and not make more of a fuss than she can identify as being what her group considers normal. But what about my group?

Your group, Baby? You don't have a group, you're just a baby.

But I'm not "just a baby," that's just one of the ideas your group has about babies. My group says that eating and sleeping isn't enough. I need quality, there are Good and Betters involved. See, I have predilections only part of which you are filling out.

My God, if I ever talked that way to my mother, she would have killed me! What is it with this? Get real.

You mean, join up with you and your mother and the others of your group? Throw in with you, identify with you? When in Rome—that sort of thing?

I'm gonna stick a pacifier in your mouth, you talk to me so fresh.

I'm not being fresh. See, my group would kill me if I defect to your group.

I'll kill you, you spoiled brat, talking that way. Who is this so-called group of yours?

Well, Mom, it's difficult to explain. But don't you think we were put on earth for a purpose?

A purpose? You have religion already?

I guess. But a purpose. You know not just eat, drink, and be merry. It's like, well, take you: see, you carried me, and you're taking care of me, holding me and stuff, why do you do it? Isn't it so that you and Dad will kind of live through me unto the generations to come? Gain your own kind of immortality?

The mouth on him! We had you because we loved you!

Yes, Mom, but don't you do a kind of triage as between how much for me and how much for yourself? I'm not complaining, but I have less of you than I did a couple of weeks ago.

You expected to stay in the womb your whole life? Of course I do less. I got to take care of myself, don't I?

But you *have* taken care of me, and very nicely too. It's just the point. Somehow you know how much is good enough—enough for me, enough for you. And it's the same with me. I gotta know how much is enough—for me and for you. Compare what I do have with what I should have.

Should have! Already you're giving your mother a should? You shouldn't talk to me that way, you're so interested in should. I woulda had my mouth washed out. Anyways, what do you know? I've had a lot more experience of life than you.

So you are of the live-and-learn school? Interesting. But what about your ideals, your sense of purpose, of destination: for example, how come you married Dad?

Don't knock your dad, honey. He may not seem like it to you, the way he tosses you in the air until you vomit, but he's a nice man, and I'm lucky to have him. I was very, very glad, I can tell you, when your father came along. I was already feeling worried: maybe I should have married the saxophone player, maybe I had tempted fate and would end up with no one.

But you did wait! You had a sense of good and better and still you waited, afraid as you were that maybe better would get in the way of good.

Did I think of it that way? I don't remember thinking that, but yes.

But didn't you ever think after you did say yes to Dad that maybe someone better might come along?

I can't believe this. I was 35, if you must know, and I wanted to have children. You, if you can imagine.

So between the not yet and the no longer, you made your compromise? Well, I have to do the same. It's part of life, as you might say. But I don't know whether I want to make the same compromise you do. See I have to be chosen also; someone has to want to marry me and have children with me. But should I be like you or better than you?

Darling, every parent wants her child to be better than she is, even your father. We want the best for you, the best schools, the best friends, yes, even the person you marry should be the best.

And I'll have the best children, who will also be the best grandchildren . . . Yes, but if I let you do your compromises with me, will I turn out to be the best person to be able to marry the best person? Maybe all I will be able to get is you.

Listen, honey, you could do worse.

Yes, but I'm not 35 yet, and if I listen to you and live and learn that is what may happen to me also.

You're telling me how I should have lived? I married, I got pregnant and here you are. And the mouth on him, thank God there is no one else in this room. Do you want to go back?

No. Of course not. And don't talk about that! It gives me nameless dread. How do I know I am one of those who is supposed to survive and flourish, anyhow? It's just that if I am to turn out I have to learn from your mistakes, learn even from what you don't consider your mistakes. Maybe you shouldn't have let your mother "kill" you. Maybe you shouldn't read Dr. Spock. See, I'm not saying you're wrong, it's just that I have to know whom to listen to, even to survive, let alone doing better than you. Oh lord, and there are the questions of getting into nursery school and a training institute and what analyst to go to. Nurse me, Mama—quick!

My poor baby. Of course you should survive, you're my precious baby. Anyone gives you trouble, you come to me and I'll give them such a. . . .

This metaphysical problem concerning when to be different and when to be like arises, I believe, out of the same comparison-contrast processes of sorting out what-is-what I was working with earlier. Both baby and mother have to be different, to be a nursing COUPLE, and have to be the same, a PAIR in agreement about what's good and what's good enough. The baby, as he or she says, has his or her own GROUPS, and they have their standards and these have been bred into them: they are in the DNA. In fact they may be part of the DNA also in the sense that he or she is driven by his genetic need to select and reproduce with the best and the fittest—if only baby can learn what and who that is. Does baby's mother know? Is Dr. Benjamin Spock reliable on those grounds? Should she be reading Nietzsche, perhaps? How will baby know, and how will baby know when he or she knows? Should baby also become thirty-five, and then settle? Maybe this father, who tosses baby around so, is implying something. Maybe baby should grow up into a girl or, no, maybe better a boy — what are saxophone players anyway? It is all confusing. Is being a mother who has a baby the same as or different from being a baby who has a mother? If different, should baby be a mother or be a baby? If the same, what difference does it make? And what differences are there to make?

I imagine I hear these debates and the dark wonders that drive the questions in the consulting room, but it would be wrong of me to say that I do hear them. I don't hear them because the baby I have portrayed will have outgrown these wonderings, probably even before he learns to talk.

A woman in her sixties remarks that when she was asked no longer to attend a particular committee, she felt "dead — deenergized, flat, as if I had run out of life. I couldn't move. I didn't have legs, or rather the stuff that makes one's legs work." Later in the session she spoke of a favorite fantasy of hers in which it is wartime and the wounded are being brought to a central clearing house, at which some will be treated, others transhipped, and, since resources are short, other will be left to die. It is her job to perform the triage. Earlier in the session she had spoken of being unable to sleep, except by taking a Valium, which she fancies I don't approve of, though she knows that as a fact, this may well be untrue. In the session previous to this one she recalled a time when she felt her father pressed a goodnight kiss onto her mouth in such a way as to render her helpless. She could only feel safe enough to sleep by sleeping out on a porch. In this session she spoke of a man at the office who stepped forward into her space. She misspoke his name and called him by the name of a former lover.

As I didn't speak, and the hour was growing late, the patient began to use her own interpretations. But as she drew to a close, she said, "All right, there is the homosexual thing with his wife [referring to the lover and the office-mate], and the castration [upon which she elaborated], but none of this seems to help. Well, it's late: the session's almost at an end. Where did all the time go? Am I late? Am I overstaying? Have you said my time is up and I haven't heard? It seems a long session now, what I was telling you about seems a thousand years ago, at the dawn of time."

As I listened, I could understand her way of construing her experience, especially as it rather faithfully amalgamated how each of us had previously understood matters so very much like that. Were the situation a COUPLE sort of thing, I would have had nothing much to add to her descriptions of hate and love and rivalry. But as I heard her out, I began to realize that she wasn't at the moment able to see the PAIR for the COUPLE; and that the thousand years ago and dawn of time linked up with the triage and her profound sense that because there isn't enough for all, some are simply expendable, therefore the only question is who and on what basis.

After the session I wondered on and off what purpose it served, if any, for her to interpret her experience in the way she did, using COUPLE concepts in lieu of those arising out of the PAIR. And I began to wonder whether guilt was preferable to the sort of nameless dread that the earliest feelings about "triage" might induce. I wondered if I should display to her how her response to dread (of being evicted from the committee; of my silence; of our death) was the search for a guilt that permitted amends to be made. Poor Oedipus had worries even before his life grew into a complex.

Still, what struck me above all was the lack of language available for the earliest PAIR experiences: how could the woman who was representing the baby who had outgrown, but not grown out of, the experience speak of it if she never had the words and she never acquired them. For as Kant (1781) said and has, thanks to Bion, become once again widely considered, though "concepts without intuitions are empty, intuitions without concepts are blind."

I saw from these reflections that I had been somewhat negligent in providing words and syntax to experiences that cannot be experienced fully without them. For example, this sudden fear of being hopelessly, dreadfully different that arose in response to being asked off the committee: Was it a threat to her manhood? Or a threat to her specieshood? What was different about her? Was she not woman enough or not person enough? Was the person in her space someone in her privates or someone in her publics? Well, of course she had a choice, but only some choice, since once she left the board into the dive, it was going to be a while. And how she experienced even her own experience of matters would depend on the point of view available to her. One point of view does not necessarily know of the existence of the other unless they are in the same field at the same time. When infants outgrow themselves too quickly they forget — are glad to forget what they hadn't the words or images to think in. But it doesn't forget them. And words are needed to perform the reintroductions, if they are to get on speaking terms.

As it happened, my patient, being, if reluctantly, experienced in the ways of self-nondisclosure began to attach her experiences to the death of her mother and herself in childbirth — viewpoints only open to the other 180 degrees of arc.

And it is to those other 180 degrees I want now to turn.

Recalling that what we are after is viewpoint, let us move closer in on the paradoxical relationship of similarity and difference — the Xs and the Os. Without Xs and Os we couldn't play tic-tac-toe, but only if we agree to let X and O represent differences can we use them to play the game. So to play, you and I have to agree — a simple X at the end of the agreement will do — to let X or O or O = You and the unused one = Me. This is a PAIR agreeing to be a COUPLE for purposes of playing or competing or going to war. But the PAIR is precedent to the COUPLE: we agree, that is we take in common, our, or our groups', standards, within which we differentiate ourselves. We then play and tote up the score: such and so many wins win. A child I saw in analysis recorded the scores for both of us. She marked an X whenever she won. She was playing for Xs. She believed them to be superior to Os. One day she said, "Well, that is the end of the Os: They're gone. Pfftt. They don't exist anymore. Zero. Now there are only Xs and all of them are mine."

Though I personally felt a little crushed, I was happy for her sake that she still knew enough about the Os to want to destroy them. That is, her other 180-degree arc was still intact. Though she felt that she could compete more successfully in a world made up only of Xs, she hadn't gone on to say, Os? What are Os? Never heard of them!

I am not fond of tic-tac-toe; I play only reluctantly and grumpily. So with the Os out of this galaxy, I dared hope I would be spared the further rigors of the game. And indeed my little patient was herself nonplussed. How could she go on acquiring her beloved Xs when there were only Xs. Xs were a drug on the market.[2] Well she was not without resources, that kid. She would play capital Xs, me lower case.

"And little Xs will be enough for you to win?" I asked, hoping I suppose to dissuade her.

"Better than nothing," she replied. "Anyways I will king them."

"Yet now you haven't left yourself a way to zero-out my Os."

Your Os don't exist anymore," she pointed out logically enough. "All you have left are little Xs."

But, thought I, what happens when the world is all Xs—isn't there such a thing as an excess of Xs? What do the Xs do with themselves. Can all the nations in the world be on one side? With whom then would nations make the intercourse of war and commerce? Or was it to be simply a homosexual world? This was during the epoch of the cold war, when the world knew and agreed on who was whose Xs and Os, more or less. It was before the mightily upheaval when everyone shifted and formed new sets of Xs and Os upon whom to wage love and war. Before strange bedfellows became fellow travelers and old allies became sources for xenophobia. *Plus ça change*. Still one knows that only so much uniformity is tolerable, and I wondered with the greatest interest how my patient was going to manage her collocation of X-ness.

Well, it was a boring time of grey sameness. I was bored and she was bored. But I cannot say we were bored together. Indeed she made noises as if she were continuing her vast pleasure in winning, and added X upon X to her

---

[2]This a poor pun, which nevertheless I mean seriously.

collection. But I felt that her pride more so than her heart was in it. Her exclamations of victory and triumph grew forced. But it didn't seem a generous act on my part to declare this inference with her. On the other hand she seemed angrier and angrier with me as the days passed and I would sometimes venture the question of whether there was something I should be doing or saying that I wasn't.

"Like what?" she would snarl, as if with that question I was about to reintroduce an O into the game. Presently it became routine for her to come in and turn her back on me, open the little satchel she carried, take out books or toys or candy, and ignore me. When she grew bored with this, she would stare fixedly at the clock as a hostage might at a passing airplane. I began to surmise that she and I were both Xs now, the remaining issue being which of us was little X and which was big. But if that were where things were at, why bigger and smaller in preference to a relationship in which she and I were different?

I asked her this. I said, "There are two Xs in this room and one is big and the other is small—"

"—*You* are small!" she interjected.

"But at least there isn't a Mommy's breast or a Daddy's penis."

"The Os," she said, and then added, "dickhead."

I apologized: "I may have surprised you, as if my head and its thoughts were a dick busting into you—almost crashing your penis and causing an 'O'."

The interesting aspect of this was her willingness to bear the great pain of being perhaps a defective X or having a therapist who was one. Because unless I were willing to be an O and look to her for intercourse, there were but two seats in the room, the better and the worse. And heaven knew my boredom was such that I was tempted to reverse the transference and take on the O-ness. Nor was she willing or able to let me be anything but a defective X or a baby O. Because if I were not, she would be, and everything she said about me would go double for her, understandably a fate no one would wish upon themselves. Still this made her very afraid of me, with her Hobson's choice of me being either an O or equally bad, a bigger X.

If I had known then what I imagine I do now, I could have put this more plainly for her, and I think the analysis might have been done more quickly, certainly more efficiently.

I would have been able to see that her dilemma was one of not knowing how to survive were she to be or become less of an X in the PAIR and GROUP of Xs to which she aspired to belong—or, to which, more accurately, she was scared to death not to belong. If it weren't her group, it would be an against-her group. And, then, on the other side be part of a COUPLE. But this was something that membership in the PAIR contradicted and precluded. An adult patient put this dilemma nicely: "The other evening it occurred to me that I might not have to die after all, so I began doing my exercises, get rid of the cellulite." What was striking was the matter-of-factness with which she said this, as if the other evening I was looking at the windows and I thought I might get some new curtains. I think she no longer knew, so envious did it make her to know that some people have to be reminded that in the midst of life they are in death.

When my little patient was playing the transference game of tic-tac-toe, she played grimly as if for dear life. She seemed to be saying, First I have to survive and then I'll worry about what to do with my life. It was the temptation of forgetting her PAIR and GROUP anxieties and getting on about COUPLING that had obliged her to empty the room of Os. She, like Odysseus, had to tie herself to the mast to get past the siren songs and safely home. I'm afraid I worried her with some interpretations about oedipal guilt and anxiety over the ricochet of split-off anxieties before she put me right.

The bit of play that finally caught my attention was simplicity itself. She had lined up a series of objects, as if dominoes, and was trying to make them hit into one another with one throw of a rag ball. But, uncharacteristically, she was missing her shots badly. I said: "You don't believe in this sort of thing, do you?"

She said, "Why should they all have to go just because one does—and I don't mean to the bathroom, either."

Then she readjusted the long grey line, so that the objects were closer front-to-back than previously. I had gone off thinking about the bathroom gibe and for a few moments I didn't catch on. The PAIR and the GROUP were now so organized as if to avoid panic and forfend against any sort of lemming impulse; they literally backed each other up and gave one another mutual support. After she had arranged them just so, she moved off to take her aim again—moved off so that her back was right against me.

"Move, you jerk," she ordered.

In the initial alignment, I thought, envy was at work: John Wayne saying, If I'm going down I'm gonna take some of them Redskins with me. This was X against X—xenophobia. In the second alignment the Os were still quiet, waiting perhaps in the bathroom: but the Xs were no longer envious but cooperative and helpful. As Machiavelli (1532) told his Prince, "It helps against internal disorders, sir, if there are enemies at our border."

In time a re-sorting takes place, although it may be truer to say that other, dormant sortings claim or reclaim the airwaves. The adversarial ethers that reek so strongly of pride and fall and that belong to the PAIR conceptualizations and the GROUP mentality seem to evaporate; they are replaced by the unmistakable pheromones of the libido at hunt.

The alternation of the two, the COUPLING and PAIRING modes, matches perfectly the mind's inherent capacity for attending to events selectively. Thus the two can be used, selectively, in preference to one another as antagonists, alternately, or in lieu of one another defensively. In adolescence, for example, the asceticism or religiosity that marks some Western young people can function both as reaction formations against their opposites and as demonstrations of affiliation with the ideals of the PAIR or GROUP. Idealizations, as the baby was earlier saying to his or her mother, are promptings: these promptings say, Remember there are betters and worses. Not just feel goods and feel bads. Freud noted this when he remarked that the superego skipped a generation: that goods and bads are strung out on generational lineages: the child develops his parents' negatives out of which he prints his grandparents' positives.

The implications of this for ourselves, as analysts, are twofold. Most of us understand our function in being part of the transference/countertransference COUPLE and of speaking aloud what we take note of in those circumstances, drawing the patients' attention to what we feel they are systematically not noticing and then the reasons for this.

We are perhaps less used to noticing the baggage we bring with us when we enter the analytic situation as a member of our GROUP. As is so often the case, such unnoticing is a residual effect of the Founder. Freud had two missions: one was innovative and organized toward discovery, the second was conservative and organized toward preservation. Which of what do we bring into the training institutes and consulting rooms? What is GROUP stuff needed for our identities and sense of belonging and which is COUPLE stuff designed to foment innovation and discovery? For example, in the Postscript to *The Problem of Lay Analysis*, Freud (1927) was responding to the call upon his selection standards for the fitness of his progeny in terms of the survival of his discoveries. But, as was his wont, he went beyond the immediate question of whether psychologists, like Reik, could represent capital-P Psychoanalysis as he intended it to be: he mused about a function he called the *Seelsorger*. This was an idea of a 7-11 or convenience-store psychoanalyst. The 1970s idea of storefront operations was very much in this tradition. But perhaps even more so than these was his idea of the *Seelsorger* as a kind of lay pastor, who makes rounds in the neighborhood or community. But, during a five-year period when I myself explored this function, I soon discovered that the people in the community assumed that persons like myself were out to change them— though we called it cure instead. And this meant that we hated them—them and their ways and values and traditions—all the PAIR and GROUP stuff. And indeed at those times when I sit stolid in my own consulting room, noting my empathy dropping like a thermometer in a cold snap, because my patient is going on and on and on with more and more and more of the same, I sometimes wonder, "Is this a mirror?" Have I so successfully converted my patient to my traditions that he or she is one of "us" now? What happened to that saucy idiopath I remember from a few months or years ago? Is what I am contemplating the so-called resistance to regression in the COUPLE? Or am I once again being part of several cultures in conflict?

The other implication is perhaps deeper and more difficult to observe. It is that what we are accustomed to think is neurotic or deviant may be the insistent hum of the DNA striking off the libido. When we are working in the transference and the making conscious of the countertransference, we will tease all this out, no matter what words we call it by. But this is not so assured, I think, when we are working with the narrative, because we are no longer present at the creation. The shaping of experiences out of events has already happened, and we are doomed to secondhand data from secondary sources. For the data we cannot get in this form is about the nothing: the absences that have been sealed over with presences, the nothings that have been created out of nothing, the sexual and emotional life which is as-if, and even while it is taking place, isn't and never was, but replaces what might have been but what, out of envy, has been so destroyed as to be gone almost without trace. How much of this is true of our stories — the narratives we call interpretations, which we tell to each other and our patients? For example, by the time I get to them almost all my students have already been taught the "as the twig is bent" story. One capable young psychiatrist was nudging her patient, who was prone to repeated bouts of insomnia during which she imagined and reimagined what it would be like to be dead, to consider the impact of her mother's death on this activity. But the patient resisted this interpretation, arguing that, as she remembered things, this had all started two years before her mother's death. This flummoxed my student because she didn't have another clue to the determinants, and she was soon upset with me because I was loath to suggest one. But how would I know? I love stories, so much so that I am willing to spend a lot of time wondering what, how and who shapes them, especially stories about facts. Really? I like to ask when it is not too tactless, how on earth did you come to that idea? I try to reserve the same tactful wonder about the stories I tell, like this one.

One other story that is told in certain circles is that psychoanalysis as a therapy is not sadistic. But it is: it is a 19th-century, racist, classist, scientifically elitist, masculinistic structure, imitative of these same qualities when they operate in medicine. It makes no difference which stranger performs this function on which other stranger, just as it makes no difference to the structurally male elements in the role whether that role is carried out by a woman or a man. Or a Freudian, Sullivanian, Perlsian, or nude marathonist. The object of this structure, the element without which it could not function, on whom it utterly depends, namely, by that or any other name, the patient, cannot but return to it the hatred it imposes. But there is a saving grace, and it is one that all the others, including its own forebears lack—it is that analysts sauce themselves with the same sauce they give the goose. We are in continual self-disclosure and self-analysis, and it is this, I believe, that represents the new departure and the reason that so far, at least, we have survived the century. Presently this will extend to our structure as a PAIR with the patient, to the GROUPS that represent us and that we represent, and to the stories we read, publish, and tell.

But in the meantime, even if we only go so far, concerning the making of interpretations, as to ask ourselves: "Why do I want to say that; how will saying that help me?" we are in the right direction.

ANALYTIC CONSIDERATIONS

That last question is, I think, especially required when working with those whose greed and circumstance were such as to make them unable to reconcile their joint memberships in the PAIR and the COUPLE and who, as a result, have grown deadly with envy.

Envy's painful nature is such that knowing who and what is envied is experienced as a tribute to the object of that envy, intolerably therewith making the object a source of even greater envy.

So the question becomes: Whose analysis is this? Not mine, says the patient, I wouldn't be caught dead in this poor excuse for an analysis. And who could blame him? The envious are connoisseurs. Though they turn their noses up, they have a keen sense of smell; they can smell an as-if analysis a mile away. I do not think a departure from an as-if analysis, one in which the therapist has begun treating the patient because the therapist cannot bear *not* to treat the patient, is a negative therapeutic reaction. These patients are bound to destroy empathy because it is precisely what their envy precludes them from having and, equally painful, reciprocating. Often the sense of growing empathic failure makes the analyst tempted either to fake it or compensate for it. But these won't do if the analysis is to be regarded as a chrysalis in which the patient can, if tumultuously, evolve from his own needs to be as-if into a capacity, himself, to tolerate being real. A patient dreams: "You were on a platform, giving a talk, but you were unable to make yourself heard. I touched you on the shoulder and whispered: "Should I get you a microphone?" You nodded yes, so I got you one. You may have gone on to finish, but I didn't see you after that."

Real people really die and must daily be prepared to do so, leaving over to other generations the wishes for immortality, salvation, and perfection that have been bred into us. The envious die a thousand deaths; it is heartwrenching, the pain they go through, because their self-preservation inclination is such that they cannot resign themselves to the one and only death. (Some, indeed, would rather kill themselves than let death take them.) What membership in what group supports the idea of early death? What is the cause worthy enough? "I propose to have a nothing of a life so that when I die it will not break my heart," said the patient whose dream I just recounted, earlier in our work when she couldn't be touched by me at all. Makes sense. Hearts can't develop calluses and still COUPLE in love and hate. But heartbreak with luck can take place in stages — particularly if someone is there to stand by and hold the remaining pieces together. That is the chrysalis. This is the analysis done when, in Bion's deceptively simple phrase, one says what he means and means what he says.

This is why it helps when the analyst comes into the analysis with as few wishes as possible for anything from the patient — or for him, *especially* that he or she flourish or get well. For to the envious this seemingly innocuous leftover ornament from the medical model means, in his or her turn, getting put into the position of exciting the appalling envy of the gods: He whom the gods wish to destroy, they first make sane. Far better, some feel, to be more and more and more of the same — and on the same side as their gods, than to venture being different.

6

THE EQUALIZING EYE

I cannot say for sure if looking or not looking is the first interposition of will and choice available to the nascent ego but it is surely among the first. No more is required than the blink of an eye or the turn of a head for the infant to establish or obliterate the potential experience in its field of vision. Smell, touch, temperature, hearing and kinesthesias are probably not so malleable in babies but their attention *can* be engaged[1]; these sensations require distractions of a more substantial sort. Each of the senses can be hypertrophied or augmented at the expense of the other by concentrating attention, not at the source, but at the receptor. Bion (1970) has observed that insofar as this activity interferes with the senses working in common, it compromises what is generally called the ability to use common sense. And because looking is more *submissive* to acts of will and ego than the other senses, it may well achieve a preeminent role as the monarch of the senses — that to which the others defer. In that capacity looking and seeing can alter the impact of the Other as it is conveyed through the senses to the Self both by becoming the

---

[1]"On the second day of birth, newborns mastered head turning to one side 83 percent of the time when sugar water was offered them after they turned. Once head turning was established, these newborns were taught to turn their heads to the left at the sound of a bell and the right at the sound of a buzzer. The task was then complicated by reversing everything. All infants were able to accomplish this in about thirty minutes" (Siqueland and Lipsitt [1966], referenced in Brazelton and Cramer [1990]).

primary mode of apprehension and, then, by becoming subject to the acts of the ego and will by which the Self hopes to shape or reshape the world of experience. When information is located *only* in the domain of the senses or only in memory, it is less difficult to diminish something's significance. The expression, "What the eye don't see, the heart don't grieve," is a case in point. It is easier to forget when memory is not prompted by sense impressions. Equally, sense impressions are easier to ignore if they do not alight memories. If only linked to the injunction, "remind me to forget," they are merely a stimulus to the practiced (and eventually) quick detour of significance from one event to the other which screens it.

This essay deals with looking and seeing in both of those respects. The basis for the thoughts I present is, however, clinical: the several patients — one in particular — have so emphatically employed aspects of looking and seeing to serve their purposes that the specifics of each became available for rudimentary generalization. What these patients seem to have revealed is a very considerable tension in having what one experiences selected for one, and the degree to which submitting to that role is a source of jagged envy and voluptuous pleasure.

EYE CONTACT

Infant observation has it that eye contact is the roadway to bonding in the first hours and days of neonatal life. Whether this is so or not is, I think, open to question. The explanatory power of the concept of bonding in human beings leaves, in my view, much to be desired[2]; but there appears to be far less doubt that infants normally recognize their mothers in a matter of hours and days after being born, can track them visually through a crowded nursery, and soon come to recognize their voices. The same holds true in the recognition of fathers. These observations were available to the naked eye of the observer, but have been augmented by videotape and computer studies. In the latter, the infant draws down differently (faster, harder, longer) on a bottle when the mother or even the mother's voice is recognized, as against the visage or voice sounds of strangers.

What is of interest is not so much that such discriminations can be made, but how they signify. For example, recognition and eye contact appear to be

---

[2]The concept of "bonding" arises out of the tradition that only observable or measurable behavior is the proper study of science; attribution of motive or subjective state is considered anthropomorphic and akin to the pathetic fallacy. Although I will not take up the matter here, I wish at least to note that this tradition arises out of deep states of mind (which it cannot itself, of course, study) and that what is and isn't scientific is a function of the psychology of the PAIR and its requirement for foresight to which I shall presently be coming.

of the very first importance to the human mother. The rapt gaze of the newborn while he or she is nursing or cuddling appears to assure the mother that the baby is in contact not just with breast or bottle, but with *her*. Indeed, I offer the thought that looking and seeing have, in this respect, the same meaning for mother and baby: that their eye contact represents a mutual recognition that they exist for one another as members of the same species, a PAIR — two of a kind. Without either of them quite realizing this, there might have been quite a bit of doubt about whether they do so exist or not beforehand and between times.

Research indicates that in any 1-minute segment of interaction, there are 4.4 cycles of attention and apparent inattention in what is called a "still-face" situation, in which mothers are instructed to keep a blank face and still torso, after a previous session of cheerful, active engagement. The consistent pattern of infant behavior in the still-face situation is of repeated attempts to elicit mother's responses, followed by somber expression, orientation away from the mother, and finally withdrawal. All this takes place in less than three minutes (Brazelton and Cramer 1990, pp. 105ff.). Should the baby in his turn present the mother with a still face, averted or evasive gaze, or turn away toward something or someone else, the effects on the mother are often most demoralizing. (Ms. A., about whom more anon, would have been around 4 months when, according to my reconstruction, she began to experiment with breaking the duet with her mother. In her particular case her mother responded by immediately weaning her. This infant's first effort of saying, "I don't care; anyway I control our interactions and so I own you, and anyway you and I may not be of the same breed" was met with a staggeringly precise riposte. Why the mother took this so hard is of interest as well: By her name and birthdate as well as a host of other less immediately obvious signifiers, Ms. A. was a "replacement" child for a younger sister of the mother's, who unaccountably drowned in early childhood.[3])

From the break of eye contact that signifies doubting and refusal, I wish to distinguish the eye contact that averts war. It is seen perhaps most clearly among animals, whose mutual acts of deference lead them each to look aside rather than to lock eyes. The locking of eyes is thus freed for use as a forerunner for hostile engagement — the locking of horns, so to speak, and of becoming visually larger in close-up as space or territorial boundaries are violated by incursion — hence a signal of a coming attack. Since staring of this sort represents a reproductive challenge, indeed foretells aggression in the instrumentation of that challenge, if the mounting of challenge is to be short-circuited, one creature, the smaller or otherwise less hierarchically dominant, will break off the locked glare and look away or down. This action

---

[3]For more in the present text concerning Ms. A., see below.

redraws the space. The continuation of "eyeball to eyeball" confrontation signals the desire of both parties to escalate the aggression—the premonitory look into further hostilities and ongoing, even murderous, tests of strength. It is important to note, however, that these hostilities are subject to rules of engagement that both creatures understand to the finest nuance, differing in this manner from hostile encounters that, for example, serve predation. (Sitting-up patients (P.) often feel that they have to adopt a strategy in this regard. They do not wish to lose the staring contest, but worse is that the therapist or analyst Ψ might lose; in either case P. feels himself to be a loser. Often therefore P. presents his challenges indirectly by acting out, or in dreams.)

Eye contact is sensitive to context: the same look may be a stare or a gaze, and as Geertz phrased it, mistaking the difference between a wink and a blink may earn one a bloody nose. Inside circumstances of intimacy, it is the instrumentality by which the most tender and trusting regard is exchanged. Outside this context the same look may be a bellicose glare. Even the interruption of a looking sequence has signal value: it can restart a sequence, end one, or become a sequence as when one looks "past" the other as if the latter no longer exists. (Looking away is more equivocal; it can, depending on the context, variously express distaste or shame, a wish to not be seen as much as not to see.) Each look one gives is easily perceived even at a distance and very rapidly—tachistiscopic exposures can be registered at speeds exceeding 1/400 of a second—and so has a language value all of its own. As I shall show, looks easily communicate whether one is in the state of mind of a COUPLE or of a PAIR. Distal language—looking toward or away or where and at what—particularly serves the needs of the individual when he or she is in the state of mind of the PAIR.[4] For example, in a commenting on *Mr. Palomar* (the eponymous Italo Calvino [1985] novel), Emery (1990) writes: "Mr. Palomar wonders about the relationship between looking, longing, thinking and their implicit relationship with the appetite and the breast." And further:

> One day Mr. Palomar walks along the beach. There, he observes in the distance the naked torso of a woman. At first he looks her way, but as fast as a thought averts his gaze toward a vague no where, so as not to see what he looks at. Between Mr. Palomar's eyes and the breast he cannot avoid but cannot see, he places a device analysts are just beginning to discover, what Mr. Palomar likes to call the "mental brassiere." [p. 8]

---

[4]Among the gestures homo sapiens shares with the apes is an eyebrow-lifting eye-widening gesture on unexpected encounter or in other situations of ambiguity as to intention. This appears to allow mutual inspection through lingering looks. President Jimmy Carter is much given to this mannerism.

From the beginning, then, there is in the infant's repertoire a bag of looks and ways of looking, which both function as and signal his states of mind. By looking he can achieve and signal engagement, signal significance and credit acknowledgment and reciprocation to his mother—and, in the merest deflection of the same gesture, do precisely the opposite. Emery's account, moreover, reveals the tensions and hubbub set up in the interval between looking and seeing: Mr. Palomar's hatred of the very fascination the figure is exerting on him: her selection of where his gaze will fall. It is Mr. Palomar who snatches up the "brassiere." Parents, needless to say, spend hour upon hour attempting to elicit reciprocal responses from their infants. They doubtless do this for a variety of reasons, but surely among them must be their intuition that their little ones may not always be disposed to join in the game of mutual acknowledgment and response. Given the relative dearth of the infant's other socially signifying skills, looking and seeing (or their opposites) must surely count heavily when weighed for their value in conveying some *effect* upon mother and others: Some effect back, that is—for it is by no means clear that infants always wish to offer the regard the parent seeks: "He does not know at first," Winnicott writes, "that the mother he is building up through his quiet experiences is the same as the power behind the breasts that he has in his mind to destroy" (Winnicott 1958, p. 151). To give that recognition constitutes at least the beginnings of the recognition that the breast or the symbolic breast or the feeding, hunger and satiety itself, belongs to the mother in a way that infant's thumb does not. Winnicott goes on:

> . . . the baby has instinctual urges and predatory ideas. The mother has a breast and the power to produce milk, and the idea that she would like to be attacked by a hungry baby. These two phenomena do not come into relation with each other till the mother and child *live an experience together*.
>
> I think of the process as if two lines came from opposite directions, liable to come near each other. If they overlap there is a moment of *illusion*—a bit of experience which the infant can take as *either* his hallucination *or* a thing belonging to external reality. [Winnicott 1958 p. 152.]

External reality and hallucinosis meet at a crossroads every bit as fateful as that at which Oedipus and his father met. Recognition of external reality— that is, allowing the presence behind the illusion to select one's mental acts as ones obtaining to perception and memory—arises issues in the Depressive position, the realization of ruthlessness and the need to find and make reparation. Illusion permits the baby nicely to settle in with paranoia and splitting.

> P., who came to analysis about being unable to endure the prospect of carrying and caring for a baby she otherwise so much wanted, came in time to bring first

one and then the second of the babies she was later able (in both senses) to bear to her sessions. There were many motives for this, but perhaps above all she wished to display to Ψ the regard she was given by her daughters' often unswerving gaze. These were tonic to her: "I never felt alive before!" Later on, after the work had terminated, she came back for a few visits prompted by the fear that she would slap the living daylights out of her elder daughter "for not looking at me when I speak to her." Interpretations reminding her that this had been her experience with her own mother (something she had learned to "give back") helped. In what was then to be her last session of this refresher she said, knowingly, "See you around."

But where does the infant's visual attention go when it is *not* here or there? Brazelton and Cramer (1990) quote Jorge Luis Borges (1964) on the subject: "A book that does not contain its counterbook is considered incomplete." What Borges means is what Lacan (1949) means when he says: "I think where I am not, therefore I am where I do not think. . . . I am not wherever I am the plaything of my thought: I think of what I am where I do not think to think" (p. 166). This is the problem awaiting one when one wonders about the alternatives to looking or to seeing while looking.

I want to add to my discussions a different axis, one that concerns not only who has what, but who chooses — who selects. The power to select is perhaps the truest expression of the concept of power, after all, and reprieve from having their responses selected is of profound importance to babies when they feel greedy. To assure themselves freedom from being mesmerized by good experiences and even more by the enduring frustration of bad ones, infants rummage through their side-real world of the no-things.

We too must revisit the nightmare world where good experiences "go" when they aren't (there). (I took this issue up previously in my elaboration of Bion's concept of the No-thing and in other essays of this series, but I am about to come at it differently.) I trust the odd distinction between the choosing of a whole object by another for some sort of relationship and that of one object being subject to selective fashioning by others will gain meaning in the remarks that follow. Fortunately, certain patients provide some information along these lines. My theme here is the stutter-step phasic and interpersonally interactive relationship involved in looking and seeing — a tension at the edges of choosing and being chosen. I will try to show that there is a significant emotional difference between the sense that one is the agent of the choice and the recipient of the choice. As usual the situation is complicated: to be chosen is at once necessary (to feel unchosen is dire) and narcissistically gratifying. However, to be chosen is not necessarily one's own to choose, and this can make the chosen feel shriven, abjectly and intolerably envious.

P. was one such. The situation simply was that until P. rediscovered, step-by-step, what Ψ told him, he felt invaded and nullified as if by internal erosion. Before he could bear to use them, P. had to replicate the process by which Ψ arrived at interpretations and *make them his own*. Close to the root of this was the quite awful feeling that Ψ, by selecting from among what he, P. presented, was murdering bits of him in favor of other bits. Also, of course, there was his envy of Ψ as the selector. P. wanted to create himself as artists want to create their works.

This tension shall occupy much of what I have to say. As the materials I furnish from the consulting room unfold, I hope the reader will feel a comfortable familiarity with it as psychoanalytic data and, as I did, feel jostled by a variety of interpretations available from the traditional interpersonal and intrapsychic understandings, based as these are on theories concerning the COUPLE. For example, I hope to convey how at first blush the behavior and associated memories and feelings seemed almost entirely within the compass of the usual issues of scopophilia and its inhibitions and tensions as these arise with the "swank and swagger" of phallic excitements and enticements (the words are Winnicott's, 1989, pp. 166–167).

But I further want to convey something of the qualities that reach to other, earlier tensions which involve the need to look before one sees—a line of tensions that follow from a selection principle operating in the psychology of the PAIR and GROUP.

FROM THE CONSULTING ROOM

P., for a longish time, did not think herself to be attractive. Indeed she sometimes contemplated cosmetic surgery. She spent more than usual (at least for people in an analysis!) on clothes and was attentive to diet and exercise; but for all of this she felt that her breasts were too small and rendered her unattractive to men. Yet, for someone so modest, she would complain from time to time that Ψ did not watch her the entire way from door to couch. Her practice was to enter, flash Ψ a smile, and then proceed to the couch. Presently Ψ became aware that if Ψ failed to watch P. every step of the way, she would, as if she had eyes in the back of her head and could see him fail to do this, herself become busily occupied with looking about the consulting room—to the point where she knew it so well that in an instant she could tell if the slightest change had been made (a chair a hair off from where it was the day previous, a book out of place in the bookcase). Thus in not looking at Ψ, although there was a very precise tit-for-tat quality (you don't look at me/I don't look at you) there was also an assertion that while in Rome she did *not* have to do as the Romans did; she was not going to be blinded.

Among her conscious recollections was that of seeing her father in his underwear (she couldn't take her eyes off him) and his practice of feeling free to walk into the bathroom if she had been there "too" long. She felt angry at the intrusiveness of both experiences. She also remembered bathing with her mother, thinking how ugly the mother's pubic hair was and hoping that she would not have such hair upon herself.

Another patient looked squarely at Ψ each session as it began, but past him thereafter. As Ψ tended to look directly at her when she talked, the only time she permitted herself to look again at Ψ was when he talked and, while doing so, looked off to search for a thought. So adept was she at this that it might have been several years before Ψ's and her eyes met. When P. was 6 she noted one day that, contrary to previous custom, her father had fig-leafed himself with a washcloth while she visited him in his bath. He was, in any case, reputedly a most handsome man, and she was later to find herself sometimes in a veritable swoon while looking at him. In seamless disconnection with these experiences, P. had spent long hours in front of a tilting full-length mirror looking at her "smoosh" to see if anything was growing yet.

P. was not only abruptly banished from the bathroom (in her case, while her father urinated) but soon thereafter, to her infinite humiliation, found that the keyhole had been plugged. Later she was to describe "that certain look men get . . . Now I think of it, the look my father got on his face when looking sometimes at my mother at the stove. It is an emasculating [sic] look, fawning, as if they lost everything that made them a man. Imagine letting a woman have an effect like that!"

Another patient once had to return to the consulting room to use the telephone and took that opportunity to look around. She had sought treatment because of anxiety attacks, which were stimulated by two basic situations: one was when she was seen by unseen lookers; the thought of this would make her anxious, whereupon the thought of being seen to be anxious would precipitate a full-blown attack so great as to bring on fainting. The second situation was one in which she would come upon something unawares, particularly a patient whose chart she had not yet read and whose condition was therefore unknown to her. In the transference there emerged powerful impulses to spy upon Ψ inhibited only — but decisively—by fears that she would be caught doing this. P. burned with curiosity, but feared learning anything about Ψ which she could at the same time not control. Once she thought that an interpretation Ψ was giving was going to reveal whether or not Ψ was married, and she blanched. At a costume party she saw a man enter who was dressed as a shepherd carrying a crook and wearing a laurel crown. She thought: "In Greek, 'man with a stick' means something phallic," so she immediately removed her eyeglasses.

P. hallucinated that "men's penises" were showing out of the flies of their trousers and often thrusting themselves upon him in the manner of dog's nuzzling one with their muzzles. He saw and felt this on the couch, it was to turn out, most especially at those times when one might have thought that ideas and feelings concerning his mother would be making themselves manifest.

P. was an attentive and diligent sexual partner but for himself, he preferred "recreational sex." This involved leafing through a library of pictures or short films to find the image of the woman who currently interested him and employing this image to accompany masturbation. Unlike sexual contacts with actual women, in these solitary acts he could do as he pleased: he did not have to wait for the woman to inaugurate sexual activities and then, after she had made her overtures to him, thank her for her kindness in doing so by entering into penile servitude. A man who since boyhood liked to doodle, P. drew again and again a basic image. It was of an eye which might have been a breast, such that the pupil was the nipple; or an eye, the pupil of which was a breast, with the cornea serving as a nipple. In each case a dagger penetrated the eye, droplets of tears being at the same time droplets of blood. P. liked to look, better perhaps than anything, and would spend hours in voyeuristic activity. But it was imperative that he not be seen seeing. He had cultivated a way of using his peripheral vision to be able to see a woman's, clothed or unclothed, breasts while appearing to be gazing at her face. His devotion to cunnilingus was partly because he could look while the woman could not see him looking, and in any case was not likely to be disposed to notice. As for himself, there was—studiously—nothing to look at. He dressed in a daily costume of blue jeans and sweater and sneakers.

P. entered the consulting room sideways through the doors, backwards while closing them, head averted in a downward nod, eyes slitted—as if hoping, ostrichlike, to remain invisible as long as possible. Once recumbent, she removed her glasses and then covered either her head or her bosom with her arms. Only then was she ready to begin. On days when her sessions were proximate to those of students or other patients, she felt cloaked by their presence, and relieved to be but one among many. On other days she felt glad that there was at least no one else to witness her shame. She remembered her mother and her older siblings as being very critical people with decisive tastes; of these tastes she was both proud and frightened. After an illness her father required a wheelchair to get about. His defects fascinated her and she spent hour upon hour trying not to visualize them precisely.

What I wish to investigate here are the other sources for what I believe may be fairly straightforward conflicts over gender. The thread on which I string these beads is that of envy, an earlier envy already in place, and upon which envy of the power to select is built or, more precisely, into which this PAIR-located envy is secondarily elaborated.

ENVY

Once it is decided that something is very nice to have, the only remaining question is which way it should point. The breast is one case in point. The data, earlier mentioned — about which way the breast points and thus about to whom it belongs — are soon available to the infant. The breast is quite a thing: does one rather be or see one? In a state of greed, this is no small question. Should it (the breast, the penis, the vagina, the gesturing finger) point out — or in? Envy comes to be about this question. Taking satisfaction from the breast is generally thought to help reconcile the conflict, but this is by no means always so. The more the satisfaction, the greater the value: the greater the value, the greater the wish to own and possess. But not getting satisfaction is no better; the infant's hunger, when sated, helps it to forget the breast for a while. A frustrate state keeps the infant mentally and sensually riveted to the breast, which now becomes unforgettable. The breast becomes Brobdingnagian. Its presence and power — its capacity to select — inspire yet further greed. That much greed is less susceptible to an evolution into appetite, which in any case if sated, would only increase the lust for ownership and control and thus the envy. Under any of these circumstances the wish, which is to say, the illusion of *choosing* the breast, must be fulfilled. And it is here, I think, that the eyes have it.

The difficulty appears to be that there are dual purposes at work in greed — on the one hand, to cherish the differences — breast and mouth, big and small, penis and vagina, man and woman — that make desire gratifiable; on the other hand, to hate precisely those same differences and try to destroy them, if not in practice, then in mind.

There are two aspects of the matter of choice versus selection. The first concerns the duality that arises out of what I have come to regard as the differences of point of view or state of mind as between the COUPLE and the PAIR. Those differences do not initially have to be reconciled. They are entirely capable of alternation or even sometimes of synchronicity. That is, one moment the Self can savor the pleasures of those complementary sets of differences that afford it pleasures and satieties and the next moment wish to regard at them as impediments to being at one with the other as a PAIR and with others as a GROUP.

For Ψ, this is a familiar alternation. He wishes in some measure to invite P. to his side so that together they can look out and regard what P. experiences with a common viewpoint that has gradually been elaborated between them. This is often termed a state of the alliance and is thought to be a very good thing to have going in order that the degree of difference between the two partners to the analysis can be encompassed, limited, and contained by their common viewpoint and perspective. Ψ hopes this of P.: it is sometimes called psychological mindedness (the other being called perhaps bloody-mindedness) and he hopes this of himself in order that his own transferences, which are based on an absorbed interest in the patient from a COUPLING point of view, can be held to manageable proportions. Indeed his membership in the psychoanalytic (or alternative) society depends quite literally and certainly on identity in terms of carrying out approved, or even just-like, analyses, with limits on the kind and amount of COUPLING permitted. Yet if there is to be that to analyze, P. must regress libidinally in the transference, so that the archetypes and prototypes of his early attachments and their traumatic elements can become available for recapitulation. Both Ψ and P. have simultaneous COUPLE and PAIR attunements with one another, as they had and have with others in their lives.

However, since the selection principle is driven by the DNA toward making choices that will forward the *species* toward increasing fitness down the generational lineage to come, it is contra egoism in all the ways the pleasure principle is egoistic—wanting pleasure and wanting it, careless as to consequence, when and where it can find it. Yet, the selection principle, bent by vague intuitions that occur in the emotional life as hope and expectation, preconception and premonition, and which yearn toward discovering and claiming whatever is better, more or other in the particular cultural or societal environment, works through the GROUP and the PAIR. In parallel with this tropism is its other half, that of being or becoming one of the chosen—one of the right, better and more so. This so-called narcissistic urge works hand in glove with choosiness: people being choosy need others to be distinctive, for of what use is either choosiness or choice without the other?

> Ms. A. in association to a dream, which she feels is about "mutant genes" and figures a mother who is oddly Mediterranean and a baby or grandbaby, who when playing "This little Piggy . . ." is obliged to display that he has an additional finger on both of his hands, one of whose digits is "fine" and the other of which is "withered," comes in the session to understand why ever since she could remember she had hated to be called by name:
>
> > Ms. A.: I just could not bear to be confined, no—defined into any one being, into a "so that is who she is"—or, worse, into a "so that is who I am." The image of an animal alone in the desert slowly consuming his own body . . .
> > Ψ [to himself]: This is a person who mothered and fathered herself wondering anxiously if she has succeeded or whether I will have to play a role in future.

Distinctions therefore exist in the drive-valencies of the selection principle, and thus in discriminations concerning both the PAIR and the GROUP: but these differences concern *degree*. In the pleasure principle, which drives the twosome or more-some when they are occupied with the matter of being or becoming a COUPLE the important differences *are of kind*.

In the COUPLE three is a crowd; jealousy flourishes: the basic interpersonal situation is that of the Oedipus complex. In the PAIR mentality, three is a group, a subspecies or a people, and the ability to fit in dominates the sensibility. The value of distinctiveness is relegated to its function in specialization in the division of labor. At-one-ment with the aggregate, where the invidious distinctions are lost in the conglomerate entity, produces an almost manic sense of mutual admiration and omnipotence. "Put on that uniform, man," says Magic Johnson, "and you know you ain't never gonna lose."

Such competitive losing in the Oedipus complex is equated with castration. Freud (1915) thought castration was the closest approximation of death the child's mentality could come to. I think this not to be the case, though I believe it to become the case after defensive actions are taken by the ego to unknow death by knowing proportionately more about castration. But in the PAIR state of mind, dying—that is, not being among the select and thus the selected—is very much a state of mind, even a premonition, and the fear of dying and the envy of those who appear destined to live in perpetuity because they have what(ever) it takes is very much a part of psychological life in the PAIR.

Indeed, I rarely meet a patient who has not come for assistance because he or she has led a partial, small, and tentative life, a life calculated not to offend on the one hand and, on the other, to succeed as meek lives are meant to when the time comes to inherit the earth but who have lost heart or faith and become aware that life is indeed running out. "Running out" means both near-time death, the death of the individual whose life he or she is leading, and the unused propagative and generative life which in the PAIR or GROUP sense is no less an unlived life (for more on the matter of time, see Jacques 1965). Greed holds onto dual wishes—the one to have what the mother has, to have whatever "cake" it takes and use it for its own propagation; the other, to eat the "cake" and so to accept, acknowledge, and feel grateful—in an enduring, even lifelong to-ing and fro-ing as to when or whether the differences between Self and Other are going to be regarded as distinctions in degree or as differences in kind.

Regarding that tension, it is understandable that someone might want to have a look-see—to see what sort of perturbation lies in store for him. Will he, upon encountering the Other, espy a difference of kind or one instead of degree? A horse is a horse, of course, of course; so the "discovery" depends not on what is espied but the vertex or point of view from which the reconnaissance is made.

When that tension of owning and using is resolved, greed gives way to mourning and appetite ensues; appetite, unlike greed, is satisfiable. When a modus vivendi is not established by means of which the needs of Self as a member both, but variously, of a COUPLE and of a PAIR, are not reconciled, both envy and jealousy fly up, and spite and revenge take up the place where admiration and gratitude might otherwise flourish (see Boris 1985, 1986).

VISION AND VERTEX

> Oh I see, his game is that he knows
> Intimately, ardently
> . . . that there is nothing he needs,
> and nothing I can keep from him.
> Anna Akhmatova, "The Guest," 1914

P: I contract myself, I shrivel, I reduce myself to a pinprick. I have no I left. Nothing can affect me; there is no me left to affect.

Vision Metamorphoses into Vertex

There is an efficiency to this, when vision becomes as if one with point of view, the language of the eyes becomes the language of the I—widening, narrowing, becoming slitted, being eye-opening: looking at, into, past, beyond. As such, looking serves the communications of the COUPLE and the PAIR with equal, often simultaneous, ease. Indeed, an exchange of looks signals, by the look of the looks, which is to be paramount, COUPLING or PAIRING. People have to see eye to eye on whether to COUPLE or PAIR, or they will be confronting one another eyeball to eyeball. This is true both of seeing and looking as eye acts and "I" acts when the range of dilation and contraction in the pupil becomes a metaphor for the way things are mentally looked at: as the focus shifts, so shift the relationships—figure-ground, contrast-compare, near-far, and all the other relativities. As the horizon line changes, the vertex alters: different differences and similarities are espied. Even not-yet and no-longer look nearer and closer, and so time, becoming spatialized, is visualized as well. "I have a perspective on this." "Things will look clearer in time, when you can look back at them."

Perhaps it is that things *seen* can be generalized or particularized more readily than those events of other senses, or perhaps seeing is more intrinsic to such social activities as the formation of pairs and groups to which humans are subject. Or perhaps it is that, as Freud said, looking easily assumes the functions of the erotic, for the inner as well as the outer eye; perhaps because looking is a distal sense, holding the object in view and being able to shape and sculpt it as well as lovingly to regard it in rapt concentration. Perhaps it is that the very act of looking—raised eyebrows and lids are genus-specific, providing us with one of our few genuswide inherited signaling behaviors;

perhaps it is all of these. But looking soon becomes the most powerful analogue for cognitions. Much of what we know or choose to know of the world—the basic being the Xs versus or vis-à-vis the Os, COUPLE versus or vis-à-vis PAIR, the Us versus or vis-à-vis the Them—is a matter simply of actual and then mental focus and position. The social signifiers that distinguish X from O are vital; baby xs and os with their round cherubic appearances elicit particular PAIR care from adults, although sometimes they seem to include something that signals "I am a tender, harmless morsel"—and are duly eaten.[5]

Gradually, as the mind begins to mind where the eyes look, the mental vertex supersedes the perceptual point of view. For the mind, of course, has an agenda. It might be that the fetish (her stiletto heels, say, or her netted black stockings) should successfully occlude the mind's almost-remembered idea of her vaginal no-thing. Or it may be the mind's wish to coalesce history, providing itself an almost infinite number of items all of which can substitute for one another in the blink of an eye: Or mind's wish to gild the lily through idealization. Idealization is employed to improve the other half of the COUPLE so that he or she can look better from the PAIR point of view.

---

[5]Jesus Christ has become an ambiguous object in this respect. As Son of Man he was an object with whom to couple, and as Son of God he became the charismatic leader of a species-group and as such one who could only be paired with. The compromise formation was that he could be coupled with but only symbolically, via Transubstantiation in the Eucharist. Moses' difficulties with the Golden Calf prefigure this. The "Veau d'Or" was an icon, but of what? There are readings in which he himself, as might any good psychoanalyst, seems to hope to take the lissome tendrils of couple-love for him and graft them to spousal objects, and likewise to take the curlicues of hope apportioned him and crochet these instead to God the Father.

7

THE SELF TOO SEEN

In the preceding chapter, I have dealt with envy as an outgrowth of the ideas and feelings consequent upon the infant's discovery of the need to make choices among potential relationships with his or her objects (including the self as object). When, as in infancy, greed is part of the prevailing state of mind, any realization of an actuality out of the reservoir of potential choices proves to be an infuriating and outraging one — insofar as the individual is not convinced that choosing is necessary. For when choosing does not seem to be necessary, choice is experienced as a possibly crippling, even mortal attack on the wanter. In this chapter I will develop the reason for such ideas and feelings and show that the same attitude regarding choice and choosing holds true of the choices others make in respect to the self. That a child is being chosen can import associative resonance from Freud's (1919) paper of a similar name.

Regarding relationships, you will recall that I have particularized two fundamental states of mind — one, the COUPLE, following from and embodying the pleasure principle and involving the discovery and use of differences; the other, the PAIR, following from the embodying what I have called the selection principle and involving the need to discover or invent likeness in order to facilitate, through identifications, the formation of pairs and of groups. This is true of the relationship one takes with one's self and those relationships others seem to make with one's self. That this duality is paradigmatic means at one and the same time that choice is necessary and impossible. Accordingly, the dialectics of paradox become the *lingua dicta* for the study of envy.

Although I have taken note of the dread that the self (or important aspects and functions of the self, in action, as actor) will not be selected as a fit for membership in the PAIR and GROUP (see also Boris 1988), I have mostly considered the options each offers and, accordingly, featured the ego in the role of agent and chooser. Although I shall begin with that characterization of the situation, I shall go on to develop the other part of the story — that in which the ego is itself subject to selective pressures by the principles that drive us. By this shift in emphasis I hope to show how the ego is not only besieged by the id and objects of the pleasure principle, within the COUPLE, but *is seized by the "need" of the selection principle to find "its" realizations in the PAIR, GROUP* and species. By setting out the dialectics involved, I can display the genesis of envy in the selection principle and the PAIR and in the problematic aspects of choices of one state of mind or the other.

All of this activity rests (how well and for how long we shall see) on the idea that nature and natural selection has bred into us a need to take a collective hand in the survival of our own species into the afterlife of the generations to come, the guide books to which can be found in every culture's aesthetics, moral philosophy, and practical theology.

By dialectics I mean the tensions — the dynamics of conflict and compromise — between the dual sets of (psycho)logics I believe to be in our experience of our own nature (cf. Boris 1993). By writing of looking and seeing I hope to exemplify these dialectics as they occur early in life and in their later reappearance in the consulting room.

PROBLEMS FOR THE EGO

The ego comes into being in order both to know and not know aspects of experience. With what the ego chooses, it creates a world out of what once was a chaos of sense impressions and bits of memory, of preconceptions and discoveries. These acts of choice might alternatively be regarded as constituting menace bespeaking the hatred of coming to know and then being stuck with knowing what one knows and that one knows before one can re-create a chaos out of it. Although the power of the ego's choice provides it wide discretion, that discretion is not infinite. The world of objects and the domain of sense impressions have selective qualities of their own. Sensations and other information have an impact; they make themselves felt and known. Only fast footwork on the part of the ego can enable it to steer its attention away from such impressions, but not merely away, away from one source means over to another — selective attention being an either-or-affair (Boris

1991). As the ego grows accomplished, it is able to create a panoply of screens, as Freud called them, to divert its attention just as that attention is in danger of being seized by a portion of an experience the ego might just as soon not altogether know about. Even so, the success of the ego in so swiveling its attention depends on a prior condition—that the ego remain unselfconscious of the fact that it practices such diversions. When the ego is unselfconscious in its use of the quick diversion, the screen can look as if it were the real thing and not some hasty substitute thrown together for purposes of avoidance or evasion. Illusion must look real if it is not to look like illusion. Thus the ego must sacrifice the blessings of consciousness in order to do some of its most urgent work.

As is well known, there are many motives for the interposition of a selecting ego, as many motives as there are for avoidance and evasion, on the one hand, and for discovery and experiencing, on the other. An oft-repeated set of findings is the following: events take place that impose response. In many studies, the response has generally been contrived to be unpleasant or painful, like the electric shock. But there is more to the shock than the electricity. The event always turns out to be the less shocking the more predictable it is. As predictability decreases, as a function either of the stimulus or of a diminution in perspicuity, the perceptor (the ego) gradually begins to attack its own system. This seems invariant, whether considered, as Bateson has done from the perspective of the double bind, or as Pavlovian experiments have done by taking a round-good plate and a square-bad plate and moving these toward the octagon and decagon; the dog ends up biting its own tail. In other studies, stenosis of coronary and kidney arteries, or decrease in the exoimmune—increases in the autoimmune—response are noted. It is important to my thesis to note that these links are not mediated via a conscious, sophisticated set of pathways but, as things go, are fairly primitive.

In order for the ego to create a more accurate world, it has, of course, to focus and concentrate its attention; to study or fathom an experiential event, the ego cannot brook distractions. What works in the direction of learning and truth works in the same manner for deriving fallacy and untruth. Other claims on the ego must be blotted out until a verisimilitudinous version can be ensconced in their place. The practice of psychoanalysis thus necessarily consists of watching the interplay of the patients' attention and marking for them the as-ifs that are or were substituted in the place of the unnoticed or unremembered experience. Efforts to mediate, which is to say anticipate, the rudeness of the shock may not begin with the experiential system itself; they may not initially involve a dismantling of the ego or the soma. They may begin, rather, with attempts through projective identification, or by more direct means, to alter the state or status of the source of the shock. (These efforts may go on synchronously.) At some point in the sequence of trying to reduce the shock value, efforts at prediction are made—in psychoanalytic terms, renewed efforts at potency through omniscience. Explanatory stories like the just-so stories of psychoanalytic theories or interpretations (or of Dianetics, astrology or political science) are introduced as intermediaries (understanding), as anticipators (prediction), and ultimately as moderators (control) (see also Bion 1965, 1970, Boris 1991). Because our images concerning selection contain such shock, the ego's attempt at mediation requires of it that it introduce what Eliot might have called a shadow between its looking and its seeing.[1]

BEING "SELECTED"

No information is available on how Lorenz's ducklings felt when imprinted on a pair of his Wellington boots. The ducklings may have felt just fine: the Wellies may have slid into place with the kind of satisfying *thunk* that one associates with the door-closing of, say, a Mercedes. Ah-ha! So that's what mother or pack-leader or trend-setter or "We" look like! A zillion nerve cells designed precisely to record or recognize such information may have heaved a collective sigh and stopped needing to search, merely now to recall. The cortex may have called to the limbic system, and the limbic system may have replied. And all may have been as it should be.

But, then again, it might have been a different story—one more along Chicken Little lines. For the ducklings were not merely selecting the boots, the boots were selecting the ducklings. Both their cortex and limbic systems were being claimed; the Reserved sign was being torn down and a pair of Wellingtons was suddenly and irreversibly in occupation, driving out every little "could be" and "might be" in the *Anschluss*. The sky had teetered—and fallen.

Edelman, in *Neural Darwinism* (1987) has shown how clumps of cells are selected by their response value—this is, determined by their DNA, but not in a completed and unyielding way—how they multiply, lay down cluster barriers to augment their specialization from other neural cells proximally located, how they strengthen their synaptic connections as use dictates (or weaken them and their boundaries as use does not dictate), and in all respects evolve according to the main rules of a natural selection system.

---

[1]"Between the motion
  And the act
    Falls the Shadow"—Eliot (1952, p. 58).

Selection is a competitive process in which a group may actually capture cells from other neighboring groups by differentially altering the efficacy of synapses. This process, in which groups that are more frequently stimulated are more likely to be selected again, leads to the formulation of a secondary repertoire of selected neuronal groups which is dynamically maintained by synaptic alterations. [Edelman 1987, pp. 45–46]

Nature is frugal with her systems. When she finds something that works, she repeats it, micro and macro.

THE POWER OF ENCHANTMENT

In *The Comforters*, Muriel Spark (1957) writes:

A typewriter and a chorus of voices: "What on earth are they up to at this time of night?" Caroline wondered. But what worried her were the words they had used, coinciding so exactly with her own thoughts.
   Then it began again, the voices: Caroline ran out on to the landing, for it seemed quite certain the sound came from that direction. No one was there. The chanting reached her as she returned to her room, with these words exactly:
   "What on earth are they up to at this time of night?" Caroline wondered. But what worried her were the words they had used, coinciding so exactly with her own thoughts.
   And then the typewriter again: tap-tap-tap. She was rooted. "My God!" she cried aloud. "Am I going mad?" [p. 48]

In *The Flight from the Enchanter*, Iris Murdoch (1956) writes:

But to find herself still, however partially and however obscurely, fascinated by the idea of Mischa was alarming, not so much because this fascination might ever come definitively to tempt her, as because of the endless variety of torments which such a situation could promise.
   . . . and she knew, too, that she had not got the strength to escape from the power of the brothers. It was profitless to ask now whether the bond that tied her to them was love. The darkness in which those two held her was profound beyond the reach of names. She could not of her own will break the spell. [pp. 109–110]

In his essay "On Being Bored" (1993), Adam Phillips writes:

In boredom, we can also say, there are two assumptions, two impossible options: there is something I desire, and there is nothing I desire. . . . In boredom there is the lure of a possible object of desire, and the lure of the escape from desire, of its meaninglessness.

In this context what begins for the child as the object of desire becomes, for the adult, what Christopher Bollas (1979, p. 97) has described as the "transformational object." Initially the mother is, Bollas writes, "an object that is experientially identified by the infant with the process of the alteration of self experience." This earliest relationship becomes the precursor of, and paradigm for, "the person's search for an object (a person, place, event, ideology) that promises to transform the self." At this first stage, "The mother is not yet identified as an object but is experienced as a process of transformation, and this feature remains in the trace of this object-seeking in adult life, where I believe the object is sought for its function as signifier of the process of transformation of being. Thus, in adult life, the quest is not to possess the object; it is sought in order to surrender to it as a process that alters the self. . . . [pp. 76–77]

BEING SELECTED: ASPECTS OF REALIZATION

This transformation is or, must, I think, be a counterpart to what I call selection in the PAIR and GROUP. The process is one of finding realizations for the promptings and importunings of the world of preconceptions, but, at the same time not settling blindly for realizations that are Wellington boots. The ego has to validate these realizations with bits of actual experience, provide them with language and meaning, give them metynomic and metaphoric existence. The effect that comes about when a preconception meets the bit of experience that combines with it to make a conception may be likened to the Ah-ha! feeling Archimedes made famous. The urgency of the pleasure ego will certainly goad the ego into making its choice of the object that will choose it. It is, I think, in this sense that Winnicott talks of the disruptive effects of the instinctual life on the formation and consolidation of self: "There can be," he wrote, "a wide discrepancy between what we like when we are excited and what we like interim. There is a difference between the quiescent self and the excited self." Winnicott says also in this paper that instinctual life is an "interference with the exercise and enjoyment of freedom"; and that "there is but little bodily gratification, and none that is acute, to be got out of freedom" (Phillips, 1988 p. 71).

Realization takes place in the absence of a spark of passion from the pleasure principle, however important that nudge is and however susceptible it makes the self to selecting and being selected. The — click! may be onto percepts or ideations, but whichever that is, it is the way for the unthought to become thinkable. It is important to note that ideations and images may be idly passing by, idle neural firing, so to speak — when all of a sudden — click! a nose can appear in an arm. The artist in question, like the dreamer he will be that night, will not know of his role in his construction: it will appear as if given.

Whatever the merits of this critical moment view (now or never), it is plain that at moments there has to be a readiness in a category to become pregnant with an encounter—the two to form a conception. The encounterer can be discovered (in the perceptual realm), imagined (in the ideational realm), or invented (a function of both).

If the readiness in a category were sap-silly, had no defining character, and were any boot in a storm, any stray bit of event could—click! This would be like leaving a self-advancing camera in the hand of a child: any exposure could record anything; each successive exposure might record anything to add to that.

> P., when he travels, always goes to a tall place in the area from which he can, camera shooting, make a *tour d'horizon*. He brings back a 360 degree diorama of the place, each photo seamlessly abutted to the next. He thus captures the whole perimeter (of mountains, sea, etc.), which he can then reconstruct for his pleasure and presumably that of friends and relatives. This ritual is organized to keep any intrusive object from getting on the recorder and interrupting the sequence. Though it is by no means obvious from this story, the intrusive object is P.'s mother's "castration," later mastectomy. The focus on the perimeter and not on the center of the scene also represents an effort not to let the primal scene recur. These efforts, because belated, use the new record to screen against the resurgence of the old, which travel stirs up. But the old has, of course, already happened—P.'s film has a thousand and one recordings on it.

In associating, which P. is naturally reluctant to do and "does" by various kept-quiet "systems" of linkings and order, there is the constant breakthrough of the grotesque—as if his slide-show montage of mountain views suddenly revealed an elbow or a pubic mass.

There are early—clicks!, dark wildernesses that he recorded and linked up with preconceptions to form realizations, the language of which, visual and ideational, he has now long forgotten. But they remain. In his archaeological metaphor Freud referred to successive civilizations building on top of previous ones, using the latter as bases and foundation-works, thus maintaining an architectonic integrity of sorts. While it expressed his view that later manifestations were related to (and did not merely cover over) earlier ones, part of the idea was that later ones screened for or drew strength and purpose from their predecessors. I should like to emphasize this latter feature—that each successive village is a connection of the earlier attempts to build the kingdom of God. As, so the Bible tells us, the kingdom has many "manses," so too do variant cultures attempt to realize a better destiny in ways different but germane to themselves.

Thus P.'s photos are aesthetic approximations of scenes that as a youngster he could fashion only crudely. The appetitive, recurring requirement of the pleasure ego or COUPLE is in its natural quantity—whether to restore homeostasis or to propel the sluggish uncertain selection ego or PAIR formation. The nature of the impulse is attuned to attaining a peak Uhm-oh!-Ah. . . . The selection ego or PAIR formation is in some way apparently bestirred by this rising of the estrus sap, but is more generally acquisitive in the accumulation of orders of things that may be counted quantitatively but are accounted qualitatively. There is, of course, no sharp line of delineation between these; as Aristotle noted in his *Poetics*, while speaking of the particular requirements of miniatures, the domain has its own exigencies. But certainly sheer quantity is not enough to convey the implication; something more must excite the utopian imagination.

Part of the power of the object comes from anxious and guilty deposits into it of the infant's own wish to empower itself at the expense of the breast; this is a well-detailed theme in Melanie Klein's writings. This wish to enslave the breast to the infant's will and whim arises naturally out of its greed and is projected in the same spirit of greed. Rather than giving up and cutting loose the will and wish to enslave, the infant banks it in the breast, hoping there to preserve it against future need. But the adult has the power to "select"—to bring out qualities—in the child, even as the sperm selects the egg and the ovum the sperm; this power easily and inevitably becomes confused with the power of choice and beyond it of life and death. This is because the child must succumb even while at the same time it must await and be sure that the mother is the true bearer of the true message.

> P. was acutely suspicious of his mother. He felt that she was bossy, but worse than bossy, inconsistent. He felt that with her nothing was safe. Such an attitude might have suggested a paranoia of some dimension, but in fact P. was deeply depressed. It was to turn out that when P.'s younger brother was born, P. at age 3 was given a new name. His brother received P.'s original name. At age 60, P. found a certain peace of soul by becoming a policeman, complete with uniform, and strolling about the town he lived in all of his life issuing parking tickets.

The energy efficiency derives from the multiple use of the same pathways (organs, tissues, etc.) for various functions—for example, COUPLE functions and PAIR functions. Intrinsic in this efficiency however is the risk of overload and an "er"-istic competition between uses for the pathways involved, and requirement instead of choices, compromises, or priorities. Sexual intercourse, for example, can provide both pleasures to the body and a sense of at-one-ment, fusion, or wholeness for the spirit, but sometimes this very capacity of the act requires choice: what if one wants one without the other?

P. is himself the result of nine prenatal months of self-improvement (in one phase, the idea of a tail had merit) and thirty-some years of more or less

postnatal work. His successive series of selves are all fashioned as improvements on their former function and structure — sometimes done with such urgency as to be the product of revolutionary rather than evolutionary procedure. These selves are designed to bear no resemblance to their earlier drafts. The earlier drafts show themselves as deliberate absences, uses of 90 degrees or 180 degrees where much less might have done — as if the tail had not merely to be suppressed but its very partial emergence countered by an enlargement of wing bones.

We are accustomed to riffling through this photo album of the past, seeing the chubby baby turn into the slender child who takes on puppy fat at 9 and at 11 seems to be all nose, both of which however he or she grows out of or into by age 17.

> At 28, P. is newly in a love affair in "real" life. In analytic life, P. is just reexperiencing the events of a very early version of the primal scene which was very exciting, frightening, and infuriating. For example, P. can't wait to have sex with L., but when they are engaged in sex, P. feels murderous and does something to interrupt it. Then P. and L. stalk moodily about the house, still neglected children, now also thwarted parents.

The sexual activity itself also shows great disagreements between the "personalities" involved both in P. (and therefore inevitably P.'s lover) and over who does what and with which and to whom. These "personalities" are conformed around realizations. As once their realization was shopped for in fantasy and encounter in order for phantasy or preconception to reach the mental domain (if only promptly to be repressed or edited — split, sundered, condensed, displaced, etc.), it now has to be discovered. Ordinarily it can be discovered in the shock of conscious realization — a glimpse of something (really, someone) or even an intrusive thought. This is a regular occurrence during psychoanalysis.

Early conceptions have a good deal of power insofar as they are closer to the predilections of the first. They have to be grown out of. People need the time and latitude to do this. These early conceptions either evolve or lie layered as in Freud's metaphor, outgrown before they are grown out of, and thus live an enduringly questing life of their own. The older child forgets them, but not they him.

This of course belabors the ego: as if nothing it can find for the earlier formed conceptions in later time is good enough. Indeed, it enviously staves off possibilities as a wife might mistresses.

The continued life of earlier conceptions produces a state of greed, which, by definition, is inherently unsatisfiable, each conception competing with and envious of the others, most of all the present, which is felt to be the main rival and the greatest danger. The risk to the individual is to discover the conceptions in the past, where they would have to be left and grieved. Accordingly they are thrust forward in time as yet-to-be's, where they can successfully avert any real seizing of hegemony in the present.

This takes us back to the fail-safe of the original preconception and its need not to—click! and lock onto boots. It too must, as best it can, keep good—in the pleasure principle sense—from surrendering to better, in the selection principle sense, before it can reach best. Once best is known and then either found or relinquished, this need to wait and find better realization holds pleasure-taking in bondage.

Such a compilation of attributes is—click!: it is an approximation of the good but one that serves both as a holding action and a bridge until better comes along. It takes ego away from conception A (say, love of the maternal breast) and contains it until conception B comes along. If "B" does not get itself out of its quotation marks as an awaited possibility, the transitional instead becomes a kind of B minus and achieves the status of a conception. Usually this shows up in fetishes of all sorts, both in the strict and the library sense of the word fetish.

People have to "make-up" their minds about a vast array of objects of every sort that appear to have demand quality looming as—clicks! Only the capacity to wait, yet when "ready," spring into action (be prepared!) will guide the arrow to the target. A certain amount of sputter takes place—fussing, fuming. What *is* it that's OK? Is *this* it? For each object there is its alternative: for each breast its "other" (Boris 1986).

COMPROMISE FORMATIONS

Looking, for P., had become and provided the template from which both previous and future analogic formations could be sprung, with each earlier experience being re-represented by subsequent ones, quite as Freud described in his essay on the Wolf Man[2] (Freud 1918, Boris 1984). The great value of this is twofold.

Translating everything into a common denominator enables discrete phenomena to be worked with, just as it does for fractions in simple mathematics. But more than this, it enables one to denude the specific

---

[2]Although Freud meant for the Wolf Man to recover the primal scene, it seems nevertheless true that the Wolf Man was spooked by his (not Freud's) experiences of it. The state of the therapeutic alliance suffered so badly that Freud felt pairing was off and would stay off until the recovery of (from) the primal scene restored the possibility of them making a better COUPLE. In introducing his famous time-limit, he smashed to smithereens the possibility of being a PAIR, which could include a degree of envy and frozenness. From this the Wolf Man never recovered.

entity — be that object, relationship, event or experience — of its individuality and make it one of the herd. Sucking becomes looking, fucking becomes looking, everything becomes looking. Looking is a common denominator of sorts, a lingua franca: here a look, there a look, everywhere a look-look. As in mathematics, it serves as a solvent, allowing discrete events to yield up their exactness as an entity and become one of the gang. But in conducing everything to a commonality, each event, each person, each fresh, new, unique day is bowdlerized: there becomes nothing new under the sun. This is especially true of what was seen; looking becomes the obtrusive experience and the scene is forgotten.

P.:   It is obscene, something, I don't know, whatever it was.

The other aspect of re-visioning experience is to keep discrepancies to a minimum. The mind uses comparison and contrast to mark the shape and time of matters. But at some point the continuities which provide the ruler by which change is appraised break off into discontinuities. A corner is turned. New rulers (rules, and people making the rules) apply. How shall it be decided what is more of the same, as the PAIR may want it, and what has so little in common that the two events compared yield only difference and discontinuity, as the COUPLE might prefer? Should the observer stretch to embrace the events, holding on to their continuities in space and time, or does the observer, be he self or other, let the stretch snap into two?

That's *so* like him!
My, how he's changed!

Why change things?
Because things *have* changed!
No, that's just you looking at them differently!
But that is one of the things that has changed.

On and off Mommy is nice.
Mommy is always nice, it's that on and off you don't appreciate her.

These are matters of choosing; what is chosen is also selected.

8

ABOUT TIME

What we call the beginning is often the end
And to make an end is to make a beginning
                                        —T.S. Eliot[1]

INTRODUCTION

What makes experience endurable or otherwise has at least something to do with knowing that there will be a time to it. Pleasure or unpleasure alike are qualified by the time they take. Can there be any pleasure so great as to survive its being ceaseless and endless? Is there any ordinary pain that cannot be endured if one knows that there will be an end to it?

To any experience, time is therefore a party. It accompanies experience dressed variously as ever and never; no longer and not yet; as beginning, ongoing, and ending; as soon or now or later; as quick or slow; as again and again or as never again. It is by no means clear how the sense of time evolves, only that to an extent it does.[2] As analysts, we are certainly occupied with it: minutes per session, times per week, punctuality and tardiness, duration of

---

[1]T. S. Eliot, *Four Quartets*. in The Complete Poems and Plays (1952), p. 144.
[2]But see Fraser 1989, Hartocollis 1983.

the analysis, timing of interpretations, and much more. In a sense this occupation reflects the suspicion that our patients are insufficiently attuned to time — that the timelessness of the unconscious, and more specifically of the primary process that Freud dealt with at the start of his psychoanalytic formulations and of the analysis interminable that occupied him at the end, remain monitory touchstones for us. Indeed the sinuous issue of time weaves throughout Freud's work. It is in the genetic formulations, the idea of phase-development, the concept of regression, at the heart of the idea of transference, in the repetition compulsion, the death instinct, and even in the idea of Nirvana. Such ubiquity certainly underscores the frangibility of peoples' sense of time.

But no wonder: Time, after all, is a theory. If there were such a thing as actual time, it might be moving backward as well as forward, round in a circle, or traveling the perimeters of a sphere along an infinite number of vectors. (Hawking 1988 and Feynman 1965 are lucid guides to these alternative realizations.)

It is equally true that no one really comes to analysis about the past, or even the future. It is their anticipations they come about: their sense that past and present, extrapolated, *augur* the future. They do not come, that is, to cry over spilt milk (though, in time, they may). They come because the past never seems to get over and done with: old whines in new battles. And yet, as do we all, those who come for consultations know that time is the greatest healer of all.

Why, then, hasn't time healed?

TIME IN

At the beginning of the life of an individual, there is no such thing as a knowledge of time. Duration, interval, pace, rhythm are none of them as yet apprehensible. Although the heart beats and peristaltic churnings pulse and coil and breathing provides its own regularity, even as does motility more generally, like temperament itself, introduce rhythms; and although these metronomes mark pace, still there is no *scale* for these events. No hands are yet upon the clock. As Winnicott wrote, "Time itself is very different according to the age at which it is experienced" (1986, p. 5). If the duration of time is to be modified, it must be done so literally. The infant can employ only its own movements from consciousness to unconsciousness to mediate, mark, and modulate the onandonongoingness of experience.

In this lies the paradox that will prove fateful. Oblivion creates periodicity, hence intervals of duration. *But it simultaneously precludes learning about duration.* Oblivion is a narcotic that must be used sparingly. An essential

element in the good-enoughness of the Winnicottian good-enough mother
would therefore be the provision to the infant of "bite-sized" portions of
experience, ones, as with Goldilocks and the beds of the Three Bears, that are
not too hard, not too soft, but just right. (Issues of time and timing will recur
in the psychoanalysis of the people some of these infants grow up to be —
about which, more later.)

The difficulty is that infants may have their own ideas about what is right
for them. And these very greedy ideas — really, preconceptions — may not
surrender to the ministrations of the mother. The infant may have no appetite
for what the mother has to offer. Rather, it may be and remain more envious
of, than fed by, the hand that might wish to feed it. Under such circumstances, the duration of its frustration may be so great as to be unendurable.
But the duration of the pleasure it knowingly takes in the fulfillment of its
appetites may persist so long as *also* to be unendurable. The key term here is
"knowingly." It is possible for the greedy infant to accept gratification
providing it either does not know it is doing so or does not know that the
breast — the mother, really — has it to give. It may then use obliviousness to
permit itself to accept fulfillment of its sensual needs. But if it does so, the
knowledge that is required to know about and use time to alleviate the
unending fright of a duration without scale is again compromised.

The breast accordingly takes immense hegemony over the infant — a
hegemony that will or would, *if he but knew it*, be curtailed by his sense of time.
But until or unless that experience of time's nature — of limit and progression,
of staying and concluding — evolves through experience, the baby is prey to
the hegemony of the breast. This exacerbates feelings of helplessness, fears of
dominion and domination, and those feelings are attached to the image and
idea of the breast. With this conjunction of idea and feeling with sense datum,
the breast becomes a symbol as well as simply a thing-in-itself. And it
symbolizes ominousness. Winnicott terms this "W O M A N" (cf Winnicott 1986,
pp. 192–193, 252–253).

SYMBOLIZATION

In the formation of a symbol, something, X, is taken to be sufficiently like Y
as to be able to stand in for it, both in terms of self-reflective experiencing and
in communication with others. A really good symbol will at once symbolize
and be symbolical, opening its analogical references in both directions. That
is, the wolf or bear in the shadows can at once symbolize the child's sadistic
or aggressive wishes and communicate these to any one who reads the tale of
Red Riding Hood — this in the absence of the event in itself.

The construction of such symbols is not an easy task. Before symbolization, there must be realization. Our love of mathematics, music, poetry, and of the graphic and performing arts is at one and the same time that they communicate to us in fathomable, even familiar symbols *and* spread out for us an array, a veritable bazaar, of usable material for the *formation* of symbols. Without such stuff as dreams are made of, we are in the position of the blind man and the color blue. We have a readiness to see blue without a commensurate ability to visualize it. Sympathetic souls may come to us and say that blue is the color of lakes and press cool water into our palms; or that it is cold and give us ice to feel — or hyacinths to smell. Much the same may hold true of anxiety (or hope). To their child, both parents may say, "You are trembling!" but one may say, "What has made you so excited?" and the other, "What has made you so afraid and frantic?" In both cases a corollary is offered by way of helping to form a way of thinking and talking of an experience in future or past when it is absent.

Experiences, that is to say, are nascent creatures, needing realization. Encounters that provide such realization are "Aha!" events. Klein (1958), as is well known, held that the earliest encounters with the breast could become such an event. In this manner Isaacs (1952) tells the story of the toddler at the clay table looking at her bosom and exclaiming, "So those are what are biting me!" In Klein's (1961) account of an analysis of a boy, Richard, she illustrates how she regularly went about observing, in the boy's drawings and play configurations, the various items that are "in" other items and which are doing what to whom: "Daddy-Hitler's penis taking all of Mummy's breast." Once one catches on to the cryptographics, it is child's play to translate them into English. But such illustrations, brilliant as they are, do not speak to the encrypting process, only to its translation or interpretation.

For example, the breast is a clumsy container for so much to be put into because it is unwieldy and ill-defined; like Kant's empty categories, though it can be filled to the shape of the contents projected into or ascribed to it, it doesn't provide definition and dimension to the contents very much more than a sack does. In contrast, the snarl of a dog or the slippy slither of the serpent or the spikey high heel of a woman's shoe fits like a skin to experiences as yet only partially surmised. They provide realization: "So that's what — where — it is!"

One of the problems about time is how difficult its realization is, especially for the infant or child who is trying to conquer time by being oblivious to it. For example, most of us think that time is a one-way street; that we pass down it, or it us, beginning, middling and ending. But in the transference or countertransference we don't think that at all. We think that just as spatial or formal differences don't matter so that this odd sort of duck who shares some time in a consulting room with us may be the spitting image of someone we know or knew, so we think that it's as if time hasn't passed, we are (still) little and dependent on, or little and afraid of, this person or some part of this person.

With this all analysts are familiar, but not so obvious, judging from the literature, is that once time has two way traffic on it, it becomes a two way street: not only is the past re-presented, but, to accommodate the transference, the present is re-pasted. *As much as past truths are surmisable from the re-presentation of the past in current-time, so current truths are to be found in the past, a past which, before the present didn't contain them.*[3] The same holds true of falsifications: they can be created anywhere and relocated to any point in time (Boris 1989). The "real" analyst, like "real" truth provides a kernel of "fact," which can easily be used to create an old present and a new past. Textual analysis of dreams and memories, accordingly, require close attention to background detail.

But lest this falsification be misunderstood, its important feature was not the damage it did to the truth, but the truth it did to the damage. Poetic licence is not confined to poets; the need to find containers by which to make potential experiences thinkable and expressible demands either the use of the time for discovery or the gift of invention. People can run out of each or, indeed, both. There are times when, for example, the dreamer awakens because he has no more dream elements into which to pour the experiences he has so far been dreaming; his muse is otherwise bemused. And there are, to be sure, differences in the quality of the resulting symbols, about which more soon, depending on the age, the state of mind, and the conditions under which the realizations that go into symbol formation are forged.

Prior-to and beginning-with, for example, are two different experiences: the latter plainly implies a progression and requires a quality of anticipation. Freud, as it is well known, assigned the import of significance in "beginning-with" or in "as a result of" to the primary process. But it may be no less true that their hatred of not knowing induces the young and the rash to assert a narrative. This allows "next," even when they do not know what it is, and because they do not know what it is, to be contrived only out of extrapolations disguised to look not like extrapolations, but like preordinations. Preordinations are quite different from the unities of which Aristotle wrote in his *Poetics*; they serve meretricious rather than communicative needs; they foreclose rather than encourage "anxious ambiguity" (I take this phrase from Feiner 1991, p. 12).

---

[3]There is a Woody Allen story, "The Kugelmass Episode," in which the analyst explains to his patient that if he wants magic he should instead consult a magician—which the patient then does, asking to be allowed to be with Emma Bovary. Back in the present, the former patient notices how all the familiar texts on Flaubert have been changed as a result (*The New Yorker* Oct. 25, 1993, p. 89).

We, as psychoanalysts, are by no means immune to any number of these foreclosures of perspective. "As the twig is bent, so grows the tree" is one of psychoanalysis's own favorite extrapolations. It has been known in other guises: "Give me a child for seven years. . . ." But largely this has meant the shaping of mind and spirit by environmental means.

There is another idea: it is that the nature of people unfurls in a regular order, in phases and stages, each somehow better or healthier than the preceding. Words like *fixation* or *regression* therefore apply. This, taken together with the twig viewpoint, lays the hand of time heavily on the ways in which we envision our own ontogeny.

A third concept has early representations of experience giving their genes, so to speak, to later versions. In contrast to the brave claims of the environment and its cultural agents, this version puts it that later representations of experience will descend from prior ones — even if or when the actual experience or thing represented has (from the points of views of others) changed over time. In short, it is that precedent symbolization has so large a claim on the formulations of subsequent experiences as those later experiences themselves do on how they are represented. If this is indeed the case, early configurations of experience form a kind of destiny. Bion referred to it as a kind of saturation, which, when in play, leaves little room for fresh experience. (As is by now well known, he worried that his saturation with such theories would foreclose the analyst to whatever the patient was trying to communicate that might fall outside them.)

It has been put forward, largely by Melanie Klein and her school, that symbol formation is a development of signal importance and this, apart from the question of its developmental status[4] is undoubtedly true. The manipulation of symbols makes it possible to think and dream in the absence of the object itself. *But the value of that dreaming and thinking is wholly dependent on how well the symbol approximates what it is symbolic of.* A symbol, the fidelity of which is high, is as useful for mathematics as it is for art and for those and other communications between persons. A low-fidelity symbol bears false witness, or none at all.

A symbol, after all, is an analogy. If, as Bion (1970) points out, we say let a knife stand for a breast, and so a surgeon for the mothering one, not all of us will find the analogy to our taste, but we may well understand it. We will not understand an analogy that says let a knife stand for a knife. The aptness of the analogy dictates the fate of the cogitations and realizations that follow from it.

---

[4]Klein (1946) believed it to mark the arrival of the depressive position out of the previous paranoid/schizoid position. But do these positions not lie side by side in extended embrace? See, for example, Eigen's (1985) position on a related question in Bion's work.

For example, some writers feel that the quality of pleasure in an Earth-centered cosmology was such that it obliged Aristotle to avert his mind from what otherwise would have been evident to him, while Newton could not take up the idea of absolute position or space, though it was implied by his theorems, because it did not accord with his beliefs in an absolute God (Hawking 1988). Freud, too, as is well known, felt that the Copernican, Darwinian and Freudian revolutions took place only finally because of strength in the resistance to the displacement of anthropocentrism each of these lines of thought represented. A symbol system that took humankind or God as the center could only breed false conclusions in the arguments by analogy that followed from the step. The analogies that become symbols have therefore to be well approximated to what they are meant to represent, and it follows that a good approximation, like anything else, takes experience, the capacity to revise, and a relative freedom from too much turbulence. Symbols formed early, under conditions of great tumult, are, it follows, poor things with which to think and learn. Their degree of abstraction suffers from the envy under whose influence they are formed. For, in envy, the abstraction is not a loving tribute to the *Dasein*. It becomes the abstraction of a thief, one who eviscerates in order to denude the original of those of its characteristics that inspire the envy. These analogies *mis*represent the original: they are cartoons, not faithful attempts at realization. Freud noted this for us within the Irma dream—in the way he, Freud, caricatured the doctor (Fliess) who attends Irma. What has not been so clear is the degree to which the entire act of dreaming and the manner of dream representation parodies and enviously mis- or re-represents "real" life—"real" time, in particular. To be sure, dreams, being primarily visual, can do the job of representation in dramatic rather than narrative fashion, so in less time; but the elapse of time in and around a dream is always a commentary on the time things ordinarily take and the time one has for them *to* take.

Any analogy, whether it is in the strict sense representational (an Ingres or Matisse drawing) or non-representational (a Pollock or a de Stäel painting), attempts to convey an experience. In the consulting room, a groan may be used in this way, or even portions of silence. The experience is made available for direct apprehension, for interpretation, or both. Sometimes the author counts on the recipient to provide the missing portion: the recipient has to learn how to see a dream symbol, the X in an equation, a line drawing, or a painting. This is not always easy. Bion (1978) reports that it took him a matter of months to take note of the fact that a patient's periodic mutterings of "Ice Cream" meant, in fact, "I Scream." People have had that difficulty with James Joyce, who also wanted to evoke an apprehension of experience that did not fit the customary linguistic or rhetorical forms. Yet Joyce had language—for example, the word *fuck*—for what had previously been inexpressible, so something for which, understandably, he was brought to trial: when he wrote the word, *fuck* no longer meant *fuck* as it was previously known.

The value of the symbol or analogy is not altogether what it represents or stands for to the recipient, but how it puts matters in the first place for the self. Factored into attempts to learn and to think, poorly contrived symbols prove an impediment. Their main function remains, therefore, signal; they are good at being a signal, rather poorer at being a sign; poorer still at being a symbol with which to derive further information and induce further understanding.

We are familiar with these signal-symbols in the consulting room. Often they usurp the place of memories from childhood. They are rather memories *of* childhood, but not spontaneous ones. Their characteristic, rather, is emblematic. They are meant to appear to shed great light, but the light they shed is only upon themselves. The brightness of that light, while seeming to be illuminating, in fact casts dark, almost impenetrable shadows across the rest of the landscape. Though they are self-referential, their signal value is meant to suppose the idea that there is nothing else of note worth looking into. They are meant to seem seamless, sui generis. Semiotic weapons.

> P. is just coming to know of the paranoia by which she protects herself from realizing her wish to impose her will on others as if they are mere objects, put there for her delectation. She goes through the photo albums of her youth, and there she finds pictures of a mother who ignores the little girl in the picture, while looking quite chummy with others, especially, in "possessive" ways, with the little girl's father. After a long and, for her, a remarkably tedious recounting of these photos, P. complains that Ψ has not spoken to her for the entire session. "Don't tell me it is my fault again! I spent my whole childhood feeling guilty until these pictures finally reveal who the guilty one really is."

The idea that pictures may be open to interpretation or that their function in the session is akin to a word-picture filibuster, blocking free association, is not present at this time. The story P. wishes to have noted is of the signs in the photos, not in her current activity in the hour. Ψ becomes an object, her father, mediating between P.'s relationship with her mother: what was meant to be discovery, reflection, and thought has become instead recrimination of Ψ through portraiture.

Contents or dis-contents if they are to be displaced or projected, need to find a container shaped to contain them properly. One cannot ascribe tender love to a snarling animal, but one can "discover" in that visage a great deal in the way of desire or rage that might otherwise look like one's own or some one else's feelings or intentions. But of more importance, encounters with a *properly configured* container give definition to what has not yet gained shape or dimension. Though these images may be further employed as bearers of what was once something emanating from one's self now become containers of intentions coming *at* one, they can, like the punishment, fit the crime. For without such containers to provide realization to what one experiences, one experiences vapors and mists, thoughts speculative but as yet unidentifiable. Neither can delusions be formed nor phobias built—nor can anything be communicated, even to the self, because the signifier is as yet absent. This is true generally, but perhaps especially so in the case of time. Pasternak observed somewhere that abstractions concerning time and particularly the future make for poor symbols because were the future in fact to arrive, which it doesn't, it wouldn't look anything like what we imagined.

Learning to "tell" time has no bearing on learning time, because the hands or, worse, the digits, which lack even spatial dimension, move at various speeds, exactly like the unwatched pot that boils sooner than the watched one. Time has to find a container or two, so that it can be poured from one to the other, and given substance and mass. Shall it be a flowing thing, like a river, or a chock-a-block thing, like frozen hunks of ice? If a river, shall it be wide and shallow, mooching along, eddying where there is something to engage it—or shall it be urgent, pell-mell, a seeker not of the journey but of its destination? Or should it be an arc curving back upon itself, as it comes to a rim, drawn slow with the pull of gravity? Are we in or outside of time as it goes by—or is it we who go by? These are pleasant questions to muse upon (if one has time), but time ranks among the most depressing and persecutory things in the world. Concerning time, some people feel the first thing to do is act as if it didn't exist; the second, be late for it; the third, anticipate it and end it before it ends you.

"Soon" is for a long time impossible to comprehend because it has no footprints outside of the child's rampant impatience. Then it comes to mean something like "not now," which, however, provides only negative information, easily confused with something mean. "When?" "Later." "Yeah, but when?" "After supper." "But when is supper?" But "When is supper?" often means why not now or why wait? Or what for?

> How soon will I die?
> Not for a long time.
> Yes, but when?
> Not until you are old, older than grandma.
> Yes, but when will grandma die?
> Hush, we'll talk about it later.
> Later?

Defective symbols retain object status in the knife-is-to-a-knife sense mentioned earlier. Even so potentially alarming an analogy as a knife is to a breast as a surgeon is to the body opens up possibilities for inquiry and exploration not inhering in the non-analogy that passes for an analogy. The signal-symbol created under circumstances of turbulence and driven by envy has more object status than thought value. It occupies the place where abstractions that might have thought value would otherwise be. Instead of growing into a some time and a no time, it becomes a no-time, with the result that it becomes iconic: an object which — really, who — is present in all or most transactions.

The icons of time are well-known: Father Time scything the new baby of the New Year as if it were already fully grown and timely to be gathered in, is, in cheerful reverse, one of the better known. This gloomy figure, auguring memento mori, becomes the third party to every dyad, a Tiresias casting his shadow over Oedipus and Jocasta, the sly serpent, Lucifer, who having himself lost eternal proximity to the Lord, causing the Lord to take eternal life from Adam and Eve. Its status as as third party invokes a triangle with its plot of rivalry; it contributes a geometry that only awaits the arrival of the actual figures, the containers, for the casting to take place. Since so far as is known, death is a foregone conclusion of life, inescapable and immutable, it takes on an aura of omnipotence. That third party of time takes on the shape and smell of omnipotence, whatever other characteristics (avenger, harvester, detective) the casting may feature.

And needless to add — and now, at last, we come to it — the figure who occupies the role will have an envious nature. For the infant's idea is that the mother wants the (his) breast for herself: that it is her satisfaction that is at issue because it is her sense of time in which the nursing or other encounter takes place. And he maintains this idea so long as the mother acts consonantly with it. Certain anorexic patients have the idea that the analyst wishes to feed them in order to gain satisfaction from the fullness and amplitude of what he or she has to offer. The reply to this kind of narcissistic self-engorgement by the other is to create an image of the breast as an object without attachments on either side. There is an optical trick by which you can poise your index fingers with the tips nearly together, close to your face, and if you stare at them properly, a sausage will appear between your fingers, which then appears to hover in air, a creature of its own surmise. This might be called a link that isn't a link; it may serve as analogy for a breast or penis that doesn't emerge from, and be part of, and so belong to any person. Such two-dimensional images have to account for the missing dimension, otherwise what is meant to remain obliviousness of the link of belonging is likely to be recovered or remembered at any moment. Size therefore becomes a usable analogy. A big penis or big nipples or breasts seem to subsume the owners of them; they are thus useful in short-circuiting envy. The absence of the third dimension, the whole object, the other whose penis or breast it is, vaporizes into a kind of gray shadow, serving only to offer figure — ground contrast for the glitzglitter of the part object. For example, patients sometimes speak of "here" when they could as easily, and more accurately, refer, pronounally, to the person of the therapist.

TIME OUT

Nevertheless, knowledge can only be accumulated over and with the aid of time. One learns what goes together and what doesn't by repeated trials. Eventually, certain events form what has been called a constant conjunction, occurrences with regularity of correlative existence. But even for this to happen, conceptualizations have to take place. One must not only have a way of thinking but also something to think about — something mentally to manipulate and conjure with.

Psychoanalytic theories — for example, Mahler et al. (1965) — have long emphasized the immense value of this kind of "object constancy" in the separation and individuation of the infant from its mother or other primary caretaker. Theoreticians like Klein, Kernberg, Winnicott, and others likewise have spoken of the need for the infant to build up an enduring inner picture of the mother from these constant conjunctions, one that can tide him over like a keepsake, in Mother's literal or figurative absences. What is being described is a process involving recurrence and so time — indeed, *a time in itself sufficiently unchanging* as to form a backdrop against which recurrent identification of repeated patterning — can be espied, what Eliot (1952) calls

> Not the intense moment
> Isolated with no before and after
> But a lifetime burning in every minute.[5]

But what if the baby and his heirs — the toddler, the child, and so on — hate the conjunction and don't want to know about links, even those that feature himself at one end? And what, especially, if he cannot bear to be present during the time it takes to descry the conjunctions?

We have seen that time has to be held as a kind of constant, a pulsed container, if spatial configurations are to be noted: once again the mother appears in the same interval as the breast; once *again* mother, breast, and internal satisfaction occur together. It is by this same means, therefore, that in its greed and envy the baby can obliterate the conjunctions he finds inimical to his other purposes. He has simply to abort time by declining to

---

[5]"East Coker," *Four Quartets* in *The Complete Poems and Plays* (1952), p. 129.

become aware, indeed by studiously becoming *unaware* that it can unfold in an orderly fashion. If this leaves him with fragments of experience that cannot be thought because thought is a link-making activity, he is left with a host of object shards. But he evades the sense that these add up to anything—like running out of time and possibility. (For a detailed discussion of this fear as a function of being part of a PAIR under the governance of the selection principle, see Boris 1993.)

This process too is a frequent visitor to the consulting room. The analyst tends to provide regularity and predictability in (sometimes accessibility between) the accustomed intervals of the regular appointments. Some tell their patients even before the work starts that they take regular summer and winter vacations or attend specified meetings or will be off during federal or religious holidays. The analytic purpose is not so much to introduce deadly dull routines (though there is no little risk of doing just that) as a holding structure upon which the patient and analyst can count. Yet such an introduction of constancy is at one and the same time an introduction of an element alien to patients who wish to control constancy, which they perceive as carrying with it oppressive certainties, compulsive order, and the power and force of the mother-analyst's being. They counter such measures with inabilities to hear, to remember, to arrive on time or at all: in short, with disorderly conduct. What they are disrupting when they can do so, is the limpid, predictable flow of time in which spatial conjoins can be located. The analyst, at such times or with such patients, may feel himself wanting to say, "As I already . . ." or, "As we discovered on Thursday . . ." or even the dread, "Again: I . . ." or "To repeat . . ."

These versions of disjuncture are used by the successors of babies who use distraction to introduce elements of obliviousness or oblivion into the dyadic interplay of which early communication, learning, and "bonding" consists—that shared, rhythmic, follow-the-leader, which Stern (1977, 1985) and his followers have filmed and played back in revealing slow-motion. Of course that they do so may be a precise carry-over from emotional dysrhythmias having been initiated by the parent in a murderous (perhaps envious) attempt to drive the infant crazy. Which this is can only be discerned in the transference by an analyst who is not easily driven to being resentful of being thrown about all the time.

For these disruptures are the patient's version of time-out, which are in turn the counterpart of what is aptly called "spacing out" (and in the '60s had a drop-out/drop-in component to it, with the use of marijuana and hallucinogens prominently employed to change the internal registry of time). But although necessary, particularly for those patients who were babies who had to know too much too soon, such time lapses preclude the very learning about the way time works that could now, in the present, be useful.

Moreover, such lapses generate anxiety about what they are obliterating: perhaps what is obliterated via oblivion is worth not missing. To that end, repetition — time and time again — is employed to remedy the possibility of loss through lapse.

TIME AND TIME AGAIN

Although repetition is necessary for learning and mastery, being an activity necessary for the discovery of pattern and conjunction and for the realization of relationships, it is also susceptible to use in the opposite fashion, as a paraprocess that summons only the old and tried and false, creating old paramnesias to undiscover or hide the garbling of information or connections left by motivated amnesias — repressions, projections, and the rest. Thus the repetition-compulsion.

In the consulting room fresh experiences (more accurately fresh *re-experiencings*) are often hard won, sometimes won only to be recanted.

> What do we do today? Same old thing, I suppose. Well, might as well get started. But I did want to mention something I forget to tell you last time. Walking in the door I felt bathed in a feeling of surprising warmth. It was almost physical, like the feeling of slipping into a warm bath after a chilly walk through rain. Some kind of thought went with it. . . . I don't remember it. Something like, this is a comfortable place, that the woods are dark and peaceful, that you are awaiting me and are once again prepared to listen to whatever I have to say — something of that sort. It was very nice. I sort of hoped I would feel it again today, but of course I don't. Now where was I?

Well, back at the beginning, one might suppose, where the bad thing is yet to happen, and might yet be prevented by halting time and doing the pre-bad things over and over again. Not surprisingly, this patient prepares for the interval between going to sleep and falling asleep by reworking phantasies into stories, which are then carefully extended and reworked again, a later version of counting or naming state capitals. Such a person knows what is going to happen (because of course it already did). What he must do is to prevent it from "really" happening by taking charge of it. The experience to be altered consists, like the linguistic entity of subject-verb-and-object, of self-act-other-act-and-yet-other. The links, represented as hyphens or dashes, are the easiest elements of the experience to sever (see Bion 1963, 1965); forgetting about or altering one's idea of the link, hyphen, or verb, permits the object world to remain intact; only the acts are changed to preserve the innocent.

Thus Freud's view of paranoia:

I love him
He loves me
I hate him
He hates me.

He hates me!

Or a view of transfiguration I have previously described (Boris 1989):

She would if she could but she cannot.
She could if she would but she won't.
She won't because she is bad.
She won't because I am bad.
She won't because he is bad and won't let her.
She won't because he is better (e.g., bigger, older) than I.

To these there are emotional markers:

Would but can't: Hopelessness, sorrow and resignation: growth.
Could but won't: Hope, anger and accusation.
Won't because she is bad: Disillusionment, hatred, persecution.
Because I am bad: Hope, Guilt.
He won't let her: illusion and outrage; manic optimism.
Because he is better: narcissistic desPAIR; hope; envy or jealousy.

In his essay, "Some Character-Types Met within Psychoanalytic Work," Freud (1916) drew attention to people who did not count themselves among the norm, of which he accounted Shakespeare's vision of Richard III one. Freud saw the hump-back Richard was born with as implying to Richard that something special was due him as a result of that curse — that he might count himself as an exception to the norms and rules of ethical behavior to the precise measure that nature had made him an exception to its general rules for masculine beauty. I have in my own work found that construction an accurate one.

But I think it has a more general source. I think it arises when an infant believes that his psychological existence hangs by a thread. How many infants are born into an existential crisis I do not know, but I would hazard more of them than we might expect. I think the crisis comes about when the infant doesn't know when to be a part of a COUPLE and when a part of a PAIR. (This concept of the COUPLE and the PAIR is developed in Boris 1993.) Or it comes about when the infant starts rocketing back and forth between trying life as a member of a COUPLE and then of a PAIR, hoping each will save him from the demons and perils of the other, unable to stay with any one before zooming off again to the other. This sets up what I believe to be a case of extreme envy, and that envy then further interferes in the infant's willingness to make or sustain a choice. For the infant won't take and then the infant won't give himself, out of the fear of being taken (it was not just Barnum who believed a sucker is born every minute). Such a crisis of envy seems to set these individuals apart from those who feel that life is a natural past time, in a fundamental way to be taken for granted, the only remaining issues being how to pass the time happily and meaningfully. And as they become aware of being set apart like that, the envy these people feel increases geometrically, to the point eventually when the nameless dread with which they began also increases exponentially.

Such individuals look — how they look! — for guilt as a way out: the sins all have names (lust, avarice) and categories (e.g., mortal, venial), and these can be borrowed to provide names for the otherwise nameless dread. To name is, in this respect, to tame, and tamed, the dread feels less singular and more part of a normative or at least social condition, one, moreover, for which sanctions are available. Patients who have managed this transfiguration of nameless dread into guilt keep their lives and the analysis alive with harangues of provocation and of blame and confession. They advertise a masochistic air, turning the plodding rounds and routines of analysis into the rites of Inquisition, making their atmospherics the more convincing with each increase in their analyst's stupor or bad temper.

> P.: I feel so guilty — so guilty that I want to say "I'm sorry" a hundred times — *two* hundred times. I would like to confess nonstop for hours. [Pause] But I don't want to say I'm sorry only once. *Even* once.

Such a patient will rightly fear the journey back through or really *back into* time from where he stands now, pockets full of entitlements, for each of which he has paid amply with his guilt and the punishments this guilt has occasioned him, and which he has misunderstood as applying to his masochistic sexualized role in the COUPLE. For the backward journey will take him once more to the precipice at which the lemming-like question will be, Who stays, who goes? Such a no-thing, frightening as it may seem, is nevertheless better than nothing.

A patient dreamed of his threatening psychosis:

> I was in a car with no brakes. To stop it, I had to put it into reverse, which I did. But everything under the hood snapped. So that was that.

Slowly, slowly, then. But the "So that was that" — isn't *it* a kind of brakes full-on? Doesn't the dream say something like, "I have a headlong way of going on about things and I don't want to experience them from any other perspective, like yours for example."

"What we call the beginning is often the end."[6]

PREMATURE DISCOVERY

As the clientele for psychoanalysis has expanded, we are in some regards finding a certain subpopulation of patient who cannot, it seems, be treated at a rate commensurate with the routine. This may be a function of several factors—perhaps, for example, the background situation as the analysis proceeds; but sometimes it appears to be a function of the nature of the personality. I have in mind people who discovered experiences too early, well before they could feel them, symbolize them or think them. Without the benefit of such mediating processes—what Bion (1962) called the alpha function, by which he meant that capacity to abstract which enables people to make and then distinguish the representations of things from things-in-themselves, the latter experiences being ones that take on a certain force against which the receiver (or maker) is mentally helpless except insofar as he wishes to begin to think—people can only feel as if they *have to do* something about what they experience. Bion regarded this state of mind as a function of an inundation or accretion of beta elements and observed that the mind treats these as it experiences them—as things to be voided or otherwise projected in the interests of reducing stimulation (that is, mental pain) to endurable proportions. In the viewpoint of psychoanalytic therapies, these are "acted out." But they are enacted primarily because the patient has found action an appropriate way of doing something about actions—and why not?—and thus keeping himself from succumbing to an agglutinate of objects that he cannot represent. The more the impingement of the objects, the greater a patient's need to discharge these through remedial action.

From this it can be seen that an analysis timed to decrease its own impact would also decrease the bombardment of stimuli on the patient and the need to discharge these. The emphasis would accordingly shift from increasing the dose of discoveries to arranging them more temperately. This does not necessarily make for a longer analysis, although it may; it makes for one in which the patient may take (over) his time. I am aware that "taking his time" is not a helpful description: no analysis rushes the patient unless the analyst is having some difficulty bearing the patient. But it is in the nature of these personalities that they themselves are in a fearful rush—having had, they feel, to anticipate things before they discover them—as if that would help in

---

[6] *Four Quartets*, p. 144.

preparing to deal with them. Such a fearful haste often means that the patient, even were he to have the best will in the world, could not stand to take the time it takes to make discoveries through free association and conjoint interpretations. This then means that the patient must revert to other, more rapid methods for discovery—like figuring experiences out, borrowing interpretations, or inventing easily understood experiences.

Emotionally, the patient feels driven by anxiety that he characteristically misinterprets as impatience and a wish to progress more quickly. He does not notice that his actions confound his beliefs, for these patients are indeed slowpokes.

> P.:   As you know I am always in a hurry, and—
> Ψ: [Interrupting] Speaking for myself, I know only that you *feel* in a hurry. [P.: considers this.]
> P.:   Well, as I was saying . . ."
>   Ψ had hurried the patient.

The result of such hurrying, on whomever's part, is pseudoanalysis in which discovery is headed off, and for it is substituted any amount of learning, even of change. The patient learns (perhaps with the so-called assistance of being taught) how to anticipate events and encounters, for which he then can prepare. But such anticipation is anathema to discovery because the situation changes once it is wrapped in anticipation. Experimental conditions show the immense stress people (and animals) experience when bad things happen, like electrical shocks, and there is no way of preparing, even in retrospect. One patient who, for various reasons, refused to anticipate the consequences of which she was always being told was often taken aback by the actions and especially the reactions of others. Consonant with her need not to be intimidated by the unforeseen, she then retrospectively drew conclusions from events that were wildly off the mark. If someone had unexpectedly criticized her, she would feel brutalized, but then, in a return engagement, offer defenses and justifications that had nothing to do with either the criticism, if it was, in fact, criticism, or the reason she had been given it. But the preparation for the rejoinder was in itself an immensely reassuring activity: this time around she was damn well *not* going to be taken aback. Until of course she was.

The template for this patterning was based on discovering much too soon her own possible "castration." She had no way to consider this except as something so catastrophic as to warrant disbelief. But were she to disbelieve it, the chances were she would discover worse. For the death = castration transformation Freud noted is so: castration does, by giving partial and yet mendacious realization, defend against the dread of having to be the one selected to die—or so people like to hope, playing for time.

"HE HAS A GREAT FUTURE BEHIND HIM"

Voltaire remarked that the human race is the only species that knows it must die and that "it knows this only through its experience. A child brought up alone and transported to a desert island would have no more idea of death than a cat or a plant." Freud (1923), in a similar vein, observed: ". . . death is an abstract concept with a negative content for which no unconscious correlative can be found" (p. 58). Hence the need to accrue correlatives such as the aforementioned death = castration link.

Elsewhere Freud (1915) writes: "It is indeed impossible to imagine our own death; and whenever we attempt to do so we can perceive that we are in fact still present as spectators. Hence the psychoanalytic school could venture on the assertion that at bottom no one believes in his own death, or, to put the same thing in another way, that in the unconscious every one is convinced of his own immortality" (p. 289). But all of memory or anticipation is like this: after a certain age we look back or forward upon ourselves from the perspective of an onlooker. Our most private life is a public event. Winnicott (1986) writes: "In the total unconscious fantasy belonging to growth at puberty and in adolescence, there is *the death of someone*" (p. 159, his emphasis). As I have made clear elsewhere, I do not think this total fantasy begins at birth, rather at growth, whenever that can be said to begin.

Winnicott elsewhere adds: "Population has to be thought of another way, because we can no longer leave it to God, so to speak, to kill everybody, though of course we can have a war and people can kill each other off that way. If we're going to be logical, we're going to talk about a very difficult subject which is: what babies do we kill off?" (p. 204).

Death, moreover, is the one event that, not lived through, has no end and must therefore be provided one. *All* endings are therefore auditioned for their worth in approximating an adequate realization for death. Even non-endings are considered: "Let's take the youngest child in the family. I've found that he or she has killed all the others that didn't come after him" (Winnicott 1986, p. 206). As for the way death is represented in the unconscious, because it is not represented as something, nor can it be until it can be tolerated as such, as nothing, it is represented as a no-thing, which gathers incident, detail and indeed motive (Boris 1987). So only when the idea of nothing can be grasped can people distinguish "later" from "after," and therewith know the difference between life as rehearsal and life as the event itself.

In the meantime,

> For what *was* there none cared a jot
> But all were wroth with what was not.[7]

---

[7]From "The Art of Dying," as quoted in Enright 1983; italics added. The "not" is the presence of the absence, hence the no-thing.

9

TOWARD A NATURAL HISTORY OF ENVY

I said, "Were they long pants?"

"What does that matter?" she said. "Yes. They weren't knickers, or whatever you call 'em. They were regular pants like you get at the store. Probably not pants you would buy, or I would buy, but pants you might see at the store. Each pair was a hypothesis, a proposition, you know? They were saying things to each other."

"Talking," I said. "What were they saying?"

"They were discussing happiness," she said. "Contrasting views, comparing views, I guess. That kind of thing. Reflecting on happiness, its causes, its allure, its limitations. I don't know. They had all these great pants and that was enough for them. They were like very complex and dense, the pants were, with clues, nuances, shadings. Like logorams or ideograms, or oleographs." [Barthelme 1990, pp. 76–77]

Without it being quite described as such, envy has been considered as something so basic in the way of emotions as not to need further elaboration. This is as may be. But in my work, at least, such a view has proved rather a flat-earth thing. Useful as it is to identify a patient's envy and explore its ramifications, the question, "But why did I feel envious?" is poorly answered by, "Because you wanted one for yourself."

The same situation obtains when we ask about envy as a state of mind and an emotion. We know that envy arises out of a state of mind in which qualities and traits are looked at comparatively and possessively, but why people take that view of things is another question. Why, in any intercourse, should one person suddenly break off and contemplate what he has that the other hasn't or what the other has that he hasn't? Why that nervous, fussy, ragtime jitter between exchange and advantage?

In linking envy with the wherewithal for psychic (and physical) survival, near term and penultimate, I have suggested that people act as if it were incumbent on them to have what it takes — both for the security of their own personal fate, and for what the GROUP may need to call upon for their collective survival. (It is in the latter sense that I have come to understand "narcissism" to be rather more obligatory than egotistic; as individuals, we are meant to cultivate our assets for the greater good of the GROUP.) I do not, of course, know there to be such a belief, or if there is, whether belief is the right word for it. I infer that there is from the way people sometimes act or at any rate, the way some people sometimes act. It is, in any case, a strangely sophisticated belief to attribute to people early in their lives. And yet I think that dread attaches to some kind of permeating inner doubt concerning our status in these regards. If it were to be protested that the sophistication of the belief is such as to beggar so young and perforce undeveloped a mentality, I could only agree. Yet I would reply that the existential questions are there in larval form, and no less urgent for their being inarticulate. I think, for example, that the effort the infants make to convey themselves into the imaginative sensibility of the mother are early versions of self-reproduction through impregnation of the breast, and that inferences as to reproductive rights are being determined accordingly.

Such impressions do not necessarily become any more evolved and articulate over time because these principled issues do not necessarily become conscious. In fact, there is an absence of direct and particularized language for these questions. And *because* there is an absence of a referentially explicit language for these powerfully emotional questions, we are, as it were, subject to our belief. Not knowing we have it, we cannot articulate it either to ourselves or to others. Many hundreds of thousands of young women are anorexic: that is the answer; what is the question?

When I started thinking about what I am describing, I began, in a sense, to fear for my sanity. How could the idea that people act as if there were a selection program be apparent to me and yet not to everyone else? But I soon saw that a vital part of the program was to cultivate and retain an air of mystery. The individual does not experience these grave existential doubts as residing within himself — he experiences them as coming upon, one might even say, "into," him from the GROUP with which he is identified (or "dientified", as, at these junctures, my computer likes to write) through his membership in the PAIR. To be sure, the issues at stake have inevitably found *some* sort of articulation—they are within the questions concerning the perfectibility of man and our fitness for the hereafter that have long abounded in the moral philosophy and theology of many peoples. And questions of selection and salvation are everywhere in myth, art, ceremony, and music. All the same a great caul, itself invisible, has been placed over the nature of our participation in states of affairs. It is as if the state of affairs has nothing to do with states of mind, as if a state of affairs is not only an emergent phenomenon, but an orphan as well. It is as if the group enjoys an existence somehow independent of the men and women who comprise it.

Perhaps the most controversial aspect of what I have to say concerning this linkage is the supposition that as a big-brained, social species, we have been lumbered with the dim, inchoate shiver of an idea that we must take a hand in our own survival. I do not mean by this a conscious interest in genetics or eugenics. We have been competent at the breeding of our livestock for generations now, and as far as plant stock is concerned, we have it down to a science. I mean the hypothesis that there is a selection principle at work deep in our psychology that keeps us from reproducing through a random series of biological incidents, keeps us attuned to some sort of domestic structure for rearing the children of our reproductions, and makes us, through our hopes, take the long view even though we don't in any real sense know what the long view is.

But this hypothesis—that there may be such a metapsychological animal as a selection principle—is no more than a reification of a far less reaching one, namely that people act as if there were a selection program in which some are selected and some not. It is enough for purposes of thinking about the function of envy in human affairs to suppose the smaller hypothesis. That supposition could then lead to its opposite. What if people were not concerned with selection issues? If we were to meet such a person, a man therefore devoid of envy, what would he be like? It may say something that the attempt to think of such a person boggles the imagination.

HOW STANDS THE MAN WITHOUT AN ENVIOUS BONE IN HIS BODY?

He is unarched by hope, unbent by despair, unbowed by hopelessness, unriddled by depressions that no-things fashion where something that isn't was meant to be. This is the gamboling man, nature's sunlit child, the man who could "go gentle into [his] good night," with only tears to speak his loss of those he came to love and pleasured in. Disinterested in his standing vis-à-vis others, he would be guided by appetite, untormented by greed. Without greed, there would be no resentment, no lust for spite and revenge.

Frustrations, of which he would have his share, would of course disappoint him, but that disappointment would be far more blue with sorrow than red with rage. His failures to find satisfaction would not be taken personally by him. They would not reflect on him in his own eyes, nor would he imagine they did in the mirroring eyes of others. Lacking egotism, he would be absent of shame and indifferent to grandeur. Though at times of high frustration he might claim that those who frustrated him could have done otherwise if they had but chosen to, his lack of ego-involvement would make it far easier for him to mourn the other's inclemency and move on to new and different people.

He would feel jealousy, of course, in the same measure that he would feel unrequited love and longing. How could he not wish that whom he wanted would come to him and not to some other? And he would fiercely compete, but only up to that point at which what he might lose of himself or hurt in the other was not worth what he might find elsewhere. He would not fear hopelessness. So what a keen sense of the market would he have, with no hot fumes of performance anxiety to cloud his lens!

Having bred by happenstance and propinquity, he would know too it is the wise man who knows his own children. But as to that part of nature's mandate for propagating successfully by making offspring who will live and flourish and amount to something, surely he would want that and do what he could to teach his children what he knew of the craft and art of living to achieve it. But what would he know of the right stuff, he to whom each day's good and evil sufficed and left no tally?

It would be the mother of their children who would know something quite different. She would know that only the best would do, and even if he thought he chose her, or that it was mutual, she would know it was she (or the elders of her people or the gods) who chose him. In selecting him as the person who could get her children off to the best start, she would have to know more about wherewithal than he, and would naturally be more choosy—more selective.

Yet even he would be alive to those distinctions that a cognition capable of comparison and contrast necessarily yields, and doubtless he would enjoy aesthetic preferences. But those categories of good and bad, better and best would yield him tender choices: I like this more, this less, the value not taken as residing in the object, but in the pleasuring self. Thus upon encountering the elegance of truth and the appositeness of beauty, such a person will laugh aloud with delight.

This child of nature—from whose womb could he have sprung? Who would have given him suck? In the tradition of the Golden Age, it would not matter whose womb gave him birth, for directly he was dry, or even before, each woman of his tribe, if she could, would give him suck. He would be known as one of theirs, a collective view that would follow him to marriage and beyond. If his own mother could not feed him, someone else would, and if his mother could not take him as her mate, someone else would, and he would be passed from one regretful one to another until someone would be there to give him what he wanted. Thus that emotionally arthritic spine that the envious person has had to grow old with—that to him spells backbone, determination, and resolve—would stay a sapling, a sinew, the inner flexibility mirroring the flexibility found without.

HOW COMES BY THIS MAN WITHOUT ENVY?

We are rather a new species still, and anxieties are bound to dapple even so sunkissed an existence. What occurs when this baby or child feels those inner dark clouds that undiscover the sun? Does he too make every attempt to conjure himself up in the mothering one's imagination—her "reverie," as Bion has called it—and convey to her his dark and incoherent fears?

The fate of these initial, inaugurating attempts by the infant or child to PAIR does much, I believe, to determine whether envious or vicarious identifications will ensue. The loving child will send subsequent feelers out to find relief, the envious one to leave them there. In the case of the unenvious soul, we will have to assume that something comes back that can be experienced as reassurance. Will this, however, be the result of an act of empathy? Or can it be a passing gesture, innocent of imagination, yet not devoid of caring? Does it make a difference whether the mother doesn't get it or doesn't *want* to get it? Does this difference reside primarily in the child's disposition toward the mother, or in the mother's disposition toward the child?

Winnicott (1956) made much of this question; it was at the core of his ideas concerning "primary maternal preoccupation": indeed it was a source of no little despair to him that Klein said she also agreed on the importance of this preoccupation, but in his view neither got it nor would agree to know that she didn't get it. I use the word *despair* advisedly. His letters (1987) are filled with this theme. He writes of this to her (letter of November 1952), and to Joan Riviere (letter of February 1956) who, after James Strachey, was his analyst. But like the baby who cannot get through to its mothering one, he feels himself unable to make a dent in Klein's and Riviere's unshakable conviction that Klein and her followers (Segal, Heimann Joseph, for example) are no less sensitive than he to the crucial effects on the baby when it cannot make a dent in its mother. Winnicott's failures to make a dent on them in this regard plainly revivified feelings he had when young. To his recurrent despair, with Klein and Riviere, history repeated itself.[1]

In contrast to them, the inventor of the "squiggle" game provided to his analytic children just such a means of eliciting spontaneous responses. It is not "mirroring" he wished to provide them, but the revelation of the vapor trail, the path which the neutrino, itself too minute to be seen, leaves in the medium through which it has passed. In the same spirit, he is alert to that spontaneous gesture, the slip of the tongue. This too is a squiggle of a sort, and he wants right away to respond with an interpretation, with an active kind of receptivity akin to reciprocity. Though this is about psychoanalytic repair, it describes the situation obtaining between parent and child.

The inability or unwillingness on either part, baby or mothering one, to afford the other reciprocal receptivity is sufficient to stimulate envy. For it marks the first and most enduring failure of what can later be spoken of *un*-metaphorically as cross-fertilization. Neither party can reproduce himself in the experience of the other. Efforts on the part of each to do so in the absence of a disposition to be receptive on the part of the other are felt by the latter to be intrusive, even rapacious, involving as they do projections that are each time (in the words of the song) a little bit louder and a little bit worse. The not unreasonable inference drawn by the unsuccessful projectionist is that the other is filled either with himself or with some third party or object, in what Klein described as the primitive or archaic Oedipus complex. And such an empowered other, one who is believed could help but will not, becomes at once the bad and the enviable object.

As later the envyless person will not envy those privileged with rights of first refusal to be the belle of the ball or the best of the lot, he will earlier in life have allowed there to be a breast unspoiled by envy and resentment. The remembered presence of that breast (what is sometimes misleadingly called the internalization of) will have spared him the almost nameless dread that arises when one cannot elicit vicarious identifications in the mother. But when envy clouds the scene, the baby spoils and de-selects the breast, which doesn't like being spoiled (as who does?). With that spoiled, half-dead breast in the picture, his feelers risk retaliation. The more he cries out, the more the spoiled and envious breast goes on alert. The more the good breast comforts him, the more cagey and alert the other breast becomes. He is soon subject to its revenge for not submitting quietly, trying instead to make an end run around

---

[1]The story is told of Klein that when Clare Winnicott's mother died, Klein responded with something like: "Well, she's dead; there's no use talking of her. There's nothing you can do." Grosskurth, who repeats this story, observes that Klein was working on her autobiography at the time (Grosskurth 1986, p. 59). Was the terrifying blankness of Klein's response a reflection of her own despair vis-à-vis her own mother re-remembered in the recall work of the autobiography?

it to Mommy, Teddy or 911. Soon the screams are inside out and silent ones—the baby could pass for dead; passing for dead, the baby can only wait to be rescued through no initiative of his own.

The Elysian life he who is without envy leads depends then not only on the kindly, generous, collective care he receives in the COUPLE, doting when it can be, regretful when it can't, but his fate in the PAIR. When those distempers of the spirit, unconfusable with colic, arise as they are bound to, there must be days in which fear does not turn into loathing and trembling into grandiose disdain. And this depends not only on how good the help he receives is, but how good he can allow it to be. Since he is free of envy, he has not, out of his envy, made the breast envious, and he need not fear and loathe it. Thus his inner landscape is fresh and untrammeled; the life he traverses is serene and idyllic.

I am aware that such a life is not to everyone's taste. What may be serene may also be as bland as white bread, idyllic, devoid of meaning, halcyon, lacking in that frisson of angst that makes many feel fully alive, stretched, and at the cutting edge.

But one thing is certain: the unenvious life is life in the Age of Plenty.

LIFE IN THE AGE OF SCARCITY

And envy is, of course, *par excellence*, the Child of Scarcity.

For of what meaning is the need to be selective, to make selections, and to be selectworthy if not within a landscape of scarcity—of space and of time and of goods? He who is spared envy knows nothing of this. His tomorrows do not creep in petty pace; his days are occupied merely with delights and sorrows. The envious soul, on the other hand, being ever hopeful, ever fearful, lives on a gradient: each day takes him up, takes him down, or doesn't count for anything. On each accounting, he is closer to being selected and elated, further from it and deflated, or no account and numb. Propelled by his biology, he is driven *at once to be and to have* the biggest and the best, whether these are the best and the brightest, the richest and most powerful, or the meekest and most community minded. His preoccupations with his position and status relative to others is often mistaken for self-love. But it is not; it is his sociable expression of his membership in the species.

Indeed there is something profoundly hateful to him about the selection process (the rat race) to which he must submit: his egoism must submit to endless transgressions. The idyllic life of the unenvious person is sequestered from him—not by pushy parents or society, as he often thinks, but by those forces in his nature that will not let him be. It can get to the point where he cannot have a moment's peace, not a thought of his own. As the sleeper cannot get free of the need to dream, so those pursued by the harpies of their envy cannot get free of the daily din of influences—of harrying worries, of the unrelenting pressures of time, of voices real and imagined conveying orders or crying down shame. At each behest, more egoism must be given up; more submission to selection taken on. When he is young he may feel that he is doing this for himself, that it is not a kind of spectral ancestor worship, and he may embrace it as self-fulfillment. But he may in time, if only on his death bed, wonder what it was all for and just who (or what) was being served.

Selection is the Darwinian principle: simply put, the ecology runs its fingers over the vast hoard of possible and potential responses and rewards those that work with additional opportunities to work. Thus natural selectionists speak of adaption, by which they mean that in the enormous repertoire of potential responses, there are traits and behaviors that cope with the demands put upon the organism if it is to survive to breed. A classic example is the following:

> Batches of guppies when in home waters were prey to fish which preferred fully developed guppies. Of these, some picked at random were kept in a stream where as usual predators preyed on mature fish and adults; others were transferred to waters farther downstream, where the new local predator preferred newly hatched and still small guppies. Those subject to this new predation produced fewer, but larger off-spring, which is to say off-spring indeed more likely to survive predation. This evolving—and mathematically predicted difference—took place over a mere 30–60 generations. [Kolata 1990, pp. A1, B6]

It is important to note, moreover, that so-called strong selectionists maintain that what has long been assigned to learning works on the same principle. *Education*, which means a leading out, is considered by them to be just that. Learning is not viewed by them as something taken in and, in so being, altering the mind or brain. Rather, responses already present in potential are made kinetic by the formative experiences to which one is exposed (Edelman 1992, Gazzaniga 1992, Gould 1979). One model for this comes from the learning of language. The child is considered to have the syntactic and grammatical rules for all the languages of Babel, out of which are selected and onto which are mapped the sounds and syntax of his own. This done, vast numbers of brain cells, presumably corresponding to all other languages, are sloughed off. An extension of this model is the gravitation of cells once used for one sense, say vision, to the bundles serving another, say hearing, should blindness occur. Finally, at least one person feeling itching sensations from a phantom limb found that he could get relief by scratching a particular area of his cheek (Sacks 1993).

Correspondingly, there are languages we cannot learn because they violate the particular orderliness of our circuitry and architecture and preclude category formation (Chomsky 1972). And there are other limitations as well. Of these the most important is the problem endemic to our species, as compared with the guppies mentioned above. Their changes took place in only thirty to sixty generations. Changes in our own genetic structure evolve far more slowly. Thus selection takes hundreds of thousands, even millions, of years to shape or reshape our traits and characteristics. But what *has* been selected is our overabundance of features (or flaws):

> I don't doubt for a moment that the brain's enlargement in human evolution has an adaptive basis mediated by selection. But I would be more than mildly surprised if many of the specific things it can now do are the product of direct selection "for" that particular behavior. Once you build a complex machine, it can perform so many unanticipated tasks. [Gould quoted in Gazzaniga 1992, p. 88]

Although many biologists have gone astray when they argue that such and such trait has an adaptive value, and propose therefore that that is the reason it was selected, qualities of function can be selected for behaviors for which they haven't been designed—"exdapted," to use Gould's (1983) term for it. Feathers, for example, are good for flying, but they functioned originally because of their thermal qualities. To suggest therefore that envy functions as the stick that helps drive us to possess that wherewithal that strikes us as the best of breed is not to suggest that that is how temperament in general and envy in particular arose in the scheme of things. But it is to suggest that we are not careless of our fates. Hope struggles with desire, potential with kinesis, ego-ism with social-ism. Our behavior is principled.

The unenvious soul, as I have been imagining him, is a sybarite. Wandering life's bazaars, his nose canted forward aquiver with interest, sampling, tasting, moving on or lingering as fancy dictates, he walks the horizontal plane. Envy follows from comparing this with that along the vertical axis. The envious soul abhors the horizontal. His nose is turned up, the better to smell what lies ahead, the worse to smell what is in front of his nose. The nettle of envy provides the sting that drives him toward the top of the heap, where our biology wants him.

His nature, moreover, is such as to require a position in society. For he does not want merely to mate, but to breed well. And for that he needs to be a part of something greater and more potent than himself. Where I AM cannot succeed, IBM often can. To this end, he throws in his lot with the GROUP (the *right* group, of course) and to it he subordinates his egoism. He may have to play second fiddle or second base, but he does so for the greater good of the enterprise. What is good for the GROUP is good for him. For the GROUP psychologically embodies the biology of the species. And if he is selected, as any dinosaur can attest, his future is assured. For by throwing his lot in with the GROUP—that is, by PAIRING through identifications, he exposes himself to the brutal fact that the best contribution he can make to the society of his fellows is to make himself scarce. To include himself out. To die in behalf of the cause. When, then, he asks himself what it's all for and dimly surmises the spectral presence of his ancestors, he is not far wrong. They are with him all right, but not just in the traditions of his culture. They are in his very genes. And those genes, like all living things, want to make more of themselves, no matter who or what.

I have noted that the ambiguities between personal or egoistic and collective or social-istic survival are present from the very beginning of life. One can help by one's personal success at being good or different. And/or one can help by getting out of the way. (If you're not part of the solution, you're part of the problem.) What I want to add now is some reflection upon the ramifications of the tensions in this ambiguity. One may after all prefer to be good rather than different, or one may prefer not to be made redundant.

The word *stress* is a portmanteau word. At present it enjoys use by those who wish to refer to the emotional life of a person without quite wishing to be so unscientific as to imply the person has one. Thus everything from losing one's job to losing one's spouse is stress. But degrees of misfortune can be rated as to severity. When this is done, stress has turned out to be less the unfortunate event than one's helplessness in regard to it. (Even among animals, electroshocks, that durable staple of stress, are physiologically worse when the animal cannot either predict them or offset them.) For many people, indeed, the threat of catastrophe—such as dying or going mad—is often far worse than being mad or committing suicide.

What discussions of stress ordinarily lack is a conjunction with the conscious or unconscious fantasy life of the afflicted individual. The "Why has this happened to me?" feeling rushes into the vacuum of an event in an effort by the victim to make sense of something that otherwise would seem random and meaningless.

Looked at closely, events are stressful in the degree they are felt to imply to the afflicted person that he or she is being unselected. Of course sometimes that is plainly the case. Being fired or thrown over in favor of some other suitor are commonplace examples. But sometimes it is not so clear. Having a patient skip or forget an appointment can exact such a feeling, and two or more in the same day can turn anxiety into black and brooding feeling as to whether one is in the right field or is the right person for the job. For some a phone call to a friend is enough; even if all they are getting is a wake-up call, the susceptible have to work hard at not succumbing to the job of going about their dying.

There is a good deal of evidence, though of variable quality, that somatic changes follow from this kind of stress, though that they do should hardly be surprising. One would expect the body to adjust to its new psychosocial circumstances. Among the baboons, for example, a male overthrown from his rank in the troop undergoes hormonal changes opposite to those he underwent when an assertive, breeding male. It is important to note that these follow rather than precede his change in status. Changes in the same direction also take place in the brain. Correlated with these changes are atherosclerosis, hyperlipidemia, decreases in immune function, and a host of signs of aging correlated with status, uncorrelated with age. These, although less systematically studied, have been noted in people under stress. When deselection begins to occur in our own species, however early, I think degrees of psychological marasmus follow, in consequence of which a physiological aging, more accurately, a dying process, then ensues.

Deselection is a fact, and it is also an interpretation of a fact. As a supremely social fact, it is mediated in the PAIR and the GROUP. One turns to a friend when one's patients seem to be ganging up on one. In conditions of anomie there is no group to save the individual from his interpretation of his setbacks and pitfalls. Suicide, as Durkheim (1933) years ago recognized, was more common among such individuals. There are other self-destructive behaviors — alcoholism is one — that also require mediation by the GROUP. As is well known, AA is far and away the best treatment for alcoholism. Indeed, *supportive* group therapies are more helpful to the chronically ill than are individual therapies, and probably more helpful than interpretive therapies in a group. It is as if only the GROUP, providing it is the "right" GROUP (religion enters here), can undo what the GROUP has wrought and provide new assurances that the misfortunate event need not be understood as a message.

But how do we know the right GROUP from the wrong? From which do we take the message, secure that we're not tracking down the wrong garden path? Since we cannot know this, we are ever subject to doubt and uncertainty. The way out of this dilemma comes when the people we would otherwise envy find us and ours enviable. To be envied is the best anodyne for envy.

Self-possession is a critical element in the idea of what is enviable. Its insignia is not being found wanting — in both senses of that word. For when one has been selected to be among the elect, what more need one want? There need be no afterlife to the life hereafter. In this there is a genetic idea. Selection can cease once the species is perfected. As Goldilocks maintained, there is such a thing as just-right.

I have previously alluded to Kellman's and Spelke's work (1983). They report, for example, that infants at 4 months, when presented with a screen from the sides of which protrude two small cylindrical blocks, evince surprise when the screen is removed and there are two blocks. When, however, the screen is removed and they espy a rod—a single piece—they evince no surprise. The infant comes equipped with theories of how things are or should be. When they are he seems to lose interest, when they're not he sits up and takes notice. But he too is noticed.

10

ENVY IN THE
PSYCHOANALYTIC
PROCESS

To pay their respects to the Lord came three men. As befit his station in life, the one who was arrayed in gold was the first to present himself at the altar. "Forgive me, O Lord," he prayed. "I am nothing."

The second man then stepped forth. He was arrayed in silver. "O Lord, forgive me. I am nothing," he prayed.

The third man then came to the altar. He was disheveled, his robes tattered and torn. "O Lord," he prayed. "Forgive me. For I am nothing."

At this, the first man nudged the second: "Look who's calling himself nothing!"

Although analysts of all persuasions attend to them intuitively, the dynamics of envy have not (until now, perhaps) been available for systematic therapeutic investigation and relief. In this chapter I hope somewhat to remedy that omission. Unlike other writers, I do not regard envy as primary. I shall therefore focus on fantasies concerning selection, on hope, and on that handmaiden of hope, time.

The explicit role of envy in the therapeutic endeavor has for the most part been confined to the analysis of the negative therapeutic reaction. In his encyclopedic work, *The Fundamentals of Psychoanalytic Technique*, Etchegoyen (1991) provides a summary of these contributions beginning with Freud. In "Remembering, Repeating and Working Through" (1914), he warned that the patient's worsening condition might be used for his own ends. In "The

Economic Problem of Masochism," Freud (1924) changed his terms some-what; rather than the sense of guilt Freud refers to the need for punishment. In 1923 in *The Ego and the Id* Freud links the condition to guilt generated by the superego; the patient, who ought to have the right to improve, worsens because the superego does not assign this right to him.

Abraham (1919) wrote that such patients cannot understand that the aim of the treatment is the cure of their neurosis and indicates that narcissism, competitive rivalry and envy are important impelling forces. Horney (1936) noted the paradoxical nature of the backward movement. There is a puzzling worsening of the patient when there should be progress. Horney wrote of the narcissism and sadomasochism of the patient, which distort the reactions to interpretation and make the patient a rival of the analyst. Joan Riviere (1936) proposed that, in the advent of the depressive position, the anticipation of a depressive catastrophe is particularly intense and that feelings of omnipotence figure large in the manic defenses employed to control the analyst and the analysis. She pointed out that such patients come not so much to have themselves cured as to find a cure for their damaged internal objects. Reflecting on the curious mix between entitlement and dread which I have myself emphasized, she observes a conflict between conscious egotism and unconscious altruism.

Homer tells the story of Penelope awaiting the return of her husband, the father of her son. As Queen, she is under vast pressure to consider her long overdue husband Odysseus dead, to remarry, and give order and continuity to the monarchy. Pressed, finally, to stipulate a time by when she will do this, she promises to do so when she has finished the robe, the winding sheet, she is weaving for Odysseus' sick and dying father, Laertes. It is as if in this she asks only to put a wrap on her former marriage.

> "So spake she," recounts Antonious, "and our high hearts consented thereto."

But what Penelope wove in daytime, she unraveled by night.

> "Such wile as hers we have never yet heard that any of the women of old did know. . . . Not one of these in the imaginations of their hearts was like unto Penelope." (*The Odyssey*, pp. 18–19)

The generosity of this estimation was doubtless prompted by Antonious's effort to save face among the wooers who, for more than three years, were taken in by her. Penelope had higher hopes, almost higher even, it was to turn out, than for Odysseus. But in fact undoing what was done in order to rearrive at square one is a device probably as old as time itself.

Regarding time, Adam Phillips (1993) puts the pith of the traditional psychoanalytic view, which regards the intervals (frustration, absence) between being contentedly with the object and being with it again as at once the source and seat of mental life. One could ask the following "slightly absurd question, Is the first thought the absence of mother or the presence of time?" (p. 91). "I think where I am not, therefore I am where I do not think," writes Lacan (1977, p. 166). Indeed—but this is time in the COUPLE. I begin with time, but time in the PAIR.

Many of those who harbor doubts as to whether or not, or to what extent, they are meant to flourish, feel that it is only a matter of time before their status as one of the unselected will come into view. But that is only part of it. There is in these instances a need to be reborn or otherwise transformed consonant with one's hopes (see Bollas below). Such travelers cannot long tarry. If therapy were a place they could be out of before all was discovered or before time ran out on hope, that would be one thing. Failing that, there are not many options. They can leave (sometimes at a moment's notice). They can make it look as if they are there against their will (this is not tactically disconnected from the first). Or they can continually reset the clock to zero. (This makes schedules a favorite battleground with rules coming a close second, particularly those concerning coming late and leaving early, and rescheduling; if the therapist has a taste for skirmishes, all he needs are a few rules.) Whichever way they take, they cannot but envy the comfortably vast sense of time that psychoanalysts enjoy (as expressed, for example, in the aphorism "These things take time."). Envy's need to disestablish time and continuity is acute or acutely chronic. Through all of these, of course, runs the anguished argument—who decides?

The patient's often covert anxiety about getting well, becoming better, being different, indeed, becoming or getting anything, must occupy the center of the analysis, if there is to be one. At the core of this is the patient's use of analogs to decrease feelings of being tormented by differences he can neither use nor forget. These analogues serve (often enviously) to blur distinctions and so at once reduce desire and increase similarity. They thus serve the PAIR at the expense of the COUPLE. When distinctions are heightened, the loss of these fondly fashioned analogies represents, accordingly, not one, but two frightening events; a sense of being at one with the group is jeopardized and the now-no-longer-just-like-me portion or person becomes open to relationships featuring either xenophobic attack (stranger anxiety) or abject desire, both of which had been finessed by blurring the vast distinctions between "more than" and "different from." There then, after a long interval, lurks a renewal of the awesome otherness of the other.

How hard people who fear the pain of feeling envious work to make the analysis someone else's and not their own! When they arrive it is because they are sent. While they are here it is to assist the analyst with clear or obscure purposes of his own, for which he never seems sufficiently grateful since he is always carping about something or other. When at length it begins to dawn on very envious patients that they may just possibly be here for purposes of their own, they threaten to leave, wait to be dissuaded, and then resume their care of their needful analyst. After each interval the question seems to arise anew: if I have to want, or know I want, it won't be you I choose. Analysts who themselves need a sense of alliance are often tempted to regain one by filling out the space the patient is leaving. And indeed if one doesn't, one's own serenity and dispassion seem so enviable as to inspire havoc. Rather than succumb, the patient might rather die or starve or give himself or herself to others. Part of the difficulty is that people justly fear selection; they know that the more ardent their desire the fewer the choices. They sense, correctly, that the analyst is making selection after selection, choosing this aspect of the patient over that. What will they be like when they are over?

P.   You know, when I sleep around like this I am at risk of contracting AIDS.
Ψ   Yes. But not, at least, of contracting aid.

P.   When I was little we played tag. Being the smallest, I was often "it." And being little often I could not catch the others, so I had to stay "it" for a long time. [silence.]
Ψ   My turn to be "it."

P.   Can you hear me?
Ψ   Only when you make yourself audible.
P.   But you could hear my question?
Ψ   I can hear you when you make yourself audible. I can "hear" you when you make yourself "heard."
P.   [Inaudible] Did you hear that?
Ψ   I "heard" that.
P.   But did you hear it?
Ψ   Some choice!

But as in any argument, there is the equal and opposite position. The famished wish to control time propels an intent to own it. And the surest sign of owning something often seems to be that the owner can do anything he wants with what he owns. Furious at being spooked by time, the envious patient makes waste hastily. Nothing takes too long, and there would be time for everything were the therapist not so impatient. In his novel *Mr. Palomar*, Italo Calvino (1985) writes:

"If time has to end, it can be described, instant by instant," Mr. Palomar thinks, "and each instant, when described, expands so that its end can no longer be seen." He decides that he will set himself to describing every instant of his life, and until he had described them all he will no longer think of being dead. At that moment he dies. [p. 126]

Then too there is what Calvino approvingly (elsewhere — 1988) quotes from Carlo Levi. Levi is speaking of Laurence Sterne's *Tristram Shandy*.

The clock is Shandy's first symbol. Under its influence he is conceived and his misfortunes begin, which are one and the same with this emblem of time. Death is hidden in clocks, as Belli said; and the unhappiness of individual life, of this fragment, of this divided, disunited thing, devoid of wholeness: death, which is time, the time of individuation, of separation, the abstract time that rolls toward its end. Tristram Shandy does not want to be born, because he does not want to die. Every means and every weapon is valid to save oneself from death and time. If a straight line is the shortest distance between two fated and inevitable points, digressions will lengthen it; and if these digressions become so complex, so tangled and tortuous, so rapid as to hide their own tracks, who knows — perhaps death may not find us, perhaps time will lose its way, and perhaps we ourselves can remain concealed in our shifting hiding places. [p. 47]

Thus when envy is acute there is also a therapist who must be prepared to live with nothing being settled. Indeed, if the therapist *is* so unwary as to permit himself a sigh of relief now and then because things seem to be going better, he will soon enough come to feel his sigh was overheard, for it is promptly followed, as if by magic, by the recrudescence of old issues that have come unglued again. Under such circumstances, perfectly competent therapists can be forgiven if they turn from helping their patients understand the forces driving them to teaching, confrontation, even jeremiads — those sentences that begin with, "You know. . . ."

The envious person generally tries to rid himself of his disease by inducing the illness or trauma instead in the analyst, grafting it to whatever remnants there are of the analyst's own. This is the parasitism that characterizes the patient's idea of object relations. The patient's relation in the PAIR with his introjects is the first job of the analysis; the analyst should endeavor not to expose himself for emotional discovery until well into that work. For the patient, if he cannot flourish without exposing himself to murderous retaliation from his split-off hatred, cannot thank the analyst for leading him to this.

When the patient's greed, anxiety, and envy converge on issues of ownership, for the analyst too there is a deeper question: which of the rules and structures are necessary for the work to progress, and which the hand-me-downs of tradition maintained in therapist's professional PAIR and GROUP—the latter of which I shall call the academy. In making this distinction between function and tradition, I do not mean to say that the affiliation with tradition is not important to the therapist. The therapist needs to feel a part of things, particularly when being exposed to the relentless doubts insinuated into him by the envious patient. For perhaps the greatest pain for the analyst arises out of the patient's unrelenting assertion that the analyst has bad intentions and therefore, even if he does his best, nothing he can do will be right. Often this assertion is not made verbally, but indicated in sighs and moues, small rollings of the eyes, and quick, slight movements of the shoulders. For all that the analyst may try to understand that this unrelenting attitude contains those qualities of the survivor—backbone and resolve—the fixed quality of this stubborn asseveration can get unnerving.

All the same, the lighter the analyst travels, the less there is to protect because, when excessively envious, the patient suffers from an insufficiency of unconsciousness and so needs to enlist the therapist's resistances to augment his own. The envious patient, if he is going to look into psychoanalysis at all, is not likely also to be willing to see it—or see it through. He will do what he did as a baby, he will "cut" the analyst. He is simply not going to be found wanting; every indication of want discovered will have to be the analyst's want of him. He leaves a vacuum for the analyst to fill. The analyst finds this vacancy tempting, for certainly the life he hears about and the person he encounters seem distressed indeed. He may feel further tempted by the fact that if he does not get actively to work nothing much will seem to be happening.

Impatience, boredom, irritation, desolation, doubt all help the therapist not to listen or closely attend. By inspiring these feelings in the therapist, the patient can get the therapist to join in finding little significance to what he says. Not a few patients achieve the same ends by provoking in their analysts an increasing disbelief in the analytic process. The patient will drone on or become hit or miss, and the therapy will soon begin to seem like a no-thing. In short, the therapist will soon find himself with every reason to want actively to help his patient out or out. If he does not help, the therapist will begin to be afraid of becoming sick with uselessness, helplessness, rage, and guilt. By organizing their lives into a downward spiral, the patient dares the therapist to continue what seems to have become too little or too late. Every point at which the therapist moves away from the business at hand to pick up on something peripheral to it is a moment in which the therapy can be vitiated. This places the therapist in a cleft-stick. If he sets the therapy aside to see to the downward spiral of the patient's life, he shows his care and concern for the patient, but he also demonstrates a lack of respect for the therapeutic endeavor.

Not all patients have to split the therapist like this nor all analysts to feel split. But when, out of acute envy, the patient needs insofar as he can to sever the therapist from his therapeutic potency, the analyst needs to know his own needs. Does he need assent to what he says? Does he need progress—for the patient to get better or change—for the patient to be different? What does he need by way of cooperation—regularity, promptitude, talk? The prudent therapist will know his limitations and make his rules accordingly. If he asks for no more and no less than what he absolutely needs, it follows that the rules and structures he requires can be non-negotiable. If he can settle for what the black-pajamed patient can afford him, he will spare himself from dreading the next appointment or yearning for the end of this.

So envious can envy become that it has no interest even in the self, except an envious one—ever alert to snuff out or punish any indications that the self is flourishing. Since this means that the patient cannot get well without exposing himself (really, those he is identified with in the PAIR) to terrible abuse for doing so, the patient can only turn himself to an interest in the other and getting him more ill. (It is in this sense that Meltzer [1967] talks of analysis as being a salvage operation.) Such a self, gorged by the identifications that go to make up first PAIRING, then GROUPING, so seriously lacks the relations involved in COUPLING that it is almost choked.

> As I drew closer, I saw what was happening. She [a bag lady on the streets of NYC] was *imitating the passers-by*. . . . But it was not just an imitation, extraordinary as this would have been in itself. The woman not only took on, and took in, the features of countless people. She took them off. Every mirroring was also a parody. . . .
>
> This woman who, becoming everybody, lost her own self, became nobody. This woman with a thousand faces, works, personalities—how must it be for her in this whirlwind of identities? The answer came soon—and not a second too late (sic): for the build up of personas, both hers and others' was fast approaching the point of explosion. Suddenly, desperately, the old woman turned into an alleyway which led off the main street. And there, with all the appearances of a woman violently sick, she expelled, tremendously accelerated and abbreviated, all the gestures, the postures, the expressions, the demeanors, the behavioral repertoires of the past forty or fifty people she had passed. [Sacks 1985, pp. 117–118]

To ask the self to identify with the analyst in what is sometimes called the therapeutic alliance is a disservice. It means opening up the inclination to look for, mayhaps to lust for, the very differences of which COUPLING is made. And it means the terrible loss of the identifications out of which the self is constructed (often ingeniously and with concealed pride).

> Each individual is made up of what he has lived and the way he has lived it, and no one can take this away from him. Anyone who has lived in suffering is always made of that suffering; if they try to take it away from him, he is no longer himself. Therefore, Mr. Palomar prepares to become a grouchy dead man, reluctant to submit to the sentence to remain exactly as he is; but he is unwilling to give up anything of himself, even if it is a burden. [Calvino 1985, p. 125]

It follows that it helps very much if a patient's progress, or lack of it, is his own business, and not the analyst's. Therapists are not immune from envy; indeed some portion of their practice enacts and visits upon their patients an envy screened from view by their membership in the psychoanalytic group. If the analyst can stand for the therapy to belong to the patient, there is less reason for the patient to try to "get his own back." Envious patients often ask their analysts to help them cheapen and degrade speech, free association, personal encounter, and anything else that they cannot yet use with pleasure and confidence.

The initial experience of envy is naturally at its most acute when concentrated. The infant who can take his time about discovering the features of the breast is less traumatized by the envy with which it inflames him. That same sort of time taking will be required by the infant self as it comes into contact with the analytic provider. But when envy is rife, it dilates rapidly, and with only a brief amount of time to contain it, it quickly reaches explosive proportions. The infant self doesn't know what its successor selves know about time. But though successor selves come into being, the infant self survives until it feels able to mourn its own passing.

Many people are asked or allowed to discover their analysts far too soon. There may have to be a series of encounters at the beginning, though the fewer the better, having to do with rates, times, and other housekeeping matters. And there may have to be a series of encounters in which the analyst must demonstrate that he understands that the patient will expect him to have something to ask or even to say, before he can get back out of the patient's way. But these early interventions can be used to make manifest the analyst's conviction that psychoanalysis is a matter of talking of experiences in which both analyst and patient participate and has nothing whatever to do with talking *about* experiences, particularly those the analyst only hears about. This, when repeatedly demonstrated, helps the patient to recognize himself as the vital part of the enterprise, an experience essential to any analysis, but especially to one in which the patient's envy is a prominent feature. If the

therapist can forget about his designs on the patient, including those he has been taught are necessary and correct, the patient has a chance of forgetting about the therapist and getting on with what he came to do. This is to create, or recapture, and then display a series of half-forgotten experiences. Later on, should he feel two heads are better than one and that there is something to be said for an-"other" perspective, he will ask the analyst for an interpretation of what he has been at such pains to display. This leaves the value of having a contribution to the matter by the therapist to the patient where, of course, it belongs if it is to be his and not the therapist's therapy.

If, by the time the patient is ready to discover him, the analyst's COUPLE-relationship (his or her libidinal transferences) and the PAIR-relationship (his or her identity and work as a member of a psychoanalytic PAIR and representative of the psychoanalytic GROUP) have been thoroughly investigated by the analyst, he may indeed have something to say. For he will by then know what he wants to say — and also, no less, why he wants to say it. That is why it helps so much when therapists can, first, wait to be asked; second, be really sure what it is that they are being asked; third, be clear about what they have to say; and then be fully informed as to why they want to say it. But in such self possession, there is little foothold for the patient, who may then accordingly raise the ante by becoming ill, getting in trouble, or wanting to leave. Analysts who until then have been studies in forbearance may come undone.

> In her sexual life with her new lover, P. is not feeling realized. There are some key elements in the original primal scene that are not finding their way into her current one. She is hesitant to complain, because she feels that others, particularly her lover and her analyst, might find her ungrateful. And she is ashamed to confess that she is secretly preoccupied by the admittedly unlikely possibility that her gentle and considerate lover might suddenly hit her or force her. But little by little she is "sneaking back" to her prerelationship masturbation fantasy, the main feature of which is that others are watching her undress, dance, or have sexual intercourse until they can stand it no longer. At this point the fantasy bifurcates. In some renditions the others are envious of her sensuality and beauty; they hope by interrupting and pressing money upon her to drag her down into being a prostitute. In other renditions, they are so beside themselves with desire that they must have her no matter the cost to them in money and humiliation.

Even in the richly textured warp and woof of this material, there is no missing the bright, anguished thread of loss. Past images, past hopes are going unselected by current events. It is as if (as a dream of P.'s soon puts it) P. has become a department store where people come and pick and choose whatever they like. Her fierce, desperate wish to have a hold on them through their passions is being frustrated, and in her shame of that wish, which, after

all, concerns life and death, she cannot assert her ferocity, save by sneaking
back to her fantasies.

As the new relationship goes from good to better, and she grows daily
happier, her heart sinks. The evident contentment of her lover makes her
want to wail and gnash her teeth. Death, already implied in the unmistakable
passage of time away from her youthful imaginings, and expressed in the
cruel fates of the fantasy, now makes its appearance garbed as AIDS and as
pregnancy—each definitive, hence final, so fatal. Afraid, and furious because
she is afraid, she alters the love making with her lover until it begins to
resemble a scene in a movie in which, to practice safe sex, each person crawls
into a body-sized condom. Her lover, instead of becoming rapacious, begins
to have occasional difficulties with his potency, something that leaves P.
feeling guilty and more afraid. She becomes fearful lest her lover leave, she
feels she is now living on borrowed time.

How to put an end to ending? How, instead, to force time's own pace?

P., feeling compelled to outgrow her childish ways long before she could
grow out of them, has grown up fast. She has become an adept at developing
a taste for things before coming to an appetite for them. A young woman in
a hurry—ever impatient—it took time before she could feel convinced that
where she hurried to was wherever she could take all the time in the world.
Death too is something to be gotten over with as soon as possible. Perhaps
after the pain of death is over one can relax and enjoy life. She has long felt
that only if she were already married to him could she sit back and escape the
turmoil of a first date. It is painful for P. to leave each session; on knife's
edge, she has been unable to immerse herself in the time she has. It seems she
comes too often for what she is able to accomplish; her analysis seems to be
taking forever.

Ψ   [Suggests that deep down P. feels she should have more frequent sessions,
      but hates both ideas—of more frequent sessions and of thinking she should
      have them.]

P. Why would I want to come more often? This is such a waste of time, as it is,
      that it's only because I only come as often as I do that I can put up with it!

Is this waste cause or consequence? Had she more time, wouldn't she
need less? As this begins to occur to P., she begins to feel endangered.

P. turns from lying prone on the couch onto her side. She sees the analytic foot.
"I am allowed to see your foot. I am not allowed to look at you, but I am allowed
to see your foot." [She has earlier been talking of how she lies and steals.] "Your
shoe. Do you remember how I always want to eat your shoe. I used to think about
that a lot—that's how I realized it. I feel you are angry and impatient with me.
You looked angry and impatient when I came in today. I thought of it as a

projection. But maybe you *are* angry and impatient with me. Maybe it's you, not me. Are you? *Are* you? I buy a lot of shoes, you know." [Silence] "I am sure it is your influence, though I can't see how."

To relate is to choose. To relate certain observations by supposing, for example, that to all actions there is an opposite and equal reaction is to rule out all the other possibilities that might previously have seemed determinate. Objects are merely objects — appendages — until they are discovered to be in a relationship, whereupon they take on significance, being at once signified and signifier. It is the discovery of their role in a relationship that excites envy — or, when envy can be borne, jealousy.

A patient sighs, says:

"I hope I do not let the whole thing go haywire again." [She means the "*hole*" thing, an interpretation Ψ has used for her, so her decision not to use the phrase is today probably a proximate source of her worry.] "Today I feel it, I feel second rate and I know it is a result of my wish that K. treated me better over the weekend, that I wasn't left feeling such a slob, so defective, with this, this, and this wrong with me. And today I feel you are listening, really listening, ya know? But I know you *do* listen. But today I can say it to you, let you know I know. But I am afraid. I am afraid that this will all go physical on me — out of the realm of the emotions. Into mindland: panic attacks, nausea, fatigue. And that 'the looking funny' doesn't come back. I hate that worst of anything. I cannot control it when it happens and everything looks funny. Not funny. What is the word I want? Surrealistic, out of kilter, dislocated. Everything. You have said it is my making it 'everything' is to keep it from being any particular no-thing."

Meanwhile P.'s sessions seem to be going badly.

At length, P. remarks about her silliness in thinking Ψ could help with something that after all is between her and her lover. She suspects Ψ thinks she is being paranoid.

Ψ agrees, reminding her that Ψ often thinks this to be her defense against feeling frightened. Ψ adds that she sounds annoyed at being able correctly to guess what Ψ thinks.

P. I think *you* think I ought to come more often, but I can't, and I don't think you understand that I can't. [This is said bitterly, as if there has been or is an empathic failure on Ψ's part.]

Soon P. declines to speak, instead lying in each session as if in a pool of anger, waiting for things to change. In P.'s silence, Ψ hears this:

"I have given you all the information that anyone with an ounce of intelligence and sensitivity requires before doing something to h-e-l-p. Going back to free-associating, which I know is what you expect me to sooner or later do, would be going along with what you want — allowing you, once more, to have your way. In fact, you are probably only too anxious to interpret matters as they now stand, as if it were not you who were responsible but some distant figure from my past, now reincarnated in you. Well, I say 'only too anxious,' but in fact you believe that time is very much on your side. Not only do you get paid no matter what, but you can let me either sink or swim or to stew in my own juices until I come around to your way of doing things."

This fear enrages P.

"I will not allow myself to be subjected to these intimidation tactics, not again, not now at my age. You're running a con. You lulled me with your sympathetic, nonjudgmental manner, and I fell for it. I turned myself inside out for you, but each time it is the same: never satisfied. Well, forget it! I'm not going to be that kind of sucker, not now, not ever. D' you seriously expect me just to roll over and play dead?"

P. [Talking aloud to Ψ] "Do you expect me to just roll over and play dead? And — *don't turn this around!*"

As if in some anxiety lest Ψ do just that, P. now gets up from lying down and sits on the edge of the couch. She is calmer now, enough to look at Ψ. But something in Ψ's steadfast, musing gaze sends a lightening flash of pure rage through P. Words like "just sitting there" carom past.

P. I don't have to put up with this bullshit, you know! [P. gets to her feet, walks to the door grasps the knob.] "Well, have you got anything to say, because if you don't. . . ." P. turns the knob, opens the door slightly.

Ψ I do have something to say, but could you at least sit down?

[P. sits on the very edge of the chair that was the starting off place many months ago. The door from the consulting room to the waiting room is left slightly ajar. Ψ here goes on to say what, in the turmoil, Ψ can find to say.]

Such moments occur in some form sooner or later in any therapy in which the patient's (or the therapist's) envy has a preeminent role. The time we use to allow matters to evolve and recohere and the quiet we employ to listen for our dawning intuitions conveys menace. Since so much of this is supposed to go without saying — indeed, cannot quite be said — one must (the pregnancy analogy is deliberate) bear this in mind. One's own capacity to tolerate nothing quickly becomes an issue central to the analysis. If one can regard the torment of experience as a hateful fact, analysis is possible. If one succumbs to the temptation to replace the no-things with something — well, one soon is out of the analysis business and into the transfusion business. Envy in effect blocks anything and everything the other can do until the other does what the self wants, in this case, until Ψ does what P. wants. The end need not come abruptly, in a big bang, as in the illustration it appears to be doing. The stripping away of Ψ's potency can be gradual and chronic.

The precise event P. illustrates can be understood in several ways. That there are several hot potatoes being tossed back and forth, concerning which of the two must own up to unrespectable qualities or intentions, is apparent. P. wishes to disassociate herself from being the source of these and to reassign their ownership to Ψ, something, it seems, P. feels can only be done securely

if and when Ψ acts consonantly with them. These involve being greedy, grasping and indifferent to time. And they involve something called "turning things around".

Ψ is reluctant to act consonantly with what P. attributes to him (or her). He "holds" them, in the sense of knowing them, but only when the door opens outward does Ψ make a grab for P. Does Ψ then do what P. fears? Does he, for example, interpret the transference?

After all, much of what P. has been experiencing can be accounted for very easily by explanations having to do with transference. The transference has rules in it to the effect that displacements can fan out or contract as to objects, can split subject and object (as in "part of me" or "part of you") and can reverse, as to subject and object, wholly or in parts. It is not so much the nouns that matter but the verbs—not *who* does what and with which and to whom, but the nature of what's *being done*. You can do it to me or I can do it to you, so long as we *do* it. The transference embodies this, primarily in the exploration and exploitation of differences: in part-object terms, mouth--breast, penis-vagina and so forth; in whole-object terms, prey-predator, younger-older, man-woman and so on. Thus we can imagine that P.'s opening statement, consisting of P. lying on the couch like an unchanged infant might lie about neglected in a puddle of urine or feces, reflects the recurrence, in present time, of a very distressing state of affairs in which P. once again is waiting for someone, in the present instance Ψ, to change her— but not, of course, in any therapeutic sense. The fact that Ψ is not doing this for P. and, to make matters worse, is relying on the potency of his skills as a therapist not to have to change the dirtied, uncomfortable, neglected P., adds insult to injury—and the sheer gall or effrontery of this posture of Ψ's stimulates P.'s envy. P. intends to denude Ψ of his (or her) therapeutic powers, of his wherewithal, because these stand between P. and getting cared for.

On the other hand, P. is trying out leaving, and Ψ plainly needs to afford her the time to do so. Though tempted, Ψ may not have to tell P. such things as that he can find another Ψ for P. or that he will save P.'s hours for a while so that they are there should P. elect to return. He may instead be able to say: "*Of course* we must put a stop to what you are finding so intolerable, even if that means an end to this session, or an end even to our work. *No one* should be asked to go through what you have been going through." P. may experience this as a Trojan horse designed to insinuate Ψ's own projections or to reposit P.'s projections into P. But what if Ψ means what he says?

The tension at this juncture cannot be overestimated. P. is at the edge of discovering that she may not in fact be able to conceive and give birth to herself—that Ψ is necessary as something more than a stage property. The current disparity is one in which Ψ is onlooker, is the infant in the primal apotheosis out of which, in P.'s as yet unreconstructed history, another infant, a little boy, was indeed born. Proud P. is going this time around to mother and father the as-yet-unformed baby of herself. *And don't turn this around!*

But it is—slowly, inexorably, as if huge plate tectonics are crushingly on the move—getting turned around.

> A patient says: "I am always on my back. I am a turtle or a beetle, on my back, soft underbelly up, being or anticipating being used, fucked, or devoured. Why can't I turn over? Why do you refuse to let me sit up?"

Manifestly, this woman's language is in the COUPLE; it seems sexual in nature, inviting associations of cannibalism, rape, premorbid autopsy. It is placed there defensively, because, as the image of beetle and turtle suggest, there is a carapace to be found. Translated into the language of PAIR and GROUP, which at the moment is latent to that of the COUPLE, the issue shows its darker side. In this language the turtle might refer to the length of life tortoises enjoy, while the beetle might suggest the prolixity of the beetle among extant creatures. Beyond that, moreover, is her vulnerability to the prying eye: that eye empty of remorse or charity, that espying eye that asks, "What are you doing here? Haven't I long since told you to be dead and gone by now? Your place is with the invisible chorus, yet whom do I see— You!"

When envy is on the boil, there are only two distillates: only two positions in the world and only one → way for objects to relate. There is "it" and only more of "it." The arrow may swing, but it is the same arrow. If the arrow is down↓ up, its alternative is up↑ down, if it is I am being ← fucked, it can only invert to → you.[1] It is easy to see therefore that changes in Ψ's approach to P. can all too easily be seen not as empathic accommodation, but as a capitulation. P. consciously desires such capitulation, but unconsciously capitulations degrade Ψ in P.'s connoisseur eyes and in doing so stimulate a good deal of guilt. The patient can often only escape such guilt by persuading himself that the analyst isn't worth feeling compunction about. And he will provoke the analyst until the latter conforms to the justifiable profile. But when the patient takes relief from such disparagement he loses out on whatever remaining value there is to the analyst. A victory for envy in the PAIR is a loss to the patient in the COUPLE.

---

[1]For years the psychoanalytic literature on homsosexuality could only contemplate active and passive or male and female homosexual orientations, as if these reductionistic positions were inherent and not themselves an envious perversion of what people do together.

Such divergences of opinion come about when Ψ misunderstands the bone of contention. P. is being stubborn because her understanding from day one (whenever day one was) was that she is meant to give over and die, as a result of which she can only want to—or want to become a changed character (cosmetic surgeons do very well out of this need). It has taken every ounce of P.'s resolve not to take these orders. That resolve, moreover, has alienated P. from herself, because in the PAIR she is not meant to resist; she is meant, rather, to carry out instructions as every good soldier must. The *resolute* quality of the nonreceptive object—the object made of stone and bone—becomes itself an object of envy, for its presumptive indifference is much coveted by the personality that feels itself at sixes and sevens due to the force of influences playing upon it. But if Ψ attempts to find relief by active efforts to engage the patient, he will be shown—though he may not notice—the patient's increasing triumph and relief that it is now the analyst! who needs and wants—the tables have been wormed; the cinder is on the other foot.

In the face of a feeling one should get on about dying, any status quo can only be attractive indeed. The analyst may feel that the analysis has locked into an impasse, but what is for the analyst an impasse is for the patient an anchorage:

"I felt so scared I couldn't move," says the woman alone in the dark. "I couldn't breathe, I couldn't draw a breath."

"I shrank, I tried to make myself as small as I could without moving," says the man out late in the parking garage or the deer caught up in the headlights.

"I closed my eyes," says the little boy.

"I can't go on like this!" says the woman rent by the pea under the mattresses, but mutilated by the fear that she might want nonetheless to go on.

"I covered up my ears and made noise in them by clapping my hands over them," says the little girl.

"I began to hallucinate," says the trembling gent in the corner. "The voices took charge and started screaming orders."

There has to be some way of controlling the angel of death. The envy of the unselected is atavistic, perhaps because their anxieties are so close to the fundament. I have, for example, never worked with such a patient who did not have a secret and engorged fascination with ova-positing—that quick, passing fascination with insects that immobilize their victims and make them unwilling host to their eggs and larva. But neither would I have caught that line of fantasy had I not been alert. There is much shame to it, as one might expect, since shame itself, being a social anxiety, is a function of the PAIR, and ova-positing a violation of the precepts of the PAIR that we use one another as self-objects and sources for mutual identification. But ordinary reproduction is a function of the COUPLE, and, as such, not a remedy for the illicit and defiant determination to cheat death of its proscription against progeneration.

The initial wish, to deposit experiences not yet processable by symbol formation, thought, and affect formation turns ugly. It *must* penetrate the barrier of the self-contained (or other-containing) object. The frustration of its efforts to penetrate in a straightforward way produces a surplus of hatred and feelings of persecution. These in turn stimulate the wish to murder the object—or, failing that, at least to *be* murdered *by* it. The discovery of murderous impulses in the object is tantamount to the discovery of life where all was deadness—stone and bone. The wish to be murdered (an apotheosis) is a variation on the wish to be created/selected.

> P. [Returning to the subject] You tell me I should come more often. But my
> friends always ask me when I am going to terminate. I have to tell them you
> don't think I am done. My God, if I told them how many times a week I am
> still seeing you, they would think I was crazy—I don't mean crazy crazy, I
> mean crazy to let you make me keep coming like this. You know, you may
> be over estimating me. You may think I can go farther. But it could be that
> I have reached my limit. Maybe I don't have what it takes. Maybe I am just
> not one of those people who are cut out for deep therapy. What do you
> think? You never tell me what you think. People ask me, "When are you
> going to be through?" And I don't know what to tell them.

Though P. has not come out and said so, she is bringing public opinion to bear: "friends," "people." Size figures here: the agglutinative impulse of establishing more of the same makes many of few and more of many. The public enters as if comprised of legions. Armies. Under these circumstances it is not difficult to see why murdersome Ψ, too, might come to feel by turns murderous and its dead opposite, but in either case, ready to augment *himself* also through numbers. He will invoke his group, *his* academy. And as always the academy is ready to respond. Not only will Ψ find some analysts who, in the name, say, of Margaret Little, recommend touching, but other analysts who recommend a good old fashioned dose of reality, à la Freud's precedental work with the Wolf Man.

Eckstaedt, for example (1989), writes:

> For more than a decade, analysts in all parts of the world have noticed that
> some analyses are incomparably more difficult than others, if not impossi-
> ble. In 1972, Limentani expressed the opinion that ego-syntonic neuroses,
> as he calls these disturbances, constitute an irreversible stumbling block to

analysis. Khan provides a candid and vivid description of how he spent years working in analyses where, so far as he could tell, nothing was happening or developing until he began to notice how annoyed he was with these patients and how necessary it was to counteract the situation.[2] [p. 502]

Eckstaedt herself remarks that unless modified, such analyses are likely to be "as-if" analyses: "It is as if the analyst were assuming the role of a victim whose sacrifice is that of his analytic competence" (p. 503).

This is an ambiguous issue. Surely it would be a relief to P. to know something of the mysterious depths of Ψ's hatred and surely P. would like to know that she can affect Ψ. The capacity to affect the other is the great equalizer. It is often the way people know they are alive, are there. Thus it is probable that the more greatly P. feels affected and influenced by Ψ, the more she will insist on a turn about as no more than fair play. If, at such junctures as we are considering, P. obliges Ψ to alter his methods, limits, or boundaries, there will be a diminution of envy, to the point, moreover, that the so-called negative therapeutic reaction may be averted. It may be that Freud's imposition of a time limit upon the Wolf Man was less a confrontation — putting the heat on, lighting a fire under — with that man's frozen state than an unfreezing of Freud's usual determination to "stick coolly to the rules." This is what makes such doses of reality equivocal. It is true that many patients, feeling themselves to be in abject masochistic surrender to the sadistic analyst, can only feel that as they turn the tables, the analyst will then be in the same position relative to them. (And then in danger of another turning, which can only return them to being on their backs.) The introduction of what Eissler (1953) called "parameters" is, thus, an intricate undertaking.

As I noted, Dante placed the envious in the Inferno, where they milled about leadenly with their eyes sewn shut with leaden thread. One can discern in this a punishment for their greedy and covetous eye, for their looking for the worst, for the deadness of their presence in the light of good fortune, cheer, and levity. But in the more primitive taliation, they suffer for their attempts to blind others to their status as "illegal aliens," their impostorship, their counterfeiting of belongingness. They are should-not-haves masquerading as have-nots. In fact, of course they *are* have-nots; there is an irony here. The masquerade is that they are *pretending* to be have-nots when in fact that is exactly what they are. P. is bound and determined to see whether Ψ too

---

[2]Kahn (1974) stresses the need to bear in mind that "one of the most important nutrients is the right dosage of positive aggression and even hate by the analyst" (Khan, quoted in Eckstaedt, p. 92).

is an impostor. If Ψ is, P. will feel rampant and deprived of an opportunity to increase his wherewithal; if Ψ isn't an impostor, although P.'s envy will increase, P. can continue to believe that something may come of the therapeutic endeavor. In fact, there is no choice: P. is bound to have a nose for how Ψ moves about in the world, for no pretense is safe unless the fooler can find someone willing to be fooled.

We left Ψ in somewhat of a quandary. P. was rather stubbornly about to decamp. Moreover, P. had made clear that anything Ψ might try to say would probably be construed by her — *and in addition her GROUP* — as actions that could only make matters worse. When thinking earlier about how this worked, we saw that P. was rather successfully compromising Ψ's therapeutic potency. There is in this a condensation of death and potency, of life and generativity. If there is to be a generative relationship, it seems that it will have to be with P. as the container. Quite apart from this rousing homosexual panics in patients who are or are feeling male, it means that female patients *must willy-nilly* conceive, gestate and bear Ψ's "offspring." This spells death to each one's wishes to achieve generational life in — or also in — the inverse manner.

Suppose, therefore, that P. wants to generate something that requires Ψ to be the container. Ψ's dominion over the analytic situation requires (or seems to) that P. kill off that generative strain in herself and instead submit to Ψ's in or outpourings. For P. who is close to feeling the need to give way to death as it is, this additional requirement is likely to feel like the last straw. P.'s doorway stand can be understood as a last ditch effort to get her point of view into Ψ's container. P. first tries to put a stop to Ψ's flow: she is, as it were, halfway out the door and then orders Ψ, "And don't turn this around!" Then P. continues her outpouring of grievances intending to project them so decisively into Ψ's container that they stay there long enough to affect Ψ's contents. People whose envy is chronic may allow Ψ to pour what Ψ will into them, but they may only have the conception and change afterwards. That is, they may leave or terminate the work, seeming to be essentially unaffected by the experience, but go on to "get well" on their own or with some other, more deserving therapist.

The provisioning function of the breast — vital in the COUPLE — has, as a counterpart, a receptive function, no less vital to the PAIR, for the reception and processing of projective identifications, particularly those having to do with the infant's dread. That such sympathetic imagination is essential for the analyst goes without saying, but that this differs from empathy and understanding is not so well known. The distinction is simple: empathy and understanding are issued and taken in relation to the patient's conscious communications and feelings. Sympathetic imagination is directed to fathoming and conceiving what the patient and analyst are unconscious of. Bion (1970) put it this way:

To the analytic observer, the material must appear as a number of discrete particles, unrelated and incoherent. The coherence that these facts have in the patient's mind is not relevant to the analyst's problem. His problem — I describe it in stages — is to ignore that coherence so that he is confronted by the incoherence and experiences incomprehension of what is presented to him. . . . This state must endure until a new comprehension emerges. [p. 12]

The comprehension or conception here is of the unconscious, of preconceptions that are as yet unrealized. In Winnicott's description, it is a leading out from the unconscious (1962, p. 167). An inadequate but familiar example is the slip of the tongue. A patient is telling what she knows of what she experiences, when suddenly the slip occurs:

P.   When it comes to men, I am a shrinking violent. I mean. . . .

Although (because) the unconscious has got a word in edgewise, as often as not the patient wants to correct the slip and go on. Some analysts will bring the patient back to the slip and ask for associations: "Violent . . .?" In contrast to this linear extension of consciousness, the thrust of sympathetic imagination is toward the curve of brow or shape of belly that this new addition gives to the figure in the carpet that seems to be emerging. This will include the use to which what is told is being put — how it is designed to create or modify the analytic relationship. For example, the coalescence of the two images — violet and violence — is vivid in the way that the peace posters that featured putting a daisy into the barrel of a gun were vivid. Yet in those messages the relationship was explicit: no one could doubt that the flower was meant to replace the ammunition and nullify the violence of the gun. But can the same be said of the "violent" replacement of the flower with the word violence? In the latter instance, given the divergence of the two images, P. might have been doing violence to the analyst by making it problematic as to which associational line to follow.

To happen, the patient has to gain access to the medium, and as we saw earlier, the analyst who is unable to serve as a container for the patient will either leave the patient defeated or push him toward more and more violent ways of conveying the message into the medium. The extent to which the therapist is "saturated," as Bion called it, by his own transferences or therapeutic mission is the degree to which the analyst cannot be available to who and what the patient is. The analyst is the medium in which the patient happens. It is the patient occurring within and upon him that provides him the data. It is necessary for the analyst to ignore the patient who is in his consulting room in favor of the patient who is happening at the very center of his own inner experience.

To be so ignored does not (at least not initially) ingratiate itself with any patient, and when envy is rife the conscious self that is directing the action can only persecute the borning self that is being afforded the analyst's medium. This often stimulates a double-barreled counter-attack. Material dries up — dreams, slips, and associations give way to strictly narrated material about which the patient has all the information and the analyst none (the analyst who goes for this material finds himself asking who, what, where questions in some forlorn hope of keeping up). And the patient does whatever he can to make the analyst unable to profit from his intuitions and empathy. At such times one may find one's self feeling closed off, petulant and judgmental, and much inclined to ruminate about using special measures to confront the patient even while wondering wistfully where one's capacity for imaginative identification has fled. It is possible to so hate feeling dour that one feels tempted to reassert one's receptivity to such doubting Thomases, and so to linger late over sessions, invite telephone calls, or otherwise (by "being more human") display a good spirit. These measures only confirm to the patient that the analyst's receptivity has gone and that the analytic relationship has turned into one where both can fake it.

Faking it has an awful but compeling appeal to someone when he does not want to be recognized for who and what he is because to be so could mean exposure and humiliation or arrest and execution. The patient may persuade himself (or allow himself by the manifestation of a very accepting attitude) to believe that somehow Ψ may be able to thrust his sentence aside. Because he never sees the doorways from which the analyst emerges in the daytime and returns at night, prudence dictates that P. be ever careful of what he lets Ψ know. Such analyses spend a ferocious amount of time being trials. There are explanations, testimonials, confessions, spirited defenses, counter-accusations. The trial is the more Kafkaesque in that the examining magistrate does not exactly press charges, cross examine the defendant, or in other respects give him a case to answer. In hideous fact, he acts as if there isn't even a trial. Under the circumstances, free association is a derisive notion. The patient must bring the case material in from outside. And in any event, how can one who lives or dies by the analyst's judgment of him, dare freely to associate with him?

Poor Ψ may like to think he is a good and civil man, a Stracheyean figure, mutative in his interpretations and effects. But who knows? In any case, gods are needed: without them there can be neither apology nor confession, nor least of all redemption. Once the analyst is imbued with such powers — or, worse, cultivates them, he is secretly feared and hated. (Surely these are overtones in P.'s Salomé-like images in which the judges are finally humiliated by the power of her beauty and desirability and revealed for the Circean pigs *they* are.) The therapy becomes symbiotic. In return for his therapist's good graces, the patient, now hostage, makes his ongoing explanations, his continuing obeisance. What the patient will come to establish, reestablish, remember, or invent, is a different sort of process.

In this, as Bollas (1979) says,

> The mother is less identifiable as an object than as a *process* that is identified with cumulative internal and external gratifications. [The mother is] *a transformational object* . . . that is experientially identified by the infant with the process of the alteration of self experience; an identification that emerges from symbiotic relating where the first object is known not by cognizing it into an object representation, but known as a recurrent experience of being—a kind of existential, as opposed to representational, knowing. . . . The mother is not yet identified as an object but is experienced as a process of transformation, and this feature remains in the trace of this object-seeking in adult life, where I believe the object is sought for its function as signifier of the process of transformation of being. Thus, in adult life, the quest is not to possess the object; it is sought in order to surrender to it as a process that alters the self. [p. 97]

When Bion used the term, *capacity for reverie* he meant by it not merely the capacity for vicarious understanding, but the capacity of the other to contain in reverie what the infant self calls up *without necessarily discharging it into action*. This means that although, as Bion also said, "one must say what one means and mean what one says," the analyst should say what he says sparingly. The patient has to do his own transformational work if he is to establish a process capable of transforming him. The first process, after all, failed signally to transform the patient into someone worth selecting; this time, if one gives up faking it, there can be no mistakes.

P., in leaving or threatening to leave, tries to force some portion of herself into Ψ, the message now having reached the status of a massage. Let us be as clear as we can about what is at issue. At its simplest, she would wish Ψ to know how she feels, sadistically, perhaps, to go through what she goes through. I shall suppose that P. is afraid of having to die unfulfilled—that there is something either in the process or in the transference that makes P. feel that she is dying and has to do something quite drastic to have it stop. Is this dread of her personal death? Or is she in dread of having been fated to die before she can fulfill her destiny? Is the insinuation of her dread into Ψ all she wishes to achieve? Or does she wish to impregnate Ψ with something else as well?

In P.'s particular instance, we have seen the conjunction between AIDS and pregnancy. In this, something more is at stake than her personal demise. To the question of whether she may be borne as a child, there is the question

of whether she may bear a child. And, if not, whether she can realize that
child elsewhere. Selection in the GROUP is indifferent to the individual fate of
the particular person. Selection is concerned with the successful perpetuation
of the GROUP as species. When frustrated, the urge to be transformed turns
from symbiosis to parasitism. The self wishes to reproduce and clone at the
expense of the other — and then becomes acutely fearful of retaliation in kind.
Selection by the other is bound to be regarded as pernicious — as an attempt
at seduction, rape, or more mystical intercourse. Seepage, tendrils, infiltra-
tion — these are the fears associated with the parasite. They amount to the
hostile take over the self wishes to set in motion against the unyielding
contained object. The living–dead self wishes to invade the other and deposit
both ego and reproductive capacities in it — forcing it by stealth and strength
to breed offspring.

The remarkable ability of the therapist to take in and process material
makes him a perfect container for such "Ova." But a difficulty arises when the
therapist appears to have quite similar designs on the patient. Sooner or later
the patient's material, having been processed by the therapist, is returned to
the patient, where, to be elevated about it, it is designed to take root and grow.
Since the patient, by virtue of his projections of intent, will inevitably suspect
the therapist of harboring attempts to impregnate or gestate his ova in the
patient, conscious or unconscious attempts by the therapist to effect cure or
change will for a long and confounding time only confirm the patient's worst
suspicion — that the very marrow of him is under attack. The envious patient
wants tremendously to give birth to himself; any attempt by the therapist to
imbue him with a clone or variation of the therapist's self will be staunchly
resisted. But sharing is a very difficult matter.

A patient says:
I know I am not finished yet, that there's more to do, but I can't somehow convey
that. I can't say, "My analysis is very important to me. I am much more troubled
than I ever let on." I just can't say something like that. And it's not so much that
I am afraid someone will say, "Aren't you taking yourself too seriously?" because
I don't hear it coming from them. It comes from me — "Aren't you the serious
earnest one. . . ." Very mocking. [Momentary silence] I must be going crazy, I
swear I am going crazy, because just now, I mean just then, I heard this voice
saying, not a voice, but you know what I mean, saying, "If you tell him about last
night, I'll kill you!" Now I suppose you are going to say, "Well, what about last
night?" But do me a favor — don't.. I really can't tell you now, not if my life
depended on it.

This patient is caught in the no-person's land between academies. One
academy — speaking now of organized psychoanalysis and psychotherapy —
has standards it considers secular; many observers have noted that these

standards are not far removed from religious standards, values, and structures (Bion 1966; cf.Eissler 1965). These in turn derive from the sense of an ultimate. Given our nature as human beings, there is really no escape from a devout belief in an ultimate. As I have noted repeatedly, the ultimate is some form or fashion of an eugenic ideal, a better approximation to the divine or the natural or the philosophic ideal. Science and religion may contest the scientific method or faith, revelation or experimentation, inspiration or perspiration, as artists and engineers might dispute intuition or trial and error, fiction and fact. But none of these contest that there is something better—as in good, better, best—that makes the argument passionate and important. Even cynics and nihilists, even eclectics and other flower children have articles of faith. The academy has goods and betters in mind for itself and for its clientele. Not only do we speak of patients getting better, but we have ladders for development, others for pathology.

The envious have academies of their own, of course. These are contra-academies. They tend to emphasize either nature or nurture. The nature is genetic or biological, and that is where cure lies. The nurture is economic, ethnic, or ideological, and in changes of these is where the cure lies. It is not that these assertions are true or false, one-sided or otherwise. It is how they are used that distinguishes the scholar from the demagogue. To promote a particular point of view, one must of necessity minimize another, but there is a wide difference between minimizing and diminishing. The demagogue is a creature of arrogance in the sense Bion (1957) has used the term. That is, he would like to feel that invention serves well-being more than does discovery, and that invention is in inexorable danger from discovery by those who make discoveries. Many physicians who believe in the scientific method know that psychoanalysis is a bunch of hogwash. Envious at their certainty, I wish I knew that.

But the academy has value for the group precisely in its ability to promote assertion over proof, the more so when proof is imperceptible to others. The matter of resistance is a case in point. Resistance was first used by Freud to describe the ego's anxiety lest its reconfigurations of previous and prospective experience be undone by renewing the original experience or discovering something that would invalidate currently held experiences of experience. It was as such an intrapsychic experience concerning the return of the repressed. By various means and for various purposes, however, resistance came to mean antagonisms to the precepts of the academy. As a "No" from a patient might mark a resistance to an interpretation, so a "No [nsense]" from other academies was taken also to mark a resistance. That there is sense to this is irrefutable. Psychoanalytic findings arise from the particular methodology of psychoanalytic investigation and those using the method first on the couch, then behind it are the only ones able to attest to the validity or usefulness of those findings. But why then should others be expected to accept its findings on the basis of a simple say-so? If this has truth to it in the struggle among the academies to survive and propagate their own, surely this will have truth in the consulting room as well.

In the consulting room, an interpretation can also be an assertion of the academy. If it is, it is a statement marked by arrogance, a political statement dressed up to look like a therapeutic one. I think Ψ might not dare to say to P., whose hand is on the doorknob, if still the inside one, "You are resisting," even though, in the corrupted meaning of the word, P. most decidedly *is* resisting. If Ψ did so it would be a matter of arrogance meeting arrogance, head on, and if P. were the sort of plucky person she seems to be, her hand would soon be on the knob on the other side of the door. Yet there is a paradox here too. Ex cathedra assertions by the analyst are often employed exactly because the patient habitually diminishes what the analyst says.

"So, boiled down, what you are trying to say is. . . ."

"Yeah, well, I did what you told me to and. . . ."

"Well, last time you said—I don't remember, something about, uh. . . ."

STICKING TO ESSENTIALS

What is the alternative? What is it that we may usefully do? What is it that I mean by *the* therapy or *the* analysis? In its essence, the analytic process is a search for 'meaning—what this means and what meanings are attached to that. It is an exercise in hermeneutics. It rests on the assumption that when experience becomes intolerable and cannot be changed in the world of affairs, it is changed in the world of mind. That is, the unbearable meaning of the event is changed, and substituted for it is an alternative set of meanings or meaninglessnesses. It would be pleasant to think that the psychoanalytic process restores meaning, but it doesn't altogether; too often it must get by on supplying meanings. All the same, as the patient enters into the psychoanalytic domain, he immediately becomes meaningful, even if no one yet knows what those meanings are.

When the patient's envy is deeply rooted in feelings of being unselected as against others' ability to walk astride the earth as if they belonged there, the discovery of meaning is the fulfillment of the patient's deepest wish. In her paper on the adhesive pseudo object relationship, which deals with fantasized survival mechanisms in earliest infancy, Mitrani 1993 uses the phrase, "[He] was conceived by his mother, but not *conceived of* by her" (p. 33). With admirable concision this phrase expresses the plight of the unselected, pointing directly to the importance to being conceived of—that psychoanalytic activity, par excellence. In my view, such conceptions through the discovery of meaning need to take place in what I have called a hermeneutically sealed room. In this room there is interpretation, interpretation, and very little else. By interpretation, I join with Etchegoyen (1991) in his definition: "Interpretation . . . always indicates something that properly belongs to the patient, and of which he has no knowledge" (p. 321). The difference between interpretation, confrontation ("confrontation shows the patient two things in counterposition, with the intention of making him face a dilemma, so that he will notice the contradiction" [p. 316]), clarification ("clarification seeks to illuminate something the individual knows, but not distinctly. . . . I think clarification does not promote insight but only a re-ordering of information" [p. 321]), and information ("information refers to something the patient is ignorant of about the external world. . . . something that does not belong to him") "is very great and will serve to define and study interpretation" (p. 321).

The preoccupation with whether he is worth keeping is not easily dispelled by the discovery of meaning; indeed it occludes it. Judgment rules the day. Hardly a fact can see life without immediately acquiring a penumbra of judgmental implications. Nothing less than survival is at stake and, for the infant self, the thrust toward survival entails alteration of the eco-niche. As not many pages ago we saw with P., the infant self is a mover and a shaker, whose orientation is toward changing the environment — namely Ψ. P.'s very life-lihood seemed to depend on Ψ's valuation of her, something else she could not afford to leave to chance. Each time Ψ speaks, he seems to open a door, and behind each door there is, as always, the Lady or the Tiger. (With her hand on the doorknob, P. was quite literally turning the doors on Ψ.)

The hermeneutically sealed room requires that the analyst leave the academy at the door. The less he knows about good, better, and best, the better. Interventions other than interpretations are all too easily confusable with efforts to inculcate, recruit or convert, when one would want the patient's efforts in these regards to be prominent instead.[3]

Thus the analyst may find it helpful to treat those who consult him as

---

[3]In recounting his work at Northfield, Bion (1961) provides a detailed description of what it means to display evidence for one's findings — as opposed to asserting one's conclusions, which he also does. Briefly, he encourages the patients in the psychiatry facility to air every complaint they have concerning how their treatment keeps them from getting well and returning to the front. One by one he takes these obstacles and helps to remedy them. Finally there is but one left — the 20 percent of the men the others find to be out-and-out malingerers. Bion asserts that there are those 20 percenters everywhere, and that, now all else being remedied, the 80 percenters are using them as points of resistance. Though this is an assertion, it follows upon a careful and systematic demonstration that despite what they devoutly wish, the difficulty was not in the obstacles, now fixed, but in the men. The men are able to accept this, and form into the self-study groups that Bion later was to reestablish at Tavistock.

members of some other academy come to do some basic research. Were this research to be into a matter of physics or physiology, I doubt he would offer interpretation to his newfound colleague unless and until he or she saw interpretations as being of some possible use. Indeed, he might well not take those who consult him into analysis unless or until the need for a many-sessioned week employing free association emerges in a way that convinces them both it is worth the try. (The *DSM-III* and all it represents lives in a different universe. It is the expression of a particular academy, one that knows people from their whorls and bumps and not from themselves. There is a certain kind of psychotherapy that follows from that, but it has nothing to do with what I am talking of here.) It follows that the analyst would be ever ready to abandon the attempt when and if it proves sterile — or simply not worth the effort. I cannot emphasize too strongly that before analysis is undertaken, its potential usefulness as a method must be obvious to both parties and both must be prepared for the enormous work it entails.

When would interpretations come into it? When the transference prevents new and present experience from developing, which is to say while the past remains doggedly in the present and before it can be remembered and forgotten. The mandate for interpretations, has, I think, to be renewed on a daily basis. They must be offered only when wanted, and not when the analyst needs to alleviate his discomfort (see Boris 1991).

A patient takes a rare leave of absence from her therapy to attend a conference in her field. On her return she reports she was glad she attended because, as she hoped, the conference was of great practical value. She also reports that she has for some reason been giving a lot of thought to her mother, whom she "fired" some years ago. She begins then to speak with feeling of a precisely recollected mother, a marked contrast to what she did while her mother had been fired. But by the next session this new-won access has sealed over, and P. is beside herself with frustration and fury: "I hate the whole world and everybody in it, but most of all I hate myself!"

Ψ [waits for a while to see where P. will take this, but P. has retired into a hapless mixture of "it's no use" and "I don't give a damn." Ψ draws P.'s attention back to the "everbody" in the world the patient hates, and suggests that this must surely include her. But P. merely stares disgustedly at the ceiling.]

Ψ "You may have sought to make a compromise, by hating first your mother and now yourself in the hopes we might have something to work on. Could it be that you hoped to bring your feelings about me into it but to leave me out of it?"

P. [is outraged by this breach of her compromise and tells Ψ how much she hates Ψ's need to bring herself into everything.] "You must think the sun rises and sets because of you! Well, there are other people just as important to me as you."

Here P. goes on to speak of a male friend who was at the conference with her, ending with, "Maybe he's so sensitive because he's gay."

Ψ And the mother-me is so *in* sensitive because we are not?

Envy is here, of course, and this patient is envious even of herself. To the self, the self is an object like any other, and is treated accordingly. One has to think in terms of subject-self and object-self and, of course, other. Either of the selves can and does form relations with the other self in dynamics that are linked to their relation with the other. The other can be internal or external to the psychological surface of the skin, which surface can coincide with the actual skin or, as in skin disorders, can be a part of the one rather than the other self. (Tustin [1981] has written on this phenomenon in relation to psychological autism.) Or the one can be above the waist, the other below. Or,

P.   I think in my head that. . . .
P.   I know in my mind. . . .

Of special note is that the subject-self can envy the object-self—or fear the latter's envy in respects little different from the relations between self and other. Thus, as changes begin to take place in a therapy, especially between the subject-self and the therapist, the object-self can get quite huffy:

P.   I don't know whether I mean what I am telling you or not. I mean, I mean it, but when I say it a little voice in me says, "Oh, come off it you're just telling him what he wants to hear." Just now when I told you the dream, it kept saying, "Oh, aren't you something—such a sig-nif-i-cant dream. I'm impressed." You know, real snide.
       I wish there was some way of telling you stuff without having to do so out loud. Couldn't you read my thoughts? It's weird I say that—about you reading my thoughts. That was my worst fear when I first came here. But now it's as if—if you could read them, and I wouldn't have to say them out loud, I could tell you anything . . . every thing. But it's like I can't stand over-hearing myself. I know it's crazy, but that's how I feel!

In the consulting room it does not matter whether we are looking into the relations of the COUPLE or of the PAIR. Or into the relationship between narcissism and object love, or the death and life drives. The reader who has followed me thus far will have heard countless resonances with formulations proposed by others, for example, with Rosenfeld's dissociated duo, the omnipotent narcissistic self and the dependent infantile self, or with Fairbairn's libidinal and anti-libidinal egos, or even with Freud's super ego, Bion's super-superego, Meltzer's tyrant, these on the one side, and the id, the

object-loving or the sexual self on the other. I have, of course, distorted my
own presentation in favor of demonstrating the particular biopsychology of
selection and survival that I think opens Klein's primary envy to further
analysis. In real life analysis, the COUPLE and its passions are ever at play,
contributing eroticism (e.g., sadism and masochism) and longing in equal
measures. It must not be forgotten that P. (as a member of the COUPLE — one
might say, as a "member of the wedding") was living out in the analysis a
highly excited masturbation fantasy, one which was not finding its way into
her relationship with her love, and might otherwise have to be abandoned (in
the other sense). In this sense her interest in leaving could be understood as
a perfectly straightforward defense against the pain of loss (if she were not in
analysis, her fantasies and longings would no longer be subject to interpretation).

The COUPLE is at risk to the PAIR who is or feels itself to be at risk to the
GROUP. Insofar as the analyst becomes identified with the GROUP, as he always
must, he is a danger in the PAIR and a deeper frustration in the nascent COUPLE
than he will be when in the emerged COUPLE. For this reason it has always
seemed to me foolish to imagine the analyst as a blank screen: Analytic work
is full of risks, even for those who work only with "analyzable" patients, which
patients alive with envy barely are, and patients who feel themselves to be at
risk are bound to push beyond these to see where our troubles lie — to get to
where we are at risk. Only when they have penetrated to the center of our
dis-ease, can patients feel safe enough to trust us. (I think this is true from our
vantage point as well.) I think it quite wrong for the analyst to reveal his
dis-ease — as I have already said, the problem is that we ask that we be
discovered too soon — but not to be transparent and to be opaque are two quite
different matters. The patient must be allowed to gauge his risk, it is only
common sense that he would want to — and indeed, the worry is that too often,
armed with the arrogance of omnipotent fantasy, the patient is indifferent to
his risk. (We are inclined to think, and who can blame us, that it makes
perfect sense for a patient to come and spend his time and treasure with us
after investigations of our competence and reputation that can only be called
negligent, but at least we shake our heads when they display the same
diligence in choosing one of our weaker colleagues.)

At the door, P. was asking this question: Can you stand for me to go?
What will happen to you and to me if and when I do?

That we can stand for our patients to leave us at any time, in any
condition, is a minimal condition for being in practice. P. elected to stay with
her analyst until termination. Her termination, fortunately, was taken slowly.

Time, isn't always experienced as linear — it is sometimes felt to be
circular or to have shrunk to a flickering dot like the last image on the TV
screen before it goes blank. But when it is experienced as time's → arrow, it

provides a dimension in which things can happen. When things don't go well—foiled again!—there is an "again" there. Time is one part of a dimensional experience, of which space is a second. Space is in important ways reserved for the COUPLE: it describes degrees of proximity, of closeness, contact and intimacy. The epigram for this might be, "Together, at last!" but the live-wire word is "together." When time becomes foreshortened, it is like accordion-pleating the arrow: This develops an additional dimension: a Matisse line drawing becomes a Pollock becomes a Stella construction and so on. The once-simple arrow must now be thought of as a balloon which, when squeezed in some portion, expands proportionately in another. In psychological terms this dimension turns out to be depth. As time, or the belief in time, or the belief in time as a friend (optimism), becomes foreshortened, time contracts, as if a mass condensing upon itself, and in this new gravitas there come to be different palettes of colors, increased intensities, shadings and chiaroscuro and new dimensions of meaning. Intimations become convictions, hints become voices barking orders: thus do the no-things replace the nothings when there is an intolerance of nothing. These pockmark the smooth bland surface of what is so and infuse it with significance, meaning, implication, and staying power. The depressions that mark where what was supposed to be but is not is one example, the questions to which the answer of anorexia points are another. As Kellman and Spelke's (1983) work shows experimentally, it is as we have always known psychoanalytically: infants arrive at age three or four months with a highly evolved set of preconceptions and expectations as to how things are or should be. The two little cylinders protruding beyond either side of a screen are or should be ends of a dowel that lies hidden behind the screen: they are not two little blocks—they are *related*.

After termination P. married, moved to another city with her husband, and, returning briefly to the city for a visit, had some sessions in respect to her tensions about becoming pregnant. In these tensions was a mild resurgence of the possibility of baleful magic. Insofar as randomness, accident, chance, meaninglessnes cannot be tolerated, they cannot properly be converted into nothing, mourned and relinquished. They remain no-things, and as no-things, menace the self with the dire regalia of foreshadowings and forebodings, portents and omens, with which most of us (knock wood) are familiar only through folklore, and for which the usual cure involves elements of prophecy, ritual, propitiation, and counter-magic.[4]

That these same measures also are used in the white magic we practice to make our hopes come true shows the role of hope in resisting the conversion of no-things into nothings. It is hope, after all, that furnishes the idea that

---

[4]In our culture, litigation, suits, and counter-suits, often seem to have something of this function.

anything is possible. And it is hope that drives the substitution of no-things for nothing. This sleight of mind provides us our world of preconceptions and premonitions, at whose heed we pass so much of our lives. In the top drawer of the hope chest are a legion of woulds and coulds—the clauses for a world of contracts, according to which, since we do our parts, we know others will do theirs.[5] In the deeper drawers are the architectural plotlines for our life, the schemes by which we move from here to over there, schemes often rationalized by our belief that we have devised a plan or are following one provided by society or someone else. In a planless, contractless, analysis, such premonitory designs—unseen hands—become visible and thereby open to consideration. As P. showed, these plotlines reach beyond one generation to the next.

---

[5]Clauses and *"clauses-belli"*: when others do them, all's right with the world, but when they don't we have every right, it seems to us, to feel betrayed and vengeful or depressed and filled with refusal or apathy.

References

Abraham, K. (1919). A particular form of neurotic resistance against the psychoanalytic method. In *Selected Paper on Psychoanalysis*, chapter 15. London: Karnac.

Akhmatova, A. (1985). *Twenty Poems*. Trans. J. Kenyon. St. Paul, MN: Eighties Press and Ally Press.

Augustine, A, St. (1952). *Confessions; City of God; on Christian Doctrine*. Chicago: Encyclopaedia Britannica Press.

Axelrod, G., Frankenheimer, J. (producers), Frankenheimer, J. (director). (1962). *The Manchurian Candidate*. (Film). Hollywood: United Artists/MC.

Bair, D. (1978). *Samuel Beckett: A Biography*. New York: Harcourt Brace Jovanovich.

Barthelme, F. (1990). *Natural Selection*. New York: Viking/Penguin.

Bion, W. R. (1950). The imaginary twin. In *Second Thoughts*. New York: Jason Aronson, 1967.

_____ (1957). On arrogance. In *Second Thoughts*. New York: Jason Aronson, 1967.

_____ (1959). Attacks on linking. In *Second Thoughts*. New York: Jason Aronson, 1967.

_____ (1961). *Experiences in Groups*. New York: Basic Books.

_____ (1962). *Learning From Experience*. New York: Basic Books. Reprinted London: Karnac, 1984.

_____ (1963). *Elements of Psychoanalysis*. New York: Basic Books. Reprinted London: Karnac, 1984.

_____ (1965). *Transformations*. New York: Basic Books. Reprinted London: Karnac, 1984.

186   References

——— (1966). Book review: *Medical Orthodoxy and the Future of Psychoanalysis* by K. R. Eissler (New York: International Universities Press, 1965). *International Journal of Psycho-Analysis* 47:575–579.

——— (1970). *Attention and Interpretation*. New York: Basic Books. Reprinted London: Karnac, 1984.

——— (1976). On a quotation from Freud. In *Clinical Seminars and Four Papers*, ed. F. Bion, pp. 234–238. Abingdon, England: Fleetwood, 1987.

——— (1980). *Bion in New York and Sao Paulo*. Strathclyde, Scotland: Clunie.

——— (1982). *The Long Week-End*. Abingdon, England: Fleetwood.

——— (1985). *All My Sins Remembered*. Abingdon, England: Fleetwood.

Bollas, C. (1979). The transformational object. *International Journal of Psycho-Analysis* 60 (1): 97–107.

Borges, J. L. (1964). Tlon, Upgar, Orbis, Tertius. In *Labyrinths*, ed. D. Yates and J. Irby, pp. 3–18. New York: New Directions.

Boris, H. N. (1970). The medium, the message and the good group dream. *International Journal of Group Psychotherapy* 20: 91–98.

——— (1984a). On the problem of anorexia nervosa. *International Journal of Psycho-Analysis* 65:315–322.

——— (1984b). On the treatment of anorexia nervosa. *International Journal of Psycho-Analysis* 65:435–442.

——— (1985). Interpretation: historical and theoretical perspectives. In *Psychodynamic Psychotherapy*, ed. M. Nichols and T. Paolino. New York: Gardner.

——— (1986). The "other" breast: greed, envy, spite, and revenge. *Contemporary Psychoanalysis* 22:45–59.

——— (1987). Tolerating nothing. *Contemporary Psychoanalysis* 23:351–366.

——— (1988). Torment of the object: a contribution to the study of bulimia. In *Bulimia: Psychoanalytic Treatment and Theory*, ed. H. J. Schwartz. Madison, CT: International Universities Press.

——— (1989). Interpretation of facts, interpretation of dreams. *Contemporary Psychoanalysis* 25 (2): 212–225.

——— (1990). Identification with a vengeance. *International Journal of Psycho-Analysis* 71:127–140.

——— (1991). In quest of the psychoanalytic datum. *Psychoanalytic Dialogues* 1(2):225–237.

——— (1993). *Passions of the Mind: Unheard Melodies: A Third Principle of Mental Functioning*. New York: New York University Press.

——— (1994). *Sleights of Mind: One and Multiples of One*. Northvale, NJ: Jason Aronson.

Boris, H. N., Zinberg, N. E., and Boris, M. (1975). People's fantasies in group situations: towards a psychoanalytic theory of groups. *Contemporary Psychoanalysis* 11:15–45.

Brazelton, T. B., and Cramer, B. G. (1990). *The Earliest Relationship*. Reading, MA: Addison Wesley.

Bulfinch, T. (1855). *Mythology*. New York: Random House.

Calvino, I. (1985). *Mr. Palomar*. Trans. W. Weaver. San Diego, CA: Harcourt Brace Jovanovich.

_____ (1988). *Six Memos for the Next Millennium*. Trans. P. Creagh. Cambridge, MA: Harvard University Press.

Celan, P. (1988). *Poems*. New York: Persea.

Chomsky, N. (1972). *Language and Mind*. New York: Harcourt Brace.

Deeley, M., Spikings, B. (Producers), Roeg, N. (Director). (1976). *The Man Who Fell to Earth*. (Film). Great Britain: British Lion.

Deutsch, H. (1942). Some forms of emotional disturbances and their relationship to schizophrenia. *Psychoanalytic Quarterly* 11:301–321.

Durkheim, E. (c. 1933). *The Division of Labor in Society*. Trans. G. Simpson. New York: Free Press, 1964.

Eckstaedt, A. (1989). Ego-syntonic object manipulation. *International Journal of Psycho-Analysis* 70:499–512.

Edelman, G. M. (1987). *Neural Darwinism*. New York: Basic Books.

_____ (1992). *Bright Air, Brilliant Fire*. New York: Basic Books.

Eigen, M. (1985). Towards Bion's starting point between catastrophe and faith. *International Journal of Psycho- Analysis* 66 (3): 321–330.

_____ (1986). *The Psychotic Core*. Northvale, NJ: Jason Aronson.

_____ (1993). *The Electrified Tightrope*. Northvale, NJ: Jason Aronson.

Eissler, K. R. (1953). The effect of the structure of the ego on psychoanalytic technique. *Journal of the American Psychoanalytic Association* 1:104–143.

Eliot, T. S. (1952). *The Complete Poems and Plays*. New York: Harcourt, Brace.

Emery, E. (1992). The envious eye. *The Journal of Melanie Klein and Object Relations* 10 (1).

Enright, D. J., ed. (1983). *The Oxford Book of Death*. London: Oxford University Press.

Erikson, E. (1963). *Childhood and Society*. 2nd edition. New York: Norton.

_____ (1964). *Insight and Responsibility*. New York: Norton.

Etchegoyen, R. H. (1991). *The Fundamentals of Psychoanalytic Technique*. London: Karnac.

Feiner, A. H. (1991). The analyst's participation in the patient's transference. *Contemporary Psychoanalysis* 22:389–409.

Feynman, R. (1965). The development of the space-time view of quantum electrodynamics. Nobel Prize in Physics Award Address, Stockholm, December 11.

Fraser, J. T., ed. (1989). *The Study of Time, Part IV: Time and Mind: Interdisciplinary Issues*. Madison, CT: International Universities Press.

Freud, S. (1900). Interpretation of dreams. *Standard Edition* 4–5.

_____ (1914). On narcissism. *Standard Edition* 14:73–102.

_____ (1914). Remembering, repeating and working through. *Standard Edition* 12:147–173.

_____ (1915). Thoughts for the times on war and death. *Standard Edition* 14:275–301.

_____ (1916). Some character-types met within psychoanalytic work. *Standard Edition* 14:311–333.

_____ (1917a). A metapsychological supplement to the theory of dreams. *Standard Edition* 14:222–235.

_____ (1917b). Mourning and melancholia. *Standard Edition* 14:243–260.

_____ (1918). From the history of an infantile neurosis. *Standard Edition* 17:7–122.

_____ (1919). A child is being beaten. *Standard Edition* 17:179–204.

_____ (1920). Beyond the pleasure principle. *Standard Edition* 18:7–64.

_____ (1923). The ego and the id. *Standard Edition* 19:12–66.

_____ (1924). The economic problem of masochism. *Standard Edition* 19:159–170.

_____ (1925). Negation. *Standard Edition* 19:235–239.

_____ (1927). Postscript to "The Question of Lay Analysis." *Standard Edition* 20: 251–258.

_____ (1937). Analysis terminable and interminable. *Standard Edition* 23:216–263.

Fromm, E. (1969). *Escape From Freedom.* New York: Avon Books.

Gardner, H. (1973). *The Quest for Mind: Piaget, Levi- Strauss and the Structuralist Movement.* New York: Knopf.

Gazzaniga, M. (1992). *Nature's Mind.* New York: Basic Books.

Gould, S. (1979). Panselectionist pitfalls in Parker and Gibson's model of the evolution of intelligence. *The Behavioral and Brain Sciences* 2:385–386.

_____ (1983). *Hen's Teeth and Horse's Toes.* New York: Norton.

_____ (1991). Exaptation: a crucial tool for an evolutionary psychology. *Journal of Social Issues* 47 (3): 43–65.

Green, A. (1986). *On Private Madness.* Madison, CT: International Universities Press.

Greenacre, R. (1953). Penis awe in relation to penis envy. In *Drives, Affects, Behavior,* ed. R. M. Lowenstein. New York: International Universities Press.

Grosskurth, P. (1986). *Melanie Klein: Her World and Her Work.* New York: Knopf.

Grotstein, J. (1990a). Nothingness, meaninglessness, chaos and the "black hole." *Contemporary Psychoanalysis* 26 (2): 257–290.

_____ (1990b). Nothingness, meaninglessness, chaos and the "black hole" II. *Contemporary Psychoanalysis* 26(3): 337–407.

Hartmann, H. (1959). Psychoanalysis as a scientific theory. In *Psychoanalysis, Scientific Method and Philosophy,* ed. S. Hook. New York: International Universities Press.

Hartocollis, P. (1983). *Time and Timelessness or The Varieties of Temporal Experience (A Psychoanalytic Inquiry).* New York: International Universities Press.

Hawking, S. W. (1988). *A Brief History of Time*. New York: Bantam.

Hoffer, W. (1952). The mutual influences in the development of ego and id: earliest stages. *The Psychoanalytic Study of the Child* 7:31-41. New York: International Universities Press.

Homer. *The Complete Works of Homer*. Trans. A. Land, W. Leaf, E. Myers, and S. Butcher. New York: Modern Library.

Horney, K. (1936). The problem of the negative therapeutic reaction. *Psychoanalytic Quarterly* 5:29-44.

Isaacs, S., Heimann, P., Klein, M., and Riviere, J. (1952). The nature and function of phantasy. In *Developments in Psycho-analysis*. London: Hogarth.

Jacques, E. (1965). Death and the mid-life crisis. *International Journal of Psycho-Analysis* 46:502-514.

John of the Cross, St. (1957). In *Dark Night of the Soul,* ed. K. Reinhardt. London: Ungar.

Kant, I. (1781). *The Critique of Pure Reason*. Chicago: Encyclopaedia Britannica Press, 1952.

Kellman, P. J., and Spelke, E. (1983). Perception of partly occluded objects in infancy. *Cognitive Psychology* 15:483-524.

_____ (1991). Physical knowledge in infancy. In *The Epigenesis of Mind: Essays on Biology and Cognition,* ed. S. Carey and R. Gilman. Hillsdale, NJ: Lawrence Erlbaum.

Khan M. M. R. (1974). *The Privacy of the Self*. London: Hogarth.

Klein, M. (1946). Notes on some schizoid mechanisms. In *Developments in Psycho-Analysis*, ed. M. Klein, S. Isaacs, P. Heimann, and J. Riviere, pp. 292-320. New York: Da Capo, 1983.

_____ Some theoretical conclusions regarding the emotional life of the infant. In *Developments in Psycho-Analysis*, ed. M. Klein, P. Heimann, S. Isaacs, and J. Riviere, pp. 198-236. New York: Da Capo, 1983.

_____ (1957). *Envy and Gratitude*. London: Tavistock.

_____ (1958). On the development of mental functioning. *International Journal of Psycho-Analysis*.

_____ (1961). *Narrative of a Child Analysis*. London: Hogarth.

Kohut, H. (1968). The psychoanalytic treatment of narcissistic personality disorders. *Psychoanalytic Study of the Child* 23:86-113. New York: International Universities Press.

Kolata, G. (1990). Living and dying in the wild, guppies back evolution idea. *The New York Times,* July 26, pp. A1, B6.

Lacan, J. (1949). The mirror stage as formative of the I. In *Ecrits*. New York: Norton, 1977.

Laing, R. D, and Esterson, A. (1970). *Sanity, Madness and the Family*. Baltimore, MD: Penguin.

Leach, E. (1970). *Claude Levi-Strauss*. New York: Viking.

Levi-Strauss, C. (1966). *The Savage Mind*. Chicago: University of Chicago Press.

—— (1973). *From Honey to Ash*. New York: Harper & Row.

Limentani, A. (1972). The assessment of analyzability: a major hazard in selection for psychoanalysis. *International Journal of Psycho-Analysis* 53:351–361.

Lyons, J. (1970). *Noam Chomsky*. New York: Viking.

Machiavelli, N. (1532). *The Prince*. New York: New American Library of World Literature, 1952.

Mahler, M. S., Pine, F., and Bergman, A. (1975). *The Psychological Birth of the Human Infant*. New York: Basic Books.

Mayr, E., (1972). Sexual selection and natural selection. In *Sexual Selection and the Descent of Man,* ed. B. Campbell. Chicago: Aldine.

Meltzer, D. (1967). *The Psychoanalytical Process*. London: Heinemann.

Milgram, S. (1974). *Obedience to Authority: An Experimental View*. New York: Harper & Row.

Mitrani, J. (1993). On "Adhesive Pseudo-Object Relations" as illustrated in *Perfume*. Unpublished paper.

Murdoch, I. (1956). *The Flight from the Enchanter*. New York: Viking.

Phillips, A. (1988). *Winnicott*. London: Fontana.

—— (1993). *On Kissing, Tickling, and Being Bored: Psychoanalytic Essays of the Unexamined Life*. Cambridge, MA: Harvard University Press.

Piaget, J. (1973). *The Child and Reality: Problems of Genetic Psychology*. New York: Grossman.

Piers, M., ed. (1972). Some aspects of operations. In *Play and Development: A Symposium*, pp. 15–27. New York: Norton.

Poe, E. A. (1927). "The Cask of Amontillado." In *The Works of Edgar Allan Poe*. New York: Walter J. Black.

Riviere, J. (1936). A contribution to the analysis of the negative therapeutic reaction. In *The Inner World and Joan Riviere: Collected Papers 1920–1958,* ed. A. Hughes. London: Karnac, 1991.

Rosenfield, I. (1988). *The Invention of Memory*. New York: Basic Books.

Roth, P. (1990). *Deception: A Novel*. New York: Simon & Schuster.

Sacks, O. (1985). *The Man Who Mistook His Wife for a Hat*. New York: Summit.

—— (1993). To see and not see. *The New Yorker*, May 10, pp. 59–73.

Schafer, R. (1970). The psychoanalytic vision of reality. *International Journal of Psycho-Analysis* 51:279–297.

Searles, H. (1965). *Collected Papers on Schizophrenia*. New York: Basic Books.

Smith, M. G. (1971). *The Mortgaged Heart*. Boston: Houghton Mifflin.

Spark, M. (1957). *The Comforters*. New York: Avon, 1965.

Spitz, R. A. (1957). *No and Yes: On the Genesis of Human Communication*. New York: International Universities Press.

Spock, B. (1945). *The Common Sense Book of Baby and Child Care*. New York: Duell, Sloan and Pearce, 1957.

Stern, D. (1977). *The First Relationship*. Cambridge, MA: Harvard University Press.

_____ *The Interpersonal World of the Infant*. New York: Basic Books.

Sullivan, H. S. (1953). *The Interpersonal Theory of Psychiatry*. New York: W. W. Norton.

Tinbergen, N. (1958). *Curious Naturalists*. New York: Basic Books.

_____ (1965). *Animal Behavior*. New York: Time-Life.

Trilling, L. (1971). *Sincerity and Authenticity*. Cambridge MA: Harvard University Press.

Tustin, F. (1981). *Autistic States in Children*. London: Routledge and Kegan Paul.

Twain, M. (1889). *A Connecticut Yankee at King Arthur's Court*. New York: Harper & Row, 1965.

Wiesman, A. D. (1965). *The Existential Core of Psychoanalysis: Reality, Sense and Responsibility*. Boston: Little, Brown.

Williams, R. (1989). Carnegie Hall concert.

Winnicott, D. W. (1945). Primitive emotional development. In *Collected Papers: Through Paediatrics to Psycho-Analysis* pp. 145–156. New York: Basic Books, 1958.

_____ (1952). Anxiety associated with insecurity. In *Collected Papers: Through Paediatrics to Psycho-Analysis* pp. 97–100. New York: Basic Books, 1958.

_____ (1955). Group influences and the maladjusted child. In *The Family and Individual Development* pp. 146 –154. New York: Basic Books, 1965.

_____ (1956). Primary maternal preoccupation. In *Collected Papers: Through Paediatrics to Psycho-Analysis*, pp. 300–305. New York: Basic Books, 1958.

_____ (1960). The relationship of a mother to her baby at the beginning. In *The Family and Individual Development*, pp. 15–20. New York: Basic Books, 1965.

_____ (1962). The aims of psychoanalytic treatment. In *The Maturational Processes and the Facilitating Environment* pp. 166–170. New York: International Universities Press, 1965.

_____ (1986). *Home is Where We Start From*. New York: W. W. Norton.

_____ (1987). *The Spontaneous Gesture: Selected Letters of D. W. Winnicott*. Ed. F. R. Rodman. Cambridge, MA: Harvard University Press.

_____ (1989). *Human Nature*. London: Free Association.

Note: Boris 1970, 1975, 1984a,b, 1985, 1986, 1987, 1988, 1989, 1990, and 1991 are reprinted in Boris 1994.

Credits

The author gratefully acknowledges permission to reprint the following:

Chapter 1 "Hope," (originally entitled "On Hope: Its Nature and Psychotherapy"), *International Review of Psycho-Analysis* 3:139–150. Copyright © 1976, and Chapter 3 "Identification with a Vengeance," *International Journal of Psycho-Analysis* 71:127–140. Copyright © 1990: both reprinted by permission of the Institute of Psycho-Analysis.

Chapter 2 "Tolerating Nothing," *Contemporary Psychoanalysis* 23: (3):351–366. Copyright © 1987. Chapter 4 "Black Milk" (originally entitled "Black Milk: Unconscious Envy Part I"), *Contemporary Psychoanalysis* 27 (1):110–147. Copyright © 1991. Chapter 5 "More of the Same" (originally entitled "Fears of Difference—More of the Same: Unconscious Envy Part II"), *Contemporary Psychoanalysis* 28 (2): 228–250. Copyright © 1992. Chapter 6 "The Equalizing Eye" (originally titled "The Equalizing Eye: Unconscious Envy Part III"), *Contemporary Psychoanalysis* 28 (4): 572–593. Copyright © 1992. Chapter 7 "The Self Too Seen" (originally entitled "The Self Too Seen: Unconscious Envy Part IV"), *Contemporary Psychoanalysis*, in press. Copyright © 1993. Chapter 8 "About Time" (originally entitled "About Time: Unconscious Envy Part V"), *Contemporary Psychoanalysis*, in press. Copyright © 1994: All reprinted by permission of *Contemporary Psychoanalysis*.

Index